Applied Theology 1
'GO . . . AND MAKE DISCIPLES'

TEF Study Guides

This SPCK series was originally sponsored and subsidized by the Theological Education Fund of the WCC in response to requests from Africa, Asia, the Caribbean, and the Pacific. The books are prepared by and in consultation with theological teachers in those areas. Special attention is given to problems of interpretation and application arising there as well as in the West, and to the particular needs of students using English as a second language. More advanced titles in the list are marked (A).

General Editors: Daphne Terry and Nicholas Beddow

IN PREPARATION

TEF Study Guide 9

Applied Theology 1
'GO ... AND MAKE DISCIPLES'

A. C. Krass

First published in 1974
SPCK
Holy Trinity Church
Marylebone Road, London NW1 4DU

Ninth impression 1992

ISBN 0 281 02801 X
ISBN 0 281 02802 8 (special edition for Africa,
Asia, S. Pacific and Caribbean).

Printed and bound in Great Britain by
Hollen Street Press Ltd, Slough, Berks.

Contents

CONTENTS

ACKNOWLEDGEMENTS

The photographs in this book are reproduced by permission of Camera Press Ltd, except that the photograph on p.110 is reproduced by permission of Mark Shearman.

Author's Preface

This is a book which has arisen out of an experience, and that experience has been lived in the context of an amazingly vast Christian community. The work on which it reports was started and is still being carried out by African Christians, and it has been supported from the very beginning by an African Church, the Evangelical Presbyterian Church of Ghana, which, having heard the call of the Lord to proclaim the gospel to the peoples of Northern Ghana, has never turned back from that task but has kept its hands to the plough. A rich harvest is being brought in for the Lord, one which is only possible at the cost of faithful discipleship and rigorous stewardship. At the feet of the two Moderators of that Church during my ministry in Chereponi, the Right Reverends E. K. Galevo and A. K. Abutiate, and the Synod Clerk, the Reverend E. Y. Forson, I lay great tribute. They saw a vision and have been faithful to it. To the people of that Church in Southern Ghana, who supported the work with their prayers, their offerings, and their sons, I shall be forever indebted. Their example is one worthy of emulation.

I wish to express my appreciation also to the missionaries of the Church of Scotland who inspired me to serve with the E. P. Church in Northern Ghana, and who gave me insights and guidance in the initial stages of that work, the Reverends Tom Colvin, Colin Forester-Paton, and Bob Duncan.

The United Church Board for World Ministries (USA), which appointed us as missionaries and seconded us to the E. P. Church, and which provided a furlough year in which most of the work on this volume was done, supported the work throughout. To them, the word 'thanks' seems inadequate.

My thought has been nourished by some of the leading missionary statesmen of this century, Roland Allen—to whom so many today owe a debt of gratitude—John V. Taylor, Donald McGavran, V. S. Azariah, Lesslie Newbigin, D. T. Niles, and Adrian Hastings.

People who were of special help to me in the work in Chereponi were: the Reverend Dr Gilbert Ansre of the University of Ghana, much more than a linguistics counsellor; the Reverend Charles Hein, my guide to the field of literacy work, and the United Bible Societies and its translation consultants, in Scripture translation. Professor Robert Canfield of Washington University, St Louis, helped me understand anthropologically what went on in Chereponi. Fathers Anthony Gelinck and Joseph Connolly svd, were my constant sounding-boards for new departures in mission practice—and terribly supportive friends as well—as was my self-effacing wife, Susan Krass. None of what I did could, however, have been done except that it was done in a team with my co-workers, the Reverends W. M. Baniba and C. K. Chirifu, Mr and Mrs Robert Thelin, Mr Ben Kuma, and all the evangelists, presbyters, Church mothers, and village leaders. To one of those leaders the work is dedicated.

In the preparation of this volume certain people served unselfishly as readers and advisers: Canon Harry Sawyerr, Principal Harry Boer, Mr Modupe Oduyoye, John Poulton, Donald McGavran, James Sutton, John Mbiti, Charles Forman, and Daphne Terry. C. G. Richards was of great assistance in helping to arrange for its publication.

Others who commented on the plan of the book and on individual chapters were: Archbishop Festo Olang', Monseigneur Paul Mukasa, Principal Declan Brosnan osa, Bishop Poole-Hughes, Principal E. H. Wendland, Dr Charles Taber, Dr Alford Carleton, the Reverend Walt De Moss, the Right Reverend C. K. Dovlo, the Reverend Tom Colvin, A. P. Van den Broek, Harold Lehmann, Bruce Ganaway, O. K. Agbo, M. Neels wf, M. Pageault wf, John Baur, John Callow, E. C. Esterhuyse, Loren Bliese, Joseph Connolly svd, and Principal Stephen Kauta Msiska.

Miss Daphne Terry of the Theological Education Fund performed, as editor, the task of a tireless midwife. The finished work is very much a joint product of the two of us. Miss Gladys Burkhart typed the manuscript.

For the final product I, of course, bear all the responsibility. I only hope that those in the company of whom I have produced this volume will find it a small contribution in the outgoing work of a community whose task shall never be finished until the cry goes out: 'The kingdoms of this world have become the kingdom of our Lord and of his Christ' (Rev. 11.15).

A. C. KRASS

Editor's Note:
The plan and use of this book

The Editorial Group responsible for planning the TEF Study Guides spent much time discussing what would be the most useful form for a textbook covering the subjects rather variously included in 'Practical or 'Pastoral' Theology courses—which are sometimes the only point in a college curriculum where any opportunity occurs to integrate the biblical, historical, and systematic insights derived from other disciplines.

What must the *objectives* of theological training be today in a context of almost universal social, economic, and political change and unrest? How can the understandings and skills needed for effective ministry best be learned and taught? How valid is the customary distinction between 'traditional', or systematic, and 'practical' theology, and where is the point of contact between theological disciplines and the actual human situation? Where, if at all, does the dividing line come between the 'practical' and the 'pastoral' aspects of the ministerial function, whether 'set-apart' or lay? And how should these general considerations be reflected in the methodology of preparation for the minister's multiple task as communicator, counsellor, and enabler of worship, evangelism, and service to the community?

Even the most compendious volume could hardly provide answers directly applicable to all of the diverse cultural backgrounds and Church traditions where the TEF series is used. Apart from some discussion of the general nature and purpose of ministry, therefore, the best thing seemed to be to offer case material which teachers and students could use as a springboard for study appropriate to their own specific needs and situations. And Al Krass's vivid account of apostleship in Northern Ghana, when it came into our hands, seemed to provide just the sort of material to serve at any rate part of this purpose.

Though arising directly from experience in a rural and predominantly undeveloped area, his discussion of underlying principles will be equally relevant to those practising or preparing for a ministry in a more developed or urban situation, or where the Church has long been at work. He is, however, dealing almost exclusively with ministry to people as *groups*: with outreach to previously unevangelized *communities*, and with the upbuilding, education, and nurture of *congregations* as such.

We have deliberately not invited him to extend the scope of this volume artificially beyond the range of his functional assignment in Ghana. Instead, a second, complementary volume is planned, to deal with the distinctive aspects of ministry to people as individuals and in the more intimate concerns of home and family life. Its emphasis will be on pastoral care, counselling, personal ethics, and the spiritual life, and the material will be drawn, by contrast, from an urban and industrial background.

Taken as a whole the two-volume course will, we hope, help students to draw together the various strands of their training, and 'apply' the theology they have been doing, in the context of their forthcoming ministry.

STUDY SUGGESTIONS

Questions and suggestions for research and discussion appear at the end of each chapter of this book. They are intended to help readers to understand clearly what they have read and to check their own progress, and especially to relate the ideas and issues raised to their own particular experience.

The best way to use these study suggestions is *first* to read the chapter carefully once or twice, and *then* do the work suggested, in writing or group discussion, without looking back at the chapter except where it is suggested that you do so.

Please note that these study suggestions are only *suggestions*. Some readers may not want to use them at all. Teachers may wish to select only those which are relevant to their situation, and will almost certainly need to add or substitute questions of their own for discussion or research.

The *Key* (p. 211) will enable readers to check their own work on those questions which can be checked in this way. In most cases the Key does not give the answer to a question: it simply shows where an answer is to be found.

INDEX

The Index (p. 215) includes only the main subjects which are discussed in the Guide.

QUOTATIONS

One or two passages from the work of other authors on the subject have been paraphrased rather than quoted exactly, when this seems likely to help readers using English as a second language.

BIBLE VERSIONS

Except where otherwise indicated, the English translations of the Bible used in this book are Today's English Version (American Bible Society) for the New Testament, and the New English Bible for the Old Testament.

Bibliography

The following are some helpful books on the Church's ministry:

African Religions and Philosophy, John Mbiti, Heinemann

All-Africa Seminar on the Christian Home and Family Life, Africa Literature Centre

Christian Giving, V. S. Azariah (World Christian Books), Lutterworth

Christian Marriage and Family Life in Africa, Christian Dovlo, Accra

Church and Mission in Modern Africa, Adrian Hastings, Burns and Oates

The Communication of the Gospel to Illiterates, Hans-Ruedi Weber, SCM for WCC

Dogmatic Constitution of the Church, Documents of Vatican II

The Freedom of the Son of Man, Paul and the Corinthians, and *In the Power of the Spirit* (Bible Study Guides for Group Discussion), A. C. Krass, E. P. Church, Ho, Ghana

God's Impatience in Liberia, Joseph Wold, Eerdmans

The Healing Church, WCC

Joint Action for Mission in Formosa, C. H. Hwang, Friendship for WCC

Katigondo, R. J. Ledogar (ed.)

Laity Mobilized, Neil Braun, Eerdmans

Mission and Message, Eugene Nida

New Forms of Ministry, David Paton (ed.), WCC

The Primal Vision, J. V. Taylor, SCM

The Spontaneous Expansion of the Church, Roland Allen, Eerdmans

Teaching all Nations, J. Hofinger

Understanding Church Growth, Donald McGavran, Eerdmans

The Village Pastor, Edward Ziegler, Agricultural Missions, New York

Worship and Mission, J. G. Davies

xi

DEDICATION

TO NANA DIBOLO
of the village of Mayamam
Northern Ghana

my close friend and the one who, more than anyone,
introduced me to the history and culture
of the Chokosi people

and

TO TOMMY
who has borne more than a little
of the cost

PART 1
MINISTRY AND MINISTRIES

---

1. The Meaning of Ministry and Ministries

This is a book about ministry. It *is* a book about what we often call *'the* ministry'. But it is about the ministry as related to the whole idea of 'ministry', and all that we mean by that word.

This is a book for ministers and ministerial candidates, as well as being a book for other sorts of people whose paid work is ministry in the Church. It is not a book for all ministers, however. All God's people are ministers, and it is not written for all of them. It is written for those whose special ministry it is to minister to the people of God in their ministry.

The idea of ministry which we find in the New Testament includes many different kinds of activity. Usually, however, the Church uses the word in a more limited way, to apply only to the ordained ministry. But to do this is to take the ordained ministry out of its proper context, which is the total ministry of the people of God.

In this book we shall be studying the ordained ministry within the context of ministry itself. Unless we do this we shall not fully understand the ordained ministry as the New Testament writers understood it. And only when the Church treats its ministers as part of that wider ministry can they properly fulfil the ministry for which they were ordained.

THE MEANING OF MINISTRY

'Who is greater,' Jesus asked His disciples when they were arguing on the subject of greatness, 'the one who sits down to eat or the one who serves him?'

'The one who sits down, of course,' He answered, referring to the way in which people usually think. 'But,' He went on, 'I am among you as one who serves' (Luke 22.27).

This was a difficult thing for the disciples to understand. They knew that Jesus was their Master and they were His disciples, but now *He* was serving *them*. The Greek word, which is translated here as 'serve', is the verb *diakoneo*, to serve. A *diakonos* is a servant. *Diakonia*, a closely related word which is sometimes translated 'service', is the word which New Testament writers used for 'ministry'. The Christian faith is the

1

only religious tradition in the world in which religious officials are described as 'servants', or 'ministers'.

Why do Christians do this? It is because we believe that Jesus did what He did as an example for us to follow. In the passage just quoted Jesus told His disciples, 'The kings of this world have power over their people. . . . But this is not the way it is with you; rather, the greatest one among you must be like the youngest, and the leader must be like the servant' (Luke 22.25–26).

In the parallel passage in John's gospel, we read that Jesus said to His disciples, 'You call me Teacher and Lord. And it is right that you do so because I am. I am your Lord and Teacher, and I have just washed your feet. You, then, should wash each other's feet. I have set an example for you so that you will do just what I have done for you' (John 13.13–16).

The reason why Christians call their leaders 'ministers' is because Jesus Himself took the role of a servant, and told His disciples to do the same. This command of Jesus, however, does not apply only to leaders in the Christian Church, it applies to all Christians. All Christians are called to ministry.

Whose ministers or servants are we? We are Christ's ministers, of course, just as the 'Prime Minister' is the Queen's 'first minister'. But we are also ministers or servants of one another, and of all whom we meet.

'Who is Apollos?' Paul asked the Corinthians. 'And who is Paul? We are simply God's servants . . . Each one of us does the work the Lord gave him to do' (1 Cor. 3.5). 'You should look on us,' he went on, 'as Christ's servants' (1 Cor. 4.1). But at another time Paul said, 'It is not ourselves that we preach: we preach Jesus Christ as Lord and ourselves as *your* servants for Jesus' sake' (2 Cor. 4.5).

There are thus three ways in which Christians are servants. We are servants (1) of God, (2) of our fellow Christians, and (3) of the world, i.e. of all human beings. We are, in every relationship, to follow the example of our Lord Jesus who, though 'He always had the very nature of God . . . gave it all up and took the nature of a servant. He became like man . . . He was humble and walked the path of obedience to death' (Phil. 2.6–8). 'We find our lives not by trying to save them but by losing them' (Matt. 10.35).

THE MEANING OF MINISTRIES

When we speak of ministry, then, we are speaking of something to which all Christians are called. 'All God's people,' the writer to the Ephesians says, are to be prepared for the work of Christian service, to build up the body of Christ' (Eph. 4.12). But within that body of Christ, which is the Church, different people are given different services (or ministries) to perform, so that all God's people may be prepared for Christian service.

God's wish in calling people to service in this way, is that the Church may thus 'grow and build itself up through love' (Eph. 4.16). His plan is nothing less than that He should 'bring all creation together, everything in heaven and on earth, with Christ as head' (Eph. 1.10). God has somehow, miraculously, chosen to do this through the channel of His Church, which the writer describes as 'Christ's body, the completion of him who himself completes all things everywhere' (Eph. 1.23).

The Church has an enormously difficult task to perform. The writer to the Ephesians said that 'all men' and even 'the angelic rulers and powers in the heavenly world' will come to 'know God's wisdom in all its different forms' 'by means of the Church' (Eph. 3.9–10). How can the Church complete this ministry if it is not 'built up'? How can the Church be prepared for it, without God's help? But God has helped it, we read, by 'giving gifts' to the Church. We read in Ephesians 4.14 that 'he appointed some to be apostles, others to be prophets, others to be evangelists, others to be pastors and teachers', in order to build up the body of Christ.

This is why we need to distinguish between 'ministries' and 'the ministry'. Within the total ministry of the Church there are special ministries. These change in the course of time. The list in Ephesians is not meant to be complete (see Rom. 12.4–8; 1 Cor. 12.4–11; and the Pastoral Letters; for other lists of ministries recognized in the New Testament). The ministry of 'apostle' is one special ministry. The ministry of 'prophet' is another. The ministry of 'evangelist' is still another.

Then comes the ministry of those referred to as 'pastors and teachers', which is probably the ministry of most readers of this book. Theirs is the ministry usually referred to today when people say, 'Philip has gone into the ministry,' or 'My uncle is a reverend minister.' This ministry, like all others, is a servant ministry in the service of God, and in the service of the Church, the body of Christ. It is a ministry which God has called into existence for the sake of His Church, 'to prepare all God's people for the work of Christian service, to build up the body of Christ'.

STUDY SUGGESTIONS

WORD STUDIES

1. What do the people in your Church mean by the following expressions:

(a) 'the minister'?

(b) 'a minister' or 'a reverend minister'?

(c) 'the ministry'?

3

2. (a) What is the meaning of the title 'Minister' as given to a high government official, e.g. 'the Minister of Finance' or 'the Minister of Social Welfare'?
   (b) Why do some governments refer to their executive departments as ministries'?
3. Does the Church use the word ministry' and 'minister' in the same sense in which governments use them? If not, what is the difference?
4. How is the English word 'minister' translated into your language? What is the original meaning of that word in your language?

REVIEW QUESTIONS

5. After whose ministry is the ministry of Christians patterned?
6. It has been said that those who enter the pastoral ministry belong to 'the order of the towel'. What do you think this means?
7. How would you explain the Christian idea of ministry to someone of another religion?
8. In what ways is the Christian idea of ministry related:
   (a) to God?
   (b) to the Church?
   (c) to the world?
9. What is the difference between 'ministry' and 'ministries'?

DISCUSSION AND RESEARCH TOPICS

10. If the Church has a ministry to the world, does this mean that it should do all that the world wants it to do? (See 2 Cor. 4.5) Give reasons for your answer.
11. What evidence is there that the New Testament writers regarded various ministries, or any among them, as full-time paid professional ministries? The following passages may help you to answer: Matt. 10.5–10; Acts 1.2–7; Acts 20.28–35; 1 Cor. 9.1–18; Phil. 4.10–12; 1 Tim. 3.1–8; 1 Tim. 5.3–19; 1 Peter 5.1–4.
12. If ministries are gifts of Christ to the Church, why do we need seminaries and theological faculties to train ministers?
13. Do you think that the word used to describe ordained ministers in your language fits the New Testament idea of the ministry well? Give your reasons.
14. Do you think that most ordained ministers regard themselves as servants of the Church or as its masters? Give examples to support your answer.
15. Why does the Church ordain ministers?

4

2. The Goal of the Church's Ministry

In the Letter to the Colossians there is a great deal of information about the Church's ministry. The writer discusses ministry in the total context of God's plan for the world, about which we read in Ephesians. It is important that the Church also should have a 'plan 'in mind for its ministry. What is the Church's goal in its ministry? What is its purpose? What do we ourselves hope may happen if our ministry is effective?

GOD'S PLAN

According to the Letter to the Colossians, God's plan is that 'every man should be brought into God's presence as a mature individual in union with Christ' (Col. 1.28). God's will to have fellowship with man is the basis of Christian mission. God wants all men to come into union with Himself. But the union which He wishes is with mature men. He does not want slaves but partners, and true partnership can only be between people who are free. The purpose of God's work in Christ is thus shown to be the freeing of humanity.

What is meant by this word 'free'? God created human beings free so that they should have dominion over the world He has created, and live in fellowship with Him. But when we look at the world we see that human beings have misused the power which God has given them. We have separated ourselves from Him, and as a result we are enslaved. We are slaves of 'the power of the spiritual rulers and authorities' (Col. 2.15), of the 'ruling spirits of the universe' (Col. 2.20), of 'this world' and of 'man made teachings' (Col. 2.20–22), of 'earthly desires' (Col. 3.5), of 'the old self with its habits' (Col. 3.9), of racial and national divisions (Col. 3.11), of 'the power of darkness' (Col. 1.13).

These are the names by which the Colossians knew the outward and inward 'powers' which had ruled their lives. Other peoples at other times in history may know them by other names. The point is this: the whole of humanity is enslaved, and the goal of God's work in Christ is that all should be freed. Christ, acting on our behalf, submitted to the powers that bind us. He allowed them to do their worst to Him, and then, by rising, showed that He had overcome them: 'On the Cross Christ freed himself from the power of the spiritual rulers and authorities; He made a public spectacle of them by leading them as captives in his victory procession' (Col. 2.15).

Christ's victory is our victory too: 'You have died with Christ and are set free from the ruling spirits of the universe' (Col. 2.20). By baptism

5

Christians share in Christ's victory. In Colossians baptism is understood as participation in Christ's death and resurrection (Col. 2.12). When a person is baptized, he is told: 'You have been raised to life with Christ' (Col. 3.1).

Note that it is for *life* that we have been raised; it is for *life* that we have been freed. As we have seen (p. 3), God's concern is first of all with this life. He wants us *now* to enjoy life in union with Him. It was in order to bring all people back into life in unity with Himself that He sent His Son to die. 'Through the Son God decided to bring the whole universe back to himself. God made peace through His Son's death on the Cross, and so brought back to himself all things, both on earth and in heaven' (Col. 1.21).

Thus the Church, in its ministry, is carrying out God's will that all creation should know His once-secret plan: that all people in this life should be freed and should come to mature fellowship in union with God, and that in eternity they should share His glory (Col. 1.27). This is the goal of God's action, in Christ and in the ministry and mission of the Church.

OUR GOAL

What then should be the goal of our ministry?

1. *First, that people will come to know themselves as those who are loved by God*, as those for whom God did not even spare His Son. They will know that He already loves them, as they are and whoever they are, before they themselves do anything at all. He loves them as members of their tribe, as Africans, as Melanesians. His love does not depend upon their becoming 'detribalized' or 'Europeanized' or 'civilized'.

2. *Second, that they will come to know themselves as those who have been enslaved,* as those who are not free, as those who do not live in mature partnership with God.

3. *Third, that they will come to see that whatever bound them before need not bind them any longer:* by Christ's death and resurrection they have been freed from all they fear.

4. *Fourth, they will come to see that they have been freed for life with God,* for life as mature, free men and women in partnership with God. They will come to see that in union with Jesus Christ they can come into maturity and experience freedom and abundant life.

5. *Fifth, by becoming baptized in Christ, they will say 'yes' to all that God has done for them in Christ,* and indicate their decision to live henceforth as free men in the service of God in the fellowship of His people.

The goal of the Church's ministry is thus much larger than the Church itself. It concerns the whole of creation. The Church is not called in its

6

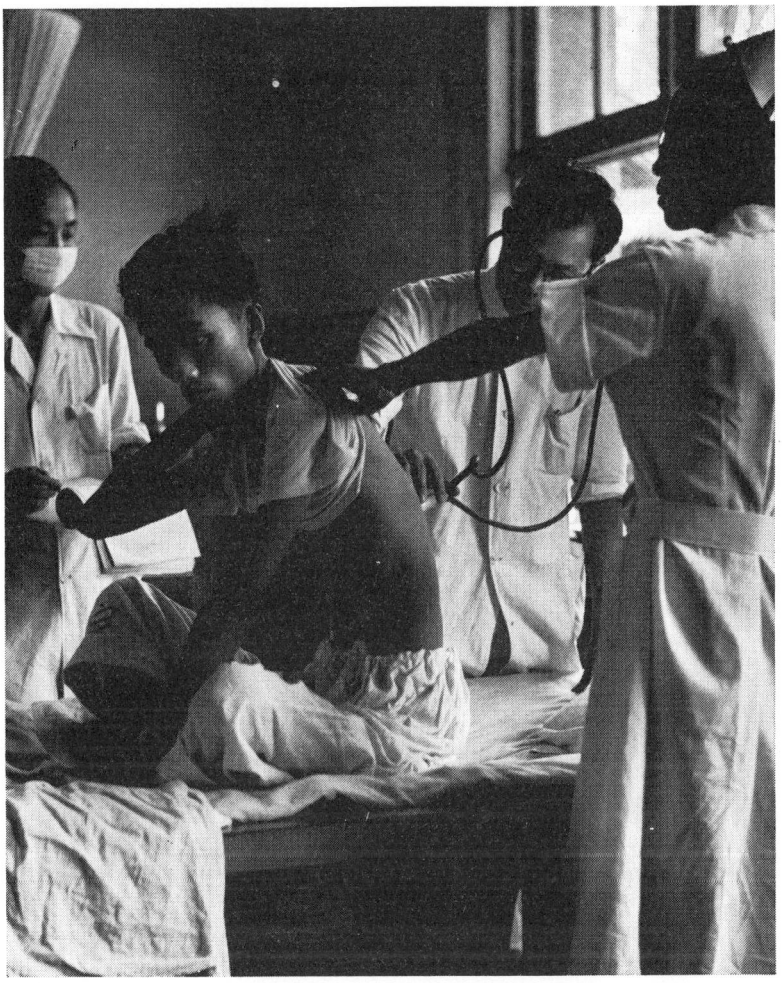

'The goal of ministry and mission is that people should be freed for life with God' (pp. 5, 6).

The goal of doctors and nurses in Taiwan is that people should be freed from crippling diseases like tuberculosis, and restored to life in the community.

In what ways is their goal and their work like—and unlike—our mission and ministry in the Church?

ministry to build itself up at the expense of the world, but to be built up for the sake of the world.

EXAMPLES OF MINISTRY

But what actually happens when the Church carries out its ministry? Has the Church always ministered in accordance with God's intention? We shall consider some examples of what *has* happened in different places where the Church has engaged in mission. The examples are fictional, but they are based on the reading of mission history.

SITUATION A

A strong pagan chief ruled the M—— tribe by means of force, inspiring fear in all his subjects, whom he kept in constant warfare with surrounding tribes. His will was law, and he and those in authority under him were held in awe—one might almost say that they were worshipped—by all his subjects.

A Christian mission was set up on the other side of the river from the chief's village. The chief hoped for personal gain from the N—— missionaries' presence, and so at first he was favourable to their being there. After a time it became clear to him that the missionaries were undermining his authority by, for example, giving shelter to those who fled from his punishment. He tried to force the missionaries out, but the missionaries called on the newly-established colonial government to defend them. This was the first time that the chief had experienced the force of colonial power, and he learned that it was something to be feared.

When the people saw how the chief was powerless, his authority over them weakened. More and more of them moved across the river and settled in the Christian village which the missionaries established. They sent their children to school, they farmed by new methods, and one by one they were all baptized and became members of the Church.

The missionaries and those who were in authority under them were held in awe by all the people. They developed a code of regulations for the village, and all who violated any law were disciplined.

Now what actually happened here? On the surface, it may seem that a tremendous transfer of allegiance took place. But when we look closer and ask what the people's allegiance was both before and after their conversion, we see that their conversion represented simply a transfer from absolute, unquestioning allegiance to the chief and his lieutenants, to absolute, unquestioning allegiance to the missionaries and their helpers. The M—— Christians did not become free, and they did not become mature and adult. They remained children, or slaves, but in another man's house. There was struggle, but it was not between the old nature of the people themselves and their new nature, it was between the old ruler and the new. Those who were ruled remained the same.

SITUATION B

The missionaries from the X—— Missionary Society were very proud of their work among the people of the Y—— tribe. They had baptized 17,000 people after only twenty years of work. Nearly every village had both a chapel and a school. The Y—— Christians sang Christian hymns with gusto, and, after only twenty years, they already supported much of the Church's work with their gifts and offerings and by means of large harvest festivals.

'In another twenty years,' the X—— missionaries reported to their home society, 'all the Y—— will be Christian. Polygamy is already decreasing, and paganism is disappearing rapidly.'

But members of the Y—— Church knew that things were not quite as the missionaries pictured them. Several of the Church members secretly had second wives—even some of the teachers did. And elders from the congregations were among those who went by night to diviners, and who made secret contributions of sacrificial animals to the priests of the earth for the annual fertility rites. Fathers took their children to Muslim medicine men for charms to help them with their school examinations.

What actually happened in this situation? Very little. Those who became Christian merely adopted a new 'religion', or rather ways of worship, which they added to the religion and customs which they practised already. There was no struggle, no break with the past. The Christian religion was merely added to what went before. The whole tribe could thus very easily become half-Christian and half-pagan, or 'Christo-pagan'.

SITUATION C

The missionaries from the Q—— mission laboured long years among the people of R—— with little success. After seventy-five years they had only 800 converts, but they were not discouraged. Their converts were all 'model Christians.' Most of them wore European dress. They all attended school, and many had gone through secondary school or the government teacher-training college. Many held positions of leadership in the civil service, and the R—— Christians were beginning to form a new middle class in the nation of S——. One had become a theologian in the university divinity faculty. The missionaries could confidently say that there were no polygamists or backsliders among them.

In 1957 one of the teacher-catechists of the Church claimed that he had had a 'revelation'. He started to gather people in his house for prayer meetings and services of healing. Some of the Christians came, at first secretly but then openly. Many of the illiterate pagans joined the movement. The catechist, who now called himself a 'prophet', baptized them, even those who were polygamists. They adopted many of the taboos of the Old Testament, and they experienced trances and spirit-possession. Within five years the movement numbered 5,000 adherents. The prophet called his Church 'The First African Assembly of the Saints of Zion, Ltd'. The members shared all their possessions and no one was in need.

What actually happened in this situation? The members of the mission Church became separate from their previous allegiances, but only by becoming not only Christianized but also Europeanized. There was both struggle and conversion: individual converts were won through painstaking decisions, long education, and the adoption of a completely different way of life. But the way of life was so different from that of the converts' parents and fellow tribesmen that few were able to adapt themselves to it. If it was necessary to become a European in order to become a Christian, then that was more than most people were able to do, or should have had to do. In other words, the people's unwillingness did not mean that they were unwilling to become Christian, for many flocked to the new Christian 'prophetic' movement. This movement, also, made great demands on them. But it spoke more to their needs and values than the mission Church did. A conversion took place in their lives, but it was limited in one respect: the people remained legalists, and instead of pagan taboos and customs, the members of the prophet's Church adopted Christian ones.

THE RESULTS OF MINISTRY

These three examples raise the question: what different sorts of results occur when the Gospel has been preached? What has been the result of the Church's ministry? Should something happen to man when he hears the message and believes? Obviously the answer is 'yes', but what?

Can we call preaching successful if its results are that a Church is planted, regardless of what type of Church? It is always right to baptize people, regardless of what their baptism means to them? Is the purpose of mission to register people's names in the Church's baptismal register and declare that X is a Presbyterian or Christian village?

The answer seems to be that our hope in ministering to the world, our hope in preaching the Gospel, is that by our ministry and by our preaching, people will be freed from their slavery to alien powers and self, and thus will be free to serve God. Our hope is that men will be freed from fear and death and selfishness, and will come to receive life.

Our hope is that men will be freed to participate in God's mission of liberation, and that they themselves will become missionaries of liberation to the world.

This is very different from the way in which many Christians and missionaries think about the Church. We often seem to think that the Church is an end in itself, and that missionary work is the way in which more members are added to it. According to this view, the world is simply the lake in which missionaries and ministers fish, from which they draw fish to place into a new artificial pond, called the Church. In this view, the goal of the fishing is to increase the number of fish in the pond, and the life which they have with one another in the pond is the goal of the activity, i.e. mission is for the sake of the Church.

But we have already seen (p. 6) that this 'fishpond' ideal of ministry and conversion is thoroughly wrong. Mission is not for the sake of the Church, it is for the sake of the world. The goal of mission, in other words, is not the Church, but the world. The Church is not an end in itself. The Church exists only for mission. The Church *is* mission. As Emil Brunner has said, 'The Church exists by mission as fire exists by burning.' If there is no mission, then there is no Church!

God's plan for the world is not that the Church will be saved. God's plan is rather to use the Church for the salvation of the world. When a man is saved, he is saved *from* the power of evil *for* the service of God. Mission which does not lead to discipleship is an abortion. Discipleship which does not take the form of mission is stillborn. Mission is the process of making more disciples to participate in mission. 'There is a great harvest, but few labourers to gather it in,' Jesus told His disciples. 'Pray to the owner of the harvest that he will send out more workers to gather in his harvest' (Matt. 9.37f).

J. C. Hoekendijk expressed the meaning of mission very well when he gave one of his books the title *The Church Inside Out*. If the Church is turned in upon itself it is not the Church of the self-emptying Lord Jesus Christ. The Church is only faithful to its Lord when it is turned outward, towards the world.

The goal of the ordained ministry within the Church is thus to make the Church better able to reach out to others. The minister serves the Church. But he does not serve the Church best by helping it to become a self-serving religious institution. He helps it, rather, to become its true self: a minister to the world for Jesus' sake.

We can see this same truth in the world of politics. Kwame Nkrumah understood the meaning of mission and ministry well when he said in 1957, as Ghana became independent, that 'the independence of Ghana is meaningless unless it is linked to the independence of all Africa.' We in the Church can learn from this. Our salvation as Christians is meaningless unless it is linked to the salvation of all mankind.

11

A man who has truly become free in Christ will want all others to share his freedom. He will not be happy so long as one other person is still enslaved by powers other than God.

The Church which sets itself up over against 'pagan' society, and feels superior to it has not been fully liberated. It is still serving itself. Pride is a wrong attitude for the disciples of the One who wept over the people of Jerusalem because they did not know where their true peace would come from (Luke 19.41–43). The Christian's goal is not just to win the prize for himself, but to bring all men to the prize of life with God in Christ. As we read in Colossians: 'We warn and teach everyone, with all possible wisdom, in order to bring each one into God's presence as a mature individual in union with Christ' (Col. 1.28).

STUDY SUGGESTIONS

WORD STUDY

1. How would you explain the idea of 'salvation' to someone of another religion?

REVIEW QUESTIONS

2. (a) What is the goal of the Church's ministry?
   (b) In what way is the ministry of the ordained minister related to this goal?

DISCUSSION AND RESEARCH TOPICS

3. (a) What if anything was wrong with the ministry of the Church in Situation A described on p. 8? In situation B on p. 9? In Situation C on p. 9?
   (b) What, if anything, could be done to change those situations for the better?
   (c) Which, if any, of these 3 example situations most nearly resembles what has happened in your own Church?
4. (a) What happens to a man when he is saved?
   (b) Some people believe that if a man is 'saved', then he can never sin again. What is your opinion?
5. What sorts of things do some pastors do, which may encourage people to have a wrong understanding of ministry and salvation?
6. If a Church runs a hospital or school, should its own members be given preference over non-Christians in getting an education or medical treatment there? Give reasons for your answer.
7. Do we minister to others only by preaching, or also by our actions? In what ways, if any, can a person's behaviour proclaim the Gospel?

3. The Source of Power for Ministry

We have considered what ministry is, and what is its purpose. Now we ask: What is the power behind ministry? How does it happen that when Christian ministers preach, people hear and believe and respond, and find new life in Christ? How does it happen that God's plan is fulfilled? Is it as a result of effective human strategies? Is it as a result of well-thought-out programmes? Is it a response to effective preaching? Is it the result of conscientious ministry? Does it arise out of self-sacrificing service?

THE MIRACLE-WORKING POWER OF GOD

The answer in every case is that it is the work of God. We cannot know exactly what happens. We only know that it does happen. It remains a mystery to us. It is the work of the Holy Spirit, the miracle-working power of God.

Just as we can only understand the creation as a miracle, so we can only understand man's re-creation as miraculous.

People awake to new life, to love, joy, peace, patience, kindness, goodness, faithfulness, humility, and self-control. This is the fruit of the Spirit. From start to finish the working of ministry is the work of the Holy Spirit. God's word does not return empty, it accomplishes its purpose:

> For as the rain and the snow come down from heaven and return
> not thither but water the earth,
> making it bring forth and sprout,
> giving seed to the sower and bread to the eater,
> so shall my word be that goes forth from my mouth;
> it shall not return to me empty,
> but it shall accomplish that which I purpose,
> and prosper in the thing for which I sent it. (Isa. 55.10f)

Ministry inspired, carried out, and fulfilled by the working of the Holy Spirit, bears fruit:

> For you shall go out in joy and be led forth in peace,
> the mountains and the hills before you shall break forth into singing,
> and all the trees of the field shall clap their hands.
> Instead of the thorn shall come up the cypress;
> Instead of the briar shall come up the myrtle;
> and it shall be to the Lord for a memorial,
> for an everlasting sign which shall not be cut off. (Isa. 55.11f)

13

'As the rain and snow water the earth, making it bring forth . . . so shall my word be . . . it shall accomplish that which I purpose' (Isa. 55.10).

This man lives in Bengal. For millions of people like him the greatest problem is how to get enough water to enable them to bring forth a harvest from the earth.

What sort of 'water' do Christian ministers need today to enable them to accomplish God's purpose? What sort of 'harvest' do they hope to bring forth?

The power behind the mission is God's own power. The sucess of the mission is the work of God's Holy Spirit. That is why Paul begins almost every one of his letters with thanks to God. In what has happened to the Churches, in their faith, and hope, and love, he can only see the work of God. He expressed these thanks in writing to the Corinthians:

> I always give thanks to my God for you, because of the grace he has given you through Christ Jesus. For in union with Christ you have become rich in all things, including all speech and all knowledge. The message about Christ has become so firmly fixed in you that you have not failed to receive a single blessing, as you wait for our Lord Jesus Christ to be revealed. He will also keep you firm to the end, so that you will be found without fault in the Day of our Lord Jesus Christ. God is to be trusted, the God who called you to have fellowship with His son, Jesus Christ, our Lord. (1 Cor. 1.4–9)

And yet we have to recognize that the response to our ministry is not the same at all times, or in all places. In some places response is immediate, in other places it comes slowly. In still other places it does not seem to occur at all. Among some tribes, movements of whole peoples to the Gospel take place: in other tribes only single households or individual people become Christian. In some tribes the movement, once started, grows steadily, or even by leaps and bounds; in others the first response slowly diminishes, and the Church no longer grows. In any one tribe, work done at one time in history may bear no fruit, but the same sort of work done twenty years later may bring forth great response.

It is not easy to explain why Christian ministry has different results at different times and in different places. If it is God's will that all men should be saved, and come to a knowledge of the truth (1 Tim. 2.4) why is the response not the same everywhere and at every time? We must look in two directions for the answer: (1) to the work of the Holy Spirit and (2) to our ministries.

THE WORK OF THE HOLY SPIRIT

The Holy Spirit works at different times in different places.

Those historians who try to find secular or historical reasons why the Christian faith grew so rapidly in the first centuries, point to a number of factors:

(a) the Roman Empire had brought peace to a wider area than had ever enjoyed peace at one time in history before.

(b) The *koine* form of Greek was a *lingua franca* (common language) throughout the Eastern Mediterranean; this made it easy to communicate ideas throughout a large area.

(c) Jews had gone out from Palestine to settle in every important city centre in the Eastern Mediterranean, thus providing a natural bridge of contacts for the early Jewish Christian missionaries;

(d) There was widespread discontent among the peoples of the Roman Empire with traditional Greek and Roman polytheistic religion. People were looking for 'something more'; many of them had attached themselves to the Jewish synagogues as 'God-fearers', and worshipped regularly with the Jews because they felt that the Jews' worship of one God was superior, and because they admired the Jews' ethical principles.

(e) Palestine, and Jerusalem in particular, were at a crossroads of commerce and communication, between Asia, Africa, and Europe.

Christians today might say that the reason why the Christian faith spread so rapidly was because of the work of the Holy Spirit, and that these other factors were not important. Some may feel that God does not need any favourable conditions for the spread of His Word. because He is able to make the very stones cry out in praise of Him (Luke 19.40). And that is true.

But we ought also to remember what we read in Colossians, about God's 'plan'—how it had been hidden from the beginning of time until just then, when God had revealed it. Why had He revealed it just then? Some Christians say that God chose that time because conditions in the world were such that people were ready to accept the Gospel. Others say that God was Himself at work in creating those conditions.

Whichever reason we give, it is not taking away from the power of God's word or from the truly creative act of the Holy Spirit. *What we are affirming is that the Holy Spirit does not work apart from the conditions of any given time and place, but within those conditions.* Some times are more favourable to His working than other. At any given time the conditions in some places are more favourable to His working than the conditions in other places. Or, to put it the other way round, the Holy Spirit works in different ways at different times and in different places, not in the same way at the same time in every place. That is what is meant in the Book of Acts where it is reported that the apostles were not permitted by the Spirit to preach in the provinces of Asia or Bithynia, but were shown that they should go to Macedonia (Acts 16.6–10). The time was not ripe for the mission to the provinces of Asia, and Paul and his partners were bound in obedience not to work there against the Spirit's will. It was not long afterwards that the time *was* ripe, and then Paul went to Ephesus and laboured long and fruitfully.

Every work is to be done at its own time. The Spirit has a plan. In seeking to carry out our ministry we must be responsive to the promptings of the Spirit, to discern where He is working and calling us to be, and where He is calling us to lay the work aside for a time. The promise stands: 'My word shall not return to me empty,' but those engaged in preaching the Word, who have received that promise, must preach it in accordance with God's plan. Provided that they do this, God promises them that their work will be fruitful.

OUR MINISTRIES

Our ministries must be responsive to the workings of the Spirit, and to the conditions of the times and places in which we minister. If we see that our work of mission is not bearing fruit, and yet we are convinced that it is God's will that we should be working in that place at that time, then we need to examine the way in which we are working. We are only the servants of the Lord, and the work is His, not ours. But even as His servants we are called to participate *responsibly* in his mission. He does not demand that we follow any special timetable or work plan. All He does is to give us gifts for ministry. He leaves it to us to discern prayerfully how and when and where to use those helps, with His promise 'I will be with you, even to the end of the age' (Matt. 28.20).

The point is this: the Spirit gives gifts which enable men to perform ministries, so we can say that these ministries are in fact given by the Spirit. In other words, He who commissions the Church to engage in mission, also gives men the ministries through which they will build up and equip the Church to minister to others.

Our responsibility is thus clear. We must use the gifts which God has given us, in ministries which he has given us, in order to fulfil the task of mission. If our work is not bearing fruit, we must ask ourselves whether we are using these ministries responsibly and faithfully.

If, for example, the Church takes a man who has the gift of apostolate and uses him for the work of administration, that Church is being unfaithful. If we take a man who has the gift of administration and use him for the work of raising funds, we are being unfaithful.

Similarly, if a man who knows that he has the gift of preaching does not exercise that gift, but instead spends all his time in being a pastor or teacher, he himself is being unfaithful. If he has the gift of directing other people but instead fancies himself an evangelist, he is not acting responsibly towards God, who has not chosen to give him that gift.

And of course a man who has been given any gift of ministry and chooses to use it for his own personal gain, or refuses to use it at all because he is leading a dissolute and immoral life, then he is destroying the work of God. Similarly, if a Church regards its own existence, wealth, and power as the supreme goal of its life, then it is not being faithful to its Lord, who emptied Himself (Phil. 2.7) and said: 'I am among you as one who serves' (Luke 22.27).

It is not always easy to recognize our own best talents, and circumstances may make it difficult for us to exercise them. But we must honestly examine ourselves, and the work we are doing, from time to time, to make sure that it really is God's work, and not just our own.

We must recognize also that, just as the Holy Spirit does not work in exactly the same way at all times and in all places, so the ministry of the Church will be different in different places at different times. *There is no one pattern for ministry. Rather we are responsible to use the ministries which we have been given creatively in each new situation.* We need to examine the society we live in, and consider the resources which God has given us, and then fit these resources creatively to our particular situation.

STUDY SUGGESTIONS

WORD STUDY

1. (a) What do you understand by the word 'power'?
   (b) Give examples from everyday life to show three different sorts of power and the ways in which they are used.

REVIEW QUESTIONS

2. What is the relationship between the Spirit and the life of the Church?
3. In what ways can the Church exercise proper stewardship of the gift of ministry which the Spirit has given it?
4. (a) Is there any evidence in the New Testament to suggest that the Church's ministries will always bear fruit?
   (b) If our ministries do not bear fruit, in what two directions ought we to look in order to discover the reason for this and to find ways of making them bear fruit?
5. What is our responsibility with regard to the different conditions in which we are called to exercise our ministry?

DISCUSSION AND RESEARCH TOPICS

6. (a) How important do you think it is for a Church to have an effective strategy for its ministry? Give examples to support your answer.
   (b) What happens if a Church has no such strategy?
7. (a) Can the Church in New Guinea or Tanzania expect to be able to use a good programme of mission which has been developed in Nigeria? Give reasons for your answer.
   (b) Give examples, if you can, of any problems which have arisen in the history of the own Church as a result of following 'imported' programmes of mission.

4. Ordination

Before we go on to see how we can match our approach to ministry to the peoples to whom we go, there are a few remaining points to consider, chiefly on the question of ordination. None of the ministries we have been studying *has* to be a professional ministry. None of them *demands* to be exercised by a fully-trained 'priest' or 'clergyman' or a paid 'evangelist', 'pastor', or 'catechist'. Each Church has to decide for itself which ministries, if any, are so urgent or important that they want to set people aside from all other work, and support them in these ministries by their gifts.

There are no set rules in the New Testament about paying people for their ministry. What rules are there about ordaining them? Ordination is the rite by which the Church sets apart, as ordained ministers, people whom it believes to be qualified for the ministry of Word and Sacrament. The laying on of hands on the ordinand's head does not mean that power or blessing is imparted: it means that he (or she) is solemnly set aside and ordained for that particular ministry. The corporate ordained ministry of the Church, acting either together or through a bishop, uses its authority to declare that authority is being given to exercise the same ministry which they have.

The main purpose of ordination is proper order. Most Churches do not limit preaching of the Word to those who have been ordained. And many Churches limit administration of the sacraments to ordained pastors, not for any theological reason, but only for reasons of order, i.e. to make sure that the sacraments are not abused.

THE FREEDOM OF THE SPIRIT

But none of this necessarily means either (a) that an ordained minister has to be a full-time paid official of the Church, or (b) that seminary or theological education is a requirement for ordination. Churches decide on practical grounds, not theological ones, who is to be ordained, and whether ordained clergy are to be paid or not.

Because no fixed pattern for the exercise of the Church's ministry is laid down in the New Testament, those Churches which lay down no absolutely fixed pattern will be those most responsible to the Spirit. As a human society, the Church is bound to take the form of an institution, i.e. it will have structure, it will have traditions, it will have customs, and from time to time it will make regulations and recognize established procedures. But the structure which the Church finds useful in one place and at one time will be different from the structure which it may need at other times or in other places. The Church takes institutional forms, but primarily it is an event rather than an institution. The Church is what *happens* in the creative meeting between God and His people. The Holy Spirit creates the Church as He encounters men and women, creates faith in them, and moves them to ministry.

Methodist hymns do not make the Methodist Church. The Presbyterian form of Church government does not create the Presbyterian Church. The Roman Catholic mass does not make the Roman Catholic Church. The Church is created by the Holy Spirit. He is its Lord. These are merely the forms which the faith and practice of the different denominations have taken in response to Him. If these forms become absolute and fixed, in any Church, it means that the Church is failing in its allegiance to the Holy Spirit, and refusing to acknowledge His lordship over its life.

The Church is something that happens, it is not something that can be pointed to or fixed. As soon as we try to imprison the happening in rigid forms, the life goes out of them. The Spirit thrives on freedom. The aim of His activity in the Church is to create life in God's people (Rom. 8.2).

The Southern Ghanaian Christians who settled in the Northern Ghana town of Chereponi prized their Presbyterian forms of Church life highly. They felt a concern to share the Gospel with the Chokosi people in whose area they lived, but they expected that if the Chokosis were to become Christian then certain things would happen. First, they expected that the Chokosis would come to their services in their chapel at 9.30 every Sunday morning. They expected them to sit on benches facing the front of the room (and each other's backs), sing European hymns, dress for services in the way in which Southern Ghanaian Christians dressed, and give offerings of money rather than goods. And they expected that the Chokosis would send their children to school, bury their dead in coffins, use European wine for communion, elect presbyters, form women's Bible classes, establish choirs which would dress in Southern Ghanaian (i.e. European) choir gowns, remain quiet upon entering the chapel, listen in silence to the sermons preached, and appoint people for the ordained ministry. They further expected that these ministers would dress in Geneva gowns and bands.

This was Christianity in the form in which Southern Ghanaians had known it. But for them to expect that Christianity among the Chokosis would take those identical forms, was to place undue limits upon the Holy Spirit. Some of the forms were good, and the Chokosis adopted them. But not one of these forms was laid down in Scripture as a form which the Church must take wherever it is found. To lay down all those conditions, based upon Southern Ghanaian Christian and European Christian customs, would have been to place obstacles in the way of the Holy Spirit. It would have been to demand that any Chokosi who became a Christian would have to become a Southern Ghanaian Christian.

Thus we see again that the Holy Spirit is the power behind Christian mission. He builds up the Church so that it may take part in mission. The Church must be responsive to His working and His leading. Although there is no one plan for mission and ministry everywhere and at all times, there is one Spirit who enables people to exercise ministry at all times and in each place.

THE ROLE OF THE ORDAINED MINISTER

As we have noted (p. 2), Christianity is the only religion which designates its officials or leaders as 'servants'. This idea of a servant ministry is difficult for the Church to communicate and for people to understand when the Church is being planted for the first time in a new culture. It is even difficult in cultures where the Church has existed for centuries. We have already considered one of the problems as a study question: What is the name by which the minister is designated in the local language? Is it appropriate to the New Testament idea of ministry?

In Ghana, the name given to a Christian minister has been an Akan word which is also used for the priest of a traditional divinity or 'fetish'. The 'fetish priest' was the one who performed sacrifices to the divinity. His role was that of a mediator between the divinity and the people who worshipped it.

Much of this traditional meaning became attached to the Ghanaian idea of the Christian minister. The Church did not *intend* this to happen. Indeed, the first Church to use this term was a Presbyterian Church, and Presbyterians do not think of their ministers as mediators—Presbyterian ministers are not 'priests'. Nevertheless, the use of the word encouraged the people—and even some ministers—to regard themselves as 'Christian fetish priests'. They simply interpreted the minister's role in the way for which their culture had prepared them. This sort of inaccurate 'translation' of Christian terms has hindered understanding in many language areas.

The Reverend C. K. Dovlo, Moderator of the Evangelical Presbyterian Church in Ghana, has asked a number of questions about the ways in which the people interpret the role of the ordained minister, e.g.:

(a) Does ordination confer certain graces without which the ministers' functions are invalid or ineffective? Or is the ordination just a means of giving ordained ministers special authority to perform certain tasks within the total ministry of all believers?

(b) How do the newly converted people look upon their ordained ministers? Do they think of them as being like the old fetish priest who has complete control over the people, including the chiefs, and whose powers are moral and spiritual as well as physical?

(c) How can ordained ministers prevent their congregations from looking on them as the source of everything? In what ways should they train the lay members of the Church to take a full share in all the activities of the Church?

How shall we today approach this problem? How can we explain to people that, though the Church allows only ordained clergy to administer the sacrament, this does not mean that ordained ministers have a 'supernatural power' to impart 'holiness' to the elements? Our present practices involve us in deep cultural problems. If we cannot change our practice, then we need at least to be aware of the problems we are creating, so that we can deal with them.

Nothing is easier than for ordained ministers to become the Christians' fetish priests, those who can 'make things holy' and mediate divinity. Ministers can only avoid this by strictly refusing to become such priests, and by constant attention to building up the spiritual power of the laity, not their own power over them. But even then people may regard them as European magicians.

The Church needs to make its theology of the sacraments quite clear. It needs to explain its theology of the ministry to the people in language they can understand. But, no matter what we explain in principle, the most important question is this: Will ordained ministers *act* like Christian fetish priests? Or, will they, by consistently and convincingly *sharing* their ministry with God's people, put aside all doubts that they are really 'the servants of the Servants of God'? Will they show that their ministry is to the people of God in their ministry to mankind as the body of Christ. The rest of this book gives examples of ways in which they can do this.

STUDY SUGGESTIONS

Word Study

1. Which of the following words would you use to explain what is meant by 'institutional'?

> static progressive responsive established
> dynamic immutable systematic organized
> lively flexible fixed

Review Questions

2. (a) What is meant by saying that the Church in its fullest meaning is an 'event' or 'happening', and not an institution?

(b) Would it be possible to have a Church which did not have an institutional form?

(c) In what ways can the Church guard against becoming too rigid or fixed in its institutional forms?

3. Compare what has been said in this chapter to the record of the 'Council of Jerusalem' in Acts 15.1–35.

DISCUSSION AND RESEARCH TOPICS

4. (a) What does your Church teach concerning the role of ordained ministers and the meaning of their ordination?
   (b) Do most of the Christians in your Church understand this teaching?
5. Give examples of some of the things that ministers do, which give people wrong ideas about the true nature of ministry.
6. Read Acts 14.8–18.
   (a) What is your opinion of the event described?
   (b) Did the disagreement between the elders and the disciples arise because of cultural differences between them?
   (c) Have you experienced similar problems of misunderstanding about the role of the Christian minister in your culture, or in the culture in which you are working?
   (d) How can such problems be overcome?
7. For what reasons are ministers sometimes tempted to accept the role which people of other religions or other cultures assign to them?
8. What is 'cultural imperialism', and what does our faith in the Holy Spirit say about it? Give examples to support your answer.

PART 2
MINISTRY TO WHOM?

5. Societies and Individuals

In Part 1 we discussed ministry and ministries. We saw that the whole Church is called to ministry in Christ's name. Our calling is to be servants of God in Christ. In our different ministries, we are servants of one another in the Church, and servants of those to whom Christ sends us out.

In Part 1, we were thinking chiefly about ourselves as Christians. In Part 2 we shall think less about ourselves and more about those to whom we are sent out. The question we shall try to answer is: To whom are we called to minister in the world? As in Part 1 we tried to understand ourselves better, so in this Part we shall try to understand the world better.

Some people may say that this is not a problem at all. The world, they may say, consists of the individual people who live in it: all the millions of Kofis and Kwames and Kojos, of Amas, and Akosuas, and Abenas, of Johns, and Susans, and Philips.

When I was sent to work in Northern Ghana, at first I looked at the people of Chereponi District in that way. Chereponi District consisted, I thought, of 25,000 individuals. I was called to minister to them. Forty of them were Christians, about 1,500 were Muslims, and the rest practised an African traditional religion. I regarded them as separate and distinct individuals.

It was true that they lived in 112 different towns and villages, but I didn't think that was particularly significant. That just happened to be where the different individuals lived, where I would find them. It was true that most of their houses contained many more people than the houses with which I was familiar in the United States. But I didn't see any particular significance in that, either. It was true that many of the men were polygamists, and that children of different mothers called one another 'brother' or 'sister'. But I didn't see what that had to do with my presentation of the Gospel to them. Whether two men who called each other 'brother' had the same mother or not didn't seem to make any difference as to how I would minister to them—each, I thought, was a separate individual.

I thus showed that I was a Westerner. I looked at Chokosi and Konkomba society through the spectacles with which European society

24

had provided me. As a European I believed that 'society' was always made up of many distinct individuals, or perhaps of small units (e.g. 'nuclear' families each consisting of one father, one mother, and their children). I was unable to see the wood, as the proverb goes, for the trees.

COMMUNITIES WITHIN SOCIETY

To the people of a particular village, however, that village is usually neither a collection of individuals nor of individual nuclear families.

Let us imagine a village called, say, Tandara. If Tandara is made up of one local clan, then its people see it as a unit. If Tandara is made up of segments of two or three local clans, they see it as a unit with two or three subdivisions. And the important thing is this: the way in which the people see their village's structure will affect the ways in which they behave. If Tandara is one, its people act as one. If Tandara is made up of two or three parts, then on some occasions they will act as separate units and on some occasions, when all the separate units are involved, they will act as one village, as a unity.

If I am to minister to the people of Tandara, I will need to understand how they see themselves. As one sent out to minister to the people of Tandara, I have a responsibility to try to understand what Tandara is. If I do not understand the people I will not be able to minister effectively to them. I will make assumptions which I should not make, and fail to make connections which I ought to make.

I remember that, after we baptized the Chokosi village of Famisa, I told the people they should appoint presbyters. I read out the characteristics recommended for Church leaders in 1 Timothy 3, and asked the villagers to select out of their number those whom they felt could serve well. Then, I said, we would vote. I asked for nominations. The chief turned to the elder of his own local clan and said 'Should we appoint Sanda to stand for us?' The elder agreed. He then turned to the head of another local clan 'Ananji, who will stand for the Fombolo people?'

I stopped him. 'You don't seem to understand,' I said. 'You are to appoint two men for the first twenty communicants and one man for every other twenty communicants. The clans and houses don't matter. There are forty male communicants in this congregation. You get three presbyters. Anyone can be nominated; and everyone will vote, and those who get the most votes will serve for a trial year.'

The chief did not understand. Nor did he try very hard. He continued to proceed as before. One man was chosen by each section of the village and no others were nominated. There was no vote. Unbelieving, I said to the people, 'Do you all agree with those who have been chosen?' They looked at me, wondering why I was so dull.

And I was dull. I just didn't see Famisa the way they did. I still thought it was a collection of individuals. I didn't realize it was a village with three parts. I didn't know what these parts were, local clans, nor how they were related to each other as a village. *The Village* had been baptized, not just the individual people. And the village, as a congregation of the Church, would be led as the village had always been led, by representatives of each of its three local clans. That was the only way in which an effective local Church council could be formed in Famisa. To try to break down these units into a collection of separate individuals, and then vote, would have been to break up the customary social structure of Famisa into an unworkable confusion. The people were very sensible when they had refused to listen to me.

A couple of months earlier, in the nearby village of Mayamam, something similar had happened. The catechist had said the people were ready to be baptized and I went to see whether this was so. 'Are you all ready to be baptized?' I asked the old headman.

'Yes,' old Dibolo replied. 'They are ready.'

'What do you mean by saying "they"?' I asked. 'Aren't you, the head, included?'

'Oh, I'm too old!' he said

'Are you too old to get out of this room if it catches on fire?' I asked.

'No, no!' he quickly replied, laughing loudly. 'I would get out!'

I convinced him he wasn't too old to be baptized, either. Anyone who repented and wanted to attach himself to Christ as Saviour and seek the new life could be baptized, no matter what his age.

Dibolo called his nephew. 'Nana,' he commanded, 'go and tell Baba and Duti and Yayu that we're all going to be baptized.'

'No, no!' I objected. 'We've only been talking about you. How can you decide for the other elders?'

He looked at me through his old blind eyes, not understanding me. He was the headman of a village which consisted of a single local clan. When he decided to do something, he made the decision on behalf of the whole village. He knew the needs of the village and the feelings of the other elders, and if he made a decision, he did it because he knew it was a good decision for the whole village. The village had always acted as one. In becoming Christian, it would continue to act as one.

As it turned out, Baba, the third elder, for personal reasons of conscience, was not baptized, but his whole house was. And even though Baba was never baptized, he always attended service and, when the congregation wanted to build a chapel, he gave a large pig to be sold to buy some roofing sheets. He was a member of Mayamam, and if Mayamam as a whole had become a Christian village, he was part of its Christianity, even though he did not himself feel able to become a Christian.

26

After my experiences in Mayamam and Famisa, I thought I had learned my lessons well. At that time we were getting good results in Sobiba, a village of the Konkomba tribe. I decided therefore to find out whether the village was ready for baptism. I was quite confident that they were, because I had developed a close personal relationship with the chief, and it was obvious that he had accepted the Gospel with all his heart and soul. He had already been to one of our Church synods, and he had been very much impressed with the fellowship which he saw on that occasion between people of different tribes and nations. He also responded readily to our Bible lessons, and was always the first to answer the comprehension questions I addressed to the group.

So I asked the question: 'Are you Sobiba people ready to begin baptismal instruction??' I then turned expectantly to the chief. He looked around. He looked at the ground. He looked at the other elders. He looked back to me. 'You know my heart,' he said.

'And what about the rest of you?' I asked, turning to the group, expecting them to say: 'You have heard our chief speak, Why do you ask us?' But it didn't happen. They looked around. They looked at the ground. One young man said: 'I will be baptized,' and nobody else said a word! If we had actually enrolled them that day, the only people to come forward would have been the chief, his three brothers, that young man, and perhaps their wives! That would have been all.

Then I began to understand that Sobiba—and all Konkomba villages —were very different from Chokosi villages. The basic unit of which the village was composed was the individual household or a group of two or three households. No decisions could be made at a higher level than those units. The chief could speak for no one except perhaps his own household. He was *obor* (chief), which we thought meant the same thing as *feme*, the Chokosi word for 'chief', but the two words were not the same at all! An *obor* was really just a 'moderator'. When outsiders spoke to him, they didn't speak directly to the village, as sometimes happened in Chokosi villages, but they spoke *through* him *to* the village, which had no overall unity. It had several separate points of authority rather than one centre.

VILLAGE STRUCTURES

If, in later years, an anthropologist looks at our baptismal register, it will help him to understand the structure of the various village communities in which we worked.

In three cases, whole villages were baptized. Two of these were villages which consisted of a single local clan, and the third, Famisa, was a village in which the three local clans were able to act with considerable unity in their response to the Gospel.

27

In other villages, all of our baptisms were of several whole houses, but of houses grouped together on one side of a road or on one end of the village's land. At the time I didn't understand why this was so; but what had happened was that in these cases we had baptized local *clans*.

In yet other villages, baptisms were of individual houses, scattered here and there. In those villages there were no strong local clans, and no strong chieftaincy. And in Konkomba villages the baptisms were of individuals, mostly of women and young men, because the elders had all rejected baptism and therefore their houses could not function as units.

I shudder to think, when I recall those first years, how many mistakes we made, how much time we wasted, and how many people may have found it difficult to accept the Gospel because of the ignorant way in which we ministered to them. It would have been much easier if I had, at the start, simply taken the trouble to learn how Chokosi and Konkomba societies functioned.

STUDY SUGGESTIONS

Word Study

1. Write a short sentence about each of the following so as to describe the differences between them.

   families   clans   households

2. If possible investigate the titles used in different languages in your area which are translated by a single English word such as *chief* or *headman*. Do the words translated in this way mean the same thing in each language, or are there differences?

Review Questions

3. In this chapter the author describes three villages, Famisa, Mayamam and Sobiba, each with a different sort of relationship between the village leaders and the people. Give a brief description of each of these three different relationships and how they worked.

Discussion and Research Topics

4. Make a list of the different groups of which your society is composed and divide them into three sorts:
   (a) Groups which are related either through blood ties or through marriage;
   (b) Groups of people related to one another because they reside together, e.g. in one village or neighbourhood or town;
   (c) Groups formed for a special purpose, e.g. work or play. Does your society also have other sorts of groups, e.g. age, sex, etc.?

5. Look at the lists you have made in answering question 4. How do these groups arrive at decisions?
6. Think of those who are Christians in your society. Do they mostly come from certain groups within the society, or are they found equally in all groups?
7. If there are several Christian denominations in your area, are they related to the groups of which society is composed in the same way, or in different ways? Can you suggest any reason for the answer? Do the different denominations use different approaches in ministering to the people?

6. The Gospel and Human Communities

Some people may argue that the differences between human communities have nothing to do with the Gospel. We are called, they may say, to preach to every individual man and woman. How people live and how society functions has nothing to do with whether they are going to respond to the Gospel or not. Each human being is personally responsible for his own decision for or against God's call. Individual people must not hide behind the decisions of their extended family or clan, either in accepting the Gospel or in rejecting it. *Groups* cannot decide to become Christians, only individuals.

So, we must ask that question: Were we wrong to allow the people of Chereponi to respond to the Gospel in the ways they chose, or in the ways which fitted their understanding of themselves? Was this an unbiblical way of proceeding? Did the Church in its very early days recognize only individual decisions for Christ?

You can only say this if you look at the Bible through modern Western eyes. The sort of society we have today in Europe and modern Africa, in which each person thinks of himself chiefly as an individual, is not described in the New Testament. It's true that the basic social unit mentioned in the New Testament (in the Book of Acts and elsewhere), when it is larger than the individual believer, is not the clan or the village or the tribe, it is the family. But that is because of the way in which society was organized in the lands around the Mediterranean in the time of the Apostles. It had nothing to do with the order of nature itself.

Where there is mention of the baptism of a man's whole family or household on the grounds of the man's own faith, the principle seems to be accepted that *the Gospel comes to men as who they are*, e.g. the Philippian jailor and Lydia, etc. (see Acts 16.30–34; Acts 16.12–15).

29

That is to say, the Gospel comes to people as they know themselves, as they have always acted, as they function in society. If Papuans or Indians or Barbadians (or Scots or Japanese) function as clans or villages or sub-tribes (or streets or neighbourhoods), then the Gospel will come to them as streets or neighbourhoods or clans or villages or sub-tribes. We can find no authority in the Bible for breaking up the social units in which people live in order to make disciples of the individuals whom we suppose to be the 'real' units of any society.

INDIVIDUALS WITHIN GROUPS

But that does not mean that the Gospel does not come to individuals. The Western distinction between individual and group breaks down here. In the Western world it is usual to distinguish clearly between the individual and the group. But we do not find this distinction in the societies of Biblical times nor in many societies which still function as they did in earlier times. In the New Testament, and in many African and other societies today, it is not a question of individual *or* group, or group versus individual. The individual leads his life *within* the group, but as a person he is *more* than simply a member of the group. 'When people start throwing rocks up in the air,' a Chokosi proverb goes, 'everyone covers his own head.'

To understand how a person is both an individual and a member of different groups, let us think of a person's relationships. Each person's relationships are, in their totality, his and only his. No other person in the whole world has exactly the same pattern of relationships as that person has. His 'mother's children' come the closest to sharing those relationships, which often go beyond the village, clan, street, or even the tribe or nation.

His 'father's children' come next, but some of them may (e.g. in a polygamous society) be related to a totally different group of people through their mother. His close kinsmen share many relationships with him, but they have many other relationships which they do not share with him, just as he has many relationships which he does not share with them.

We say that certain people are a person's 'relatives'. We mean that this 'relatedness' is a matter of sharing some relationships with other people. I am related to my brother-in-law because his sister is my wife. You are related to your first cousin because his uncle is your father. Any corporate group consists of people who are all related to other people in at least some of the same ways. As a member of a group I share in the group's corporate relatedness to others. As a member of a family I share relationships with ancestors in common with the other members of the family. But I am still an individual. I have both *community*, i.e. joint being with others, and *identity*, i.e. my own individual being.

'Identity' is that which makes us ourselves. It is what makes each human being unique, different from all others. My identity is what I am in myself. Your identity is what makes you yourself. But, if we are related, we have an identity which is partly individual and partly shared. I am who I am, both because of who I myself am, and because of what both of us together are. We are brothers because we are each children of God and disciples of Jesus Christ. We belong to the 'house' (family) of God. Our corporate unity or 'community' as Christians is stronger than the corporate unity of groups which people form simply because they want to, such as clubs or political parties. Because of our shared 'incorporation' into Christ, we are one body. As Christians we are not related only to each other, we are related to Christ, in whom we all live, as branches in a vine. When one part of the body suffers, all suffer. When one part of the body rejoices, all rejoice (1. Cor. 12.26).

When the people of Famisa became Christians—i.e. when they became related to Christ—they also became related to the people of Mayamam, who had become Christians earlier. They became brothers. It became fitting that the people of Mayamam should attend the funerals of people in Famisa (which they had never done before as a group, because they did not belong to the same clan). And when the people of Kuonu-Nansoni became Christians it was fitting that the people of Mayamam and Famisa should be there to welcome them into the fellowship, because they were becoming members of the family of the people of Mayamam and Famisa.

INDIVIDUAL AND GROUP DECISIONS

So it was, to go back to our earlier discussion, when any group in Chereponi decided to join the Church. Because the people of Chereponi place a high value on their shared group identity, the group thought of its action as a group action, a group coming into relationship with Christ and with other groups in Christ.

But we did not baptize the villages as units, nor the clans as clans. We called each man and his wife (or wives) and children in turn to come forward for baptism, and they would come forward and kneel to be baptized. Each individual's name was called: 'Simon Kojo (or whatever name), I baptize *you* in the name of the Father, and of the Son, and of the Holy Spirit.' Each person was baptized as an individual, but in the context of his immediate family, and in the larger context of the clan or village group.

Similarly, in our catechetical instruction, we did not only instruct the heads of houses, but all the people. Each man was expected to answer

'Each society has its own culture. Converts should become Christians within their own cultures' (pp. 35, 33).

These two men are both miners, working for the same purpose, in much the same conditions. But one is a Chinese, the other a Canadian.

What are some of the differences between their cultural background, and between the ways in which they might be likely to respond to the Gospel?

for himself as to what he had learned, and whether he was going to commit his life to Jesus Christ. God was confronting each man with the call to discipleship. And in the same way He was confronting the house as a whole (or the clan or the village) with the call to repent and accept the new life and follow the Way.

So we see that this matter of individuals and communities is not a question of either-or, but of both-and. To make response to the Gospel simply a group affair would have been to deny the concern for the individual child of God which we find throughout the New Testament. To make it simply an individual affair would have been to miss the important Biblical teaching that the message goes out to 'nations' (Matt. 28.19).

In Chereponi it was an individual decision *and* it was a group decision. Any individual who felt he could not make the decision—as Baba felt he could not—was free to refuse. No one came forward unwillingly, because he was forced by his father or uncle. One woman said she didn't care what her husband wanted—*she* was not going to be baptized. She wasn't. Both the traditional village structure and the teaching of the Bible leave people free to refuse to do that which, as individuals, they feel that they cannot in good conscience do. Those who came forward came of their own free will, but most of them *chose* to come forward as members of groups.

Should we have refused to accept them as groups? Should we have arranged them in alphabetical order, or at random, instead? I could see no good reason why. We had been faithful to the teaching which we found in the New Testament, and, just as Cornelius's relatives were baptized with him (Acts 10), and the Philippian jailor's household were baptized with him, and Lydia's household were baptized with her, so these African families and local clans and villages walked into the Church together.

Alan Tippett, in his book *Church Growth and the Word of God*, describes this kind of decision as a 'multi-individual decision'—not a group decision, not a mass movement, but the decision of people who remain free to make up their own minds within the group. He goes on to say something like this:

Converts should become Christians *within* their own cultures. They should not have a foreign form of Christianity imposed upon them. If a convert has to be taken out of his own culture in order to become a Christian, then he is 'acculturated' rather than converted. On the mission field we have seen converts so completely uprooted from their culture and traditions, so 'foreignized', that they are left without a home, without any social community to which they belong, and sometimes without a means of livelihood. The Lord wants converts who can live the Christian life within their own social structures.

33

STUDY SUGGESTIONS

WORD STUDIES

1. Which *four* of the following words would you use to describe an individual, and which four would you use to describe a group?
       community   personal   separate   social   mass
       sole   corporate   single
2. Give two other words which have the same or nearly the same meaning as the word 'culture' as used in this chapter.

DISCUSSION TOPICS

3. Read the story of the baptism of Lydia (Acts 16.12–15) and of the Philippian jailor (Acts 16.30–34). Why do you think Paul and Silas baptized others with them? Is there any record of the others having confessed their faith before they were baptized?
4. Why should a candidate for the ministry receive some training in anthropology and sociology?
5. In what ways is the Church, as a community, different from other sorts of human communities? Is it more like some than it is like others? If so, which ones is it like?
6. (a) As Christians, are we bound to recognize the claims of individual conscience? Give reasons for your answer.
   (b) What do missionaries and evangelists need to do in order to make sure:
    (i) that each individual recognizes that he is being confronted with the call of Christ,
    (ii) that he is responsible for the response which he is making, along with the group to which he belongs, and
    (iii) that no one is compelled to make a decision which he does not agree with?

7. Communities have Histories

An individual person is made up of different organs and limbs, and so are communities or groups of people. Just as we can study the way in which a person's organs and limbs are related to one another, and how they work together, so we can study the way in which the different parts of a community are related to one another, and how that community functions.

In the same way, we know that an individual has a history, and that if we look at that history, i.e. at the things that happen in his life, we can say how it has developed. Similarly, societies have lives. We can study how those lives develop, and we can describe their 'social histories'.

In trying to study how communities function, we shall want to understand how they function at any particular moment in time, as well as how they change as time goes on. In our work of ministering to those communities, both are equally important. Any community that we meet is a community which has an ongoing history. It is different today from what it was 100 years ago. Its membership has changed—the same people are not alive today as formerly. And also the ways in which it functions have changed. We need to understand how it is changing, as well as how it is functioning at this particular time in its history.

So we need now to consider not only the smaller groups, such as families and clans and kindreds, which we have already mentioned, but larger groups, such as whole tribes or nations, which we may refer to as *societies*.

CULTURE

Every society has its own culture. The word 'culture' is used to mean those ways of behaviour which are customary in any particular society. Some of these customs are economic, some political, some judicial, some religious, some technological. Each society has its own unique culture or set of customs. They distinguish that culture, and the society to which it belongs, from every other culture and society. Some of the customs belonging to that culture may be found in the cultures of many other societies, just as some of the lines in any person's fingerprints may be like the lines in many other people's fingerprints. But just as no two total fingerprints are alike, so no two total cultures are alike, no no matter how much they share in common. Each is particular to the society which bears it.

Cultural patterns are passed on from one generation to another through time by means of *education*. By education, we do not here mean only that sort of learning which takes place in school-rooms. That is one particular sort of education: formal school learning. All traditional societies had methods of education long before Europeans brought Western formal education to them. Some of it was formal, i.e. fixed and laid down in established patterns, as in the 'bush school' initiation rites of certain societies. Other aspects of it were informal, i.e. arising out of day-to-day situations, not predetermined. But whether it was formal or informal, the function of education was to pass on the accumulated wisdom of the society to a new generation. Every society has, in the course of its history, found ways of dealing with problems, and passes them on to its young. If, as an African, you tell

your child that the unity of the village is more important than anything else, more important even than his own individual pride, you
are educating him in the accepted ways of your culture.

There is thus no single pattern of behaviour which can be called
'culture.' Every society has its own culture. You cannot say that the
people of the X tribe are 'uncultured', whereas the people of the Y
tribe are 'cultured.' They simply have *different* cultures. Each society
educates its children in the ways of its own culture, even though the
people may not recognize this. You may not recognize that allowing
your father to make important decisions for you is part of your society's
culture, until you meet people who do not customarily do this. Then
you recognize that your parents trained you to expect this from them
when you were young.

BALANCED SOCIETIES

Why does one society behave in one way and another society in another?
We cannot always say. But we know that for each society, its own ways
must be satisfactory to it, or else it would not go on doing things that
way. Each society has, in the course of time, worked out ways of doing
things which enable its people to understand who they are and what are
their responsibilities. Having come to that understanding, they can live
peaceably together.

Anthropologists point out that every society has to solve a basic
problem: how to distribute goods and power in such a way that all the
members of the society will be satisfied, and no one will feel that the
system works against him. The society will thus be 'in balance', and
the balanced state will continue only so long as nothing disturbs it.

But no system, anthropologists say, is perfectly in balance. In every
society there are *stresses* and *strains*. There are people who aren't happy
about the way in which goods and power are distributed, or who aren't
happy about the way in which they are related to other people. Perhaps
they were once happy, but now something has happened, so that the
system is no longer working well: their needs are not met. For example,
a society in which all were once farmers may have ways of distributing
income which don't work well when some people have become wage
labourers.

When there are few such stresses and strains, there will be little
desire to change the system. But if the stress and strain becomes very
great, the balance may be upset, and people will feel disturbed. Some
people may run away, or they may encourage the leaders to change the
system. Or perhaps they may lose confidence in the system or in their
leaders. Perhaps they may even start to rebel against the system or bring
about a revolution.

THE GOSPEL AND SOCIAL BALANCE

It is very important for us, when we minister to people in different societies, to be aware of the stresses and strains which are present, for they may indicate a direction in which the society may be changing. Paths that have been closed to the Gospel may become open, or paths that have been open may close.

We have to recognize that we, in our ministry, may be contributing to such stresses and strains. Perhaps we have imported into the society where we work a new idea like the dignity of women and children, or of the rights of individual conscience, and these new ideas threaten the society. Or we may be helping a society which has been under stress and strain to achieve a new balance. Perhaps we have brought into the society a new respect for the riches of its culture, at a time when the modern world was threatening its self-respect. We are not just observers when we go out in ministry; we are participants in the ongoing history of the society. We therefore bear a heavy responsibility before God for what we do.

We must be careful, however, not to assume that the balance of each society depends on one accepted pattern only. Every culture allows for some variations in customary ideas and behaviour.

For example, Mossi society in Upper Volta is a predominantly pagan agricultural society. But Mossi villagers have for many years been allowing young men to leave their villages and become Muslims, and to trade or take jobs. This is not the dominant pattern for Mossi society, but it is a permitted alternative pattern.

In our ministry to different peoples, we need to be aware of possible alternative patterns, and not assume that the dominant pattern is the only one that is acceptable.

But the cultural patterns of a society do not exist like clouds floating on the air. They are to be seen, rather, in people's attitudes and actions. We learn about a people's culture from the way in which they behave.

In every society, certain ways of behaving are accepted as 'customary'. For example, when a person dies, watch how a whole machinery of operations is set into motion, without any hesitation or consultation. The man is buried, his funeral is celebrated, and his possessions are inherited. There are accepted ways in which to handle such affairs. In many other areas of the society's life, also, there are customary ways in which the society will operate.

How can we analyse this? Individuals have *roles*, parts which they must play in the life of society. These roles depend on their *statuses*, i.e. the positions which they occupy in relation to one another. Some have leadership roles, while the role of others is to carry out the decisions of these leaders.

DIFFERENT SORTS OF LEADERS

Leaders may be of several different sorts.

1. Some are *formal leaders*, who have titles, e.g. 'head of the village', 'judge', teacher', 'M.P.', 'priest'. They may have these titles or statuses (a) because of who they are, e.g. the oldest male may automatically be designated 'headman', or (b) because they have been elected or chosen for that position.

2. Others are *informal leaders*. These hold no office and have no title but still they exercise leadership over other people. For example, there is the chief's best friend, whom the chief consults before every decision he makes, or the influential speaker who can rally men to whatever side he advocates.

3. Still others are *opinion leaders*. These do not themselves exercise power, but people look to them for opinions on matters concerning which they are believed to have much knowledge. For example, people go to the good farmer for advice in farming, or they go to a respected teacher who, though he is not a member of the tribe, may be consulted on all affairs involving knowledge of the modern world.

LEADERSHIP AND DECISION-MAKING

The Church, in its ministry, must know who the different types of leaders are in the society or community, and how the community makes decisions. Even the Church's agents themselves may become informal leaders of the community, or opinion leaders. Similarly, a man who is an opinion leader before his conversion will, when he becomes a Christian, perhaps be quite influential in bringing others to consider the Gospel. Decisions concerning the Gospel are not unrelated to other decisions which the community makes.

The relationships between different communities within a society are difficult to understand, but anyone who has his ears and eyes open will in a short time develop a 'feel' for the way in which a community functions. He will come to understand the best way to approach his ministry to his people. The job of a minister is to be as sensitive to the existing decision-making processes as he can be. He will not necessarily bring in new ones.

There is no one 'technique' of ministry, or 'strategy' which can be applied in every situation. If we try to force one method on every people, then we are guilty of 'cultural imperialism.' And if we assume that every community will act like every other community, then we are naïve. Each community and each society is unique, and has its own ways in which it prefers to operate. What we must do, unless those ways are absolutely evil and contrary to the Gospel, is to allow the people to do with regard to Christianity, what they have done countless times before in other matters. That is, to follow their own normal process of decision-making, and arrive at a decision in the way that the Spirit moves them to respond.

The following case shows how we were able to work with a particular community's way of working. The majority clan of the village of Banjani was related to the people of the clan of Mayamam where, following old, blind Dibolo's decision, we had baptized 143 people on one day. We had had a fairly positive response to our preaching in Banjani, and we expected that the Banjani people might be ready to respond to an invitation to be baptized.

When finally the question was asked, the headman sat in silence. I asked whether, if the village was not ready to act as a unit, some individuals were. Again there was no response. I was astounded. I knew for a fact that Kwam-ba, a mature person whom I thought was an 'opinion leader', was converted in his heart. And yet, not even he responded. I went home highly disappointed.

The next day Kwam-ba came to me. 'One man can't hold up the world,' he said. 'The elders didn't agree. My brothers and I were ready, and several of the women, but when they realized that we would have to go along without the elders they lost courage.'

We talked about it, and I understood his position. He looked at the Gospel differently from the way I did. He had a need to see the whole village acting together. He did not see that a decision by an individual could be significant. He understood the village to be the vine and himself merely one of its branches.

We decided that something might be done. If the elders of Mayamam, who had been baptized, would come to Banjani to talk to the Banjani elders, perhaps they could convince them that to abandon the ancestral cult (which was the stumbling block) would not bring destruction. Perhaps they could convince them that the new way was not only one which younger men like Kwam-ba could follow, but one that elders too could adopt.

The Mayamam elders came. What happened was interesting. They did not convince the Banjani elders to be baptized, but they convinced them that the Christian faith, even if it was not to their liking, was good for the village, i.e. that it was an acceptable alternative to their customary ways. The elders gave the go-ahead, and their younger brothers and cousins and sons and wives and daughters were free to become Christians if they wanted to. Because the elders had agreed, the younger people could become Christians without threatening the unity of the village.

The second thing that happened was even more interesting. After a congregation of 38 people were baptized and had chosen Kwam-ba and another man as their presbyters, the people proceeded to make a shed for worship. And it was the headman who took charge of the project. The people understood it to be a village communal project.

Shortly after that, there was a meeting of district 'Church mothers', and we realized that Banjani had not yet elected any of these female presbyters. The headman wanted to show that, although he was not baptized, he wished to be a member of the community, and so he came to my house to offer that his new young wife should become a Church mother!

In Garinkuka, however, a Nafeba Konkomba village eleven miles further up the road, where the same number of people were baptized, the Church immediately took on the form of a separate community, unrelated to the rest of the village. The Church members acted without consulting the elders, built a chapel without asking for help from anyone, abstained without question from village rituals, and never sought financial contributions from those who had not become Christians.

The difference between Banjani and Garinkuka shows the difference between their cultural patterns. Every society is different: Konkombas are not Chokosis. The patterns of behaviour people have learned in each society, i.e. its culture, mark it off as different. If we simply assume that 'people everywhere are the same', we shall get into trouble. We must learn to observe and to listen with the 'third ear'—the ear of anthropological understanding. It is wrong to impose our own ways of doing things on other people, or even to impose one village's ways of doing things on another village, or one tribe's way of doing things on another tribe.

Similarly, we must be aware that many societies do not function today in the same way in which they functioned in earlier times. People from different tribes may now live together in larger, more complex societies, such as cities or towns. Within those cities several different patterns may exist together. The tribes or peoples who live there may each carry on their traditional ways in certain areas of life, and in their internal relationships. But they will have adopted new ways of relating to non-tribal groups. The minister must be aware of all these patterns. Ministry becomes a much more complex matter in such societies.

ALTERNATIVE SOCIAL PATTERNS

What we have said above may give the impression, however, that differences exist only *between* societies. But differences often appear also between the various ways in which a single society deals with different sorts of problems. It may deal in different ways with religious questions, economic questions, medical problems, educational problems, or agricultural questions. For some sorts of problems, group decisions may be made; for others, only individual decisions will be made; in still others, groups may make it possible for individuals to act according to their own wishes, without this causing trouble. In agriculture, we found in Chereponi that the traditional culture of most villages, both Konkomba and Chokosi, allowed great freedom to any individual who had a farm of his own. If he wanted to plant a new variety of guinea corn or rice, that was his own personal decision to make, and the society would allow him to. He alone would suffer if the innovation failed, and the society respected his right to fail if he wanted to. It was not they who would be hungry. (One village, however, did resist the introduction of pesticides, saying they would be misused to poison humans.)

In the health realm we discovered that, if we wanted our clinics for children under the age of five to be successful, we needed the fathers' support. We had only spoken to the mothers, and those mothers who agreed to come were taking to themselves a right which in that society belonged to fathers: the care of the health of the family.

Respect for the society, and willingness to work within its cultural patterns, these are what are required of us in our ministry to different peoples. In God's fulfilment of His plan to unite all things in heaven and on earth with Christ as head (Eph. 1.10), it is not His will to make all things and all people alike. Their very diversity and the richness of their varying cultures is part of their offering to His kingdom.

STUDY SUGGESTIONS

WORD STUDY

1. In the light of this chapter, explain each of the following terms, with examples.
   (a) culture   (b) education   (c) a social system   (d) stresses and strains.

REVIEW QUESTIONS

2. (a) What is meant by saying that a society is 'in balance'?
   (b) Are cultures and social systems ever *perfectly* in balance? Give reasons for your answer.
3. (a) What *three* different sorts of leaders are present in all societies?
   (b) Give examples of each sort of leader from your own society, or the society you work in.

DISCUSSION AND RESEARCH TOPICS

4. What is the difference between a 'role' and a 'status'? Make a list of the roles you play in life, and the status you possess which entitles you to play each one.
5. How does the society in which you work arrive at decisions?

6. Do you think there is any specially 'Christian 'way of arriving at decisions? If so, what makes it the Christian way?
7. What are some of the stresses and strains in societies? In the societies with which you are familiar? What do you think they show about the ways in which those societies may have to change?
8. Do you think the Church is called to bring about social change? How can it do this? How can it judge which sorts of change are desirable?
9. In what ways have you seen the Gospel bring about change in a people's ways of doing things?

8. Effects and Influence of Groups

Truly exciting things happen when the Church accepts people who come in as groups.

1. First, the whole system of kinship relation comes into the service of the Gospel. Groups who have been baptized tell their relatives and their in-laws about Christ. The Gospel message travels along lines which are already laid down for it. Donald McGavran described this process in his book *Bridges of God* (see p. 63). In Chereponi we saw it work.

After our first two years of preaching, during which time we preached in fourteen villages, we hardly ever needed to go to a village to ask the people if they would like us to preach the Gospel. Yet, at the end of five years, we were working in 54 villages! In almost every one of those forty additional villages the word had first been spread by their relatives and in-laws in villages where we had previously been working. We ought not to refuse to use such bridges of communication when they already exist. They are part of God's preparation for the Gospel.

2. Secondly, in many of the villages, there was a new sense of 'making the village a better place'. The groups who heard the Gospel began to work together in exciting new ways on community development projects, trying to defeat their age-old enemies of poor communication, poor health, and poverty (see Part 4). If the villages had not been able to act as units, this would have been much more difficult. The individual, isolated Christians of Garinkuka could say: 'Let's build a better shed for the school as a Christian service.' But when they set out to do it, they found they had few people and few resources to call upon. But when the people of Famisa, lukewarm as their faith often was, decided to build a new road to Chereponi, all of them came out and worked, and the road was completed. Famisa had been baptized as a village.

3. Thirdly, when groups became Christian, there was a tremendous

'Exciting things happen when the Church accepts people as groups: groups who have heard the Gospel begin to work together' (p. 42).

Village women in Guinea co-operate in pounding cassava.

Even in the simplest matters, people usually achieve more by working together than each for himself. What can groups of Christians achieve, that individuals working separately perhaps could not?

possibility, not only for the conversion of individuals, but for the 'Christianization' of social customs. When a number of Chokosi villages had become Christians, they were able to begin to work together toward a decision about what to do concerning the betrothal of infant girls. If they had simply been baptized as individuals, this would have been much more difficult.

This is how it happened. According to traditional Chokosi custom, if a man's wife has a baby girl, he has the right to betroth the girl to anyone he chooses, who will then start making payments until the girl is of age to be married.

For at least two centuries the Chokosi have, however, also had a custom by which girls of puberty and beyond are taken as girl friends by boys and young unmarried men.

A CAUSE OF STRESS

The existence of the two customs side by side has, for at least twenty years, been a real source of stress and strain in Chokosi society. Many of the girls have been refusing to marry their intended husbands, and have eloped with their boy friends. Most of them are caught. The majority of cases coming before the police, the courts, and the chief in Chereponi today are cases of bridegrooms suing the fathers of brides for failing to produce the wives whose price they have paid, or suing boy friends of girls for stealing their 'wives'. Many people have been beaten, whole villages have been set against one another, and an untold number have been poisoned or otherwise killed because of the hostilities.

I described this state of affairs to many non-Chokosis. A missionary advised: 'Tell the Christian girls that they should not take boy friends.' A Southern Ghanaian Churchman advised: 'Tell the fathers not to betroth their daughters to anyone, and then the girls can marry whom they like when they become of age.'

I felt that the Southern Ghanaian's advice was the best—except for the first three words. He seemed to share with the missionary the idea that I, as a pastor, should lay down rules for the Christians. I felt, however, like Paul, that I did not have a clear 'word from the Lord' on this. And I felt that, even if I did, I would have a question about the best way of speaking that word. I do not understand the Gospel as law but as grace. But, even just to be practical, I had to recognize that I could not take over the position of authority-figure from the leaders to whom authority in that society belonged. I knew that if I tried to do so, they would rightly resist. The most I could hope to achieve was that the fathers would hide from me the fact that they were still betrothing their daughters. I wanted to let the traditional authority and leadership patterns work.

I recognized, however, that the patterns had not been working well. Here was a clear case of a society whose system was no longer functioning as it once had. The young men and young women were no longer content to leave decisions to their elders and this was causing conflict. I felt that by developing an informed Christian consciousness we could help to solve the conflict.

A CHRISTIAN CONSCIOUSNESS IN SOCIETY

My first step was to learn as much as I could about marriage affairs and the custom of taking girl friends. I talked to people at all levels of society—old men and women; the chief; girls expecting to have boy friends; boys who had girl friends; the mothers and fathers of the girls; boys whose girl friends had married, leaving them heartbroken; men whose 'brides' had eloped, leaving them heartbroken; people with court cases; newly married couples.

Second, I announced an essay competition in the local newspaper. We published the thoughts of articulate young Christians, in their own language, on the subject of infant betrothal. Many people read or heard of what they had written.

Then we started discussing the subject in our presbyters' and Church mothers' retreats. I could see that many felt the answer lay in stopping betrothal of children. The women were unanimous on that, but the men did not all agree. They saw that marriage exchanges brought friendship and unity between the intermarrying groups.

At the last district conference at which I was present before leaving Chereponi, this question came on the agenda. It had been discussed at a general conference on Christian home and family life a few days before, as well. The feeling of those present at the meeting was that no decision could yet be made but that:

1. a Christian view of man meant that one could not take away from the girls the right to have some say about whom they would marry;

2. the continual strife between bridegrooms and boyfriends, and between girls and their fathers, was a danger to society;

3. the number of Christians in Chokosi society was growing so quickly that it might soon be possible for the Christians to take a stand which would influence the whole society;

4. some answer would have to be found to the problem of what to say to those who had given their daughters to your family, and were waiting for you to complete the exchange by giving one of your daughters or nieces back;

5. it was wonderful to discuss the problem openly like this, and with people from so many clans and villages present; the meeting generally felt hopeful.

I have not yet heard from Chereponi what the outcome has been. But if I understand correctly what is happening, a considered Christian consciousness is being formed there, and those people who have come to new insights are in many cases formal leaders, informal leaders, or opinion leaders in Chokosi society. Acting through the normal processes by which the society operates, they are going to solve the problem. The final solution may come from individuals who conscientiously refuse to betroth their daughters, or by a decision of the Church that 'We Christians will not betroth our daughters', or by a decision of the formal leadership of the society that betrothal should no longer be practised. I do not know.

But what is encouraging is that, because not only individuals but whole communities belong to the Church, the chance of bringing a Christian influence to bear on the relations of girls and potential husbands is much greater.

And so, in many ways, the possibilities for the Gospel are greater when the Church is willing to accept people who wish to enter the Christian fellowship as groups.

STUDY SUGGESTIONS

DISCUSSION AND RESEARCH TOPICS

1. Give at least two examples from everyday life, of problems which can be solved more easily if people make decisions as a group rather than as individuals.
2. What can be (a) the advantage and (b) the disadvantages when people make decisions as a group?
3. (a) Do groups to which you belong ever help you to make decisions? (b) Does the fact that a group to which you belong has made a decision, ever help you to be strong in resisting any sort of temptation?
4. What do most individual people do, who find themselves alone in having to make a difficult decision?
5. In what ways, if any, has the Church in your country been able to influence people of other religions? If the Church has had any influence, do you think it has been a good one?
6. For what reasons have any whole groups *not* come into the Church in your country? Do you think there is any way in which the Church could have encouraged them to come?

9. A Big Problem: Polygamy

There are some places where all that we have been saying about accepting people into the Church in groups may be meaningless because of one big 'thorn in the flesh'. This 'thorn' is the position which the Church has usually taken during the past hundred years or so, about polygamy. How can we even begin to speak of accepting whole groups into the Christian fellowship, in areas where these groups contain many polygamists? In many village communities in Africa and in South-east Asia and the Pacific, the chief and headman and elders will almost certainly be polygamists. And if we cannot bring the community's formal leaders into the Church, how can we bring in the community as a unit?

This is a widespread problem and we must not try to escape from discussing it.

When the Evangelical Presbyterian Church began its mission work in the Chereponi area, everyone assumed that the Church would not baptize polygamists. It would baptize all those other individuals who came to it, including the senior wives of polygamists, and gather them into new Christian congregations.

Three years later it became quite obvious that more than individuals wanted to come into the Church. Whole villages, or whole clans within villages, wanted to become Christian as groups. In many cases it was the village headman, like old Dibolo in Mayamam, or the senior elder of the local clan, who led his people to new life in Christ. Most of these leaders were polygamists. We dreaded the day when we would have to tell them that, though most of their people could join the Church, they themselves could not, because they had several wives. We avoided the subject, but we knew that the moment of decision drew nearer all the time.

We did not know what to do. At first I was convinced that the position of the Church was right: a polygamist could only be baptized if he gave up all of his wives but the first. As I believed that polygamy was evil, I also believed that a practising polygamist could not be a Christian.

THE BIBLE AND POLYGAMY

But I decided to study the biblical evidence, so as to be more sure of the reasons. I discovered that it was difficult to find texts in the New Testament which dealt with polygamy. The New Testament writers only refer to polygamy, if at all, by inference. They make no direct statement about it.

There is a reason for this. The silence of the New Testament writers about polygamy is like their silence concerning smoking. These problems as we know them today did not then exist. Christians did not write letters to Paul or John asking for instructions about polygamy because polygamy in general was not practised in the Mediterranean world in the first two centuries AD. As E. G. Parrinder comments:

> Both the Greeks and the Romans were monogamists by long tradition. Christianity did not need to teach them monogamy, only to heighten the ideal of marriage, and the status of women. Similarly, we have seen that the Jews also, by the time of Christ, had practically all become monogamists. Monogamy had come by itself, and was not disputed by the Rabbis . . .

We look in vain for explicit instructions about polygamy in the New Testament, for we shall not find them.

What we have to do instead is to read what *is* in the New Testament concerning marriage and personal relations. Then we can find what the starting point is, from which, *in our own personal responsibility*, we can 'build upon the foundation'. We must be ready to distinguish between those matters on which we have 'a word from the Lord', and those matters on which we can only give our own seriously and responsibly considered opinion.

Paul made this sort of distinction. He explained in his first letter to the Corinthians that there are two parts to Church work: (1) there is the laying of the foundation, and (2) there is building upon it. The foundation is Christ, and once that foundation is laid no one can change it without going against the will of God. But there is also the work which comes after the foundation has been laid, and that is the work of building, in which each man must use his own judgement as to how to build on the foundation (see 1 Cor. 3.5–15).

In Corinth Paul did not only lay the foundation. He also built. He was always careful, however, to distinguish between the times when he was laying the foundation, i.e. handing on what had been handed on to him as absolutely essential, and the times when he was building, i.e. using his own best judgement about what was needed to make the building complete. In the first case, he said 'On this matter I have a word from the Lord.' But in the second case, he would say, 'I have no command from the Lord on this.' Read 1 Corinthians 5–12 and you will see the difference.

1 Corinthians 7, in which Paul deals with questions about marriage, contains both sorts of instruction. On the matter of divorce Paul says he has a 'command from the Lord'; Jesus indeed spoke out very directly about divorce (see Mark 10.1–12). But on the matter of whether or not to marry, Paul only gives his own advice.

FOUNDATIONS OF MARRIAGE

As regards marriage then, there are three chief foundations on which we can build. These are the basic teachings about relationships between people, and about marriage, which we can find in the New Testament, and from which we can interpret what the New Testament writers would have advised us about polygamy.

1. The first of these foundation rocks is the principle which runs through the entire New Testament: *Gospel, not law.* Whatever we decide we must say concerning polygamy and marriage, we must make sure that we say it as good news concerning the new life God offers man in Christ, rather than as formal regulations like: 'thou shalt' or 'thou shalt not', as in the Old Testament.

2. The second foundation rock is the Great Commandment, upon which Jesus said, 'all the law and the prophets' are based, i.e. the commandment of love. This means the love of God, and, what cannot be separated from it, the love of our neighbour (see, e.g. Luke 10.25–28). Everything we say about relationships between human beings must be based on love. Because our Christian experience, and because God's relationship to us, is one of love alone, through His grace, we ourselves must always try to relate to others in terms of love and grace (see Matt. 18.21–35).

3. The third rock is Jesus's plain and clear teaching about God's will concerning marriage. Going back beyond Moses to the creation itself, Jesus showed that the undeniable will of God is that a man should be joined to his wife as one flesh, one body, one person. He showed that marriage creates a new interpersonal unity between a man and his wife, so that although they had been two separate people, in marriage they become one person, and cannot be separated without breaking apart what God has joined together (Mark 10.5–9).

If we look beyond these three 'foundation rocks' for other absolutely clear, unmovable bases for a Christian attitude toward polygamy, we shall not find them. Few even of the scholars who take a traditional attitude toward polygamy, base their ideas about it on the teaching in the Pastoral Epistles.

The New Testament thus gives no direct answer to the following questions, nor to many others which we may want to ask on the subject:

(a) Should we baptize polygamists? Under what conditions?

(b) Should we baptize the wives of polygamists? Some of them?

(c) Should we admit polygamists and their wives into the full membership of the Church?

Thus all we can do is to decide responsibly, from what we do know about New Testament teaching on marriage and human relations and the Church, what God is calling us to do about our relations toward polygamists in the Church in our particular situation.

A POSITIVE APPROACH

The best way is to start from *positive* proclamation. Because our message is a message of grace and not law, it must be positive. It must be proclamation, a joyous announcement of the good news of God's activity in Christ to bring new life to the world. Just as in every other area of life we have the commission to announce God's gracious plan for the renewed life for humanity, so with regard to marriage we are commissioned to announce God's loving purpose for mankind. And God's purpose in marriage is to bring men and women to a new relationship with each other in Christ, to what the All-Africa Seminar on Christian Home and Family Life called 'life-long fellowship in which there is the fulfilment and completion of husband and wife, each in the other'.

Thus we have much more to announce about marriage than a plain joyless law of 'monogamy'. In fact we do not proclaim monogamy, as such, at all, because monogamy *by itself* may or may not provide fulfilment and completion of the marriage relationship. Many monogamous marriages are less than Christian, in that they do not truly provide the deep, interpersonal fellowship of 'one flesh' to which the Gospel points us. It is not mere monogamy that we announce.

What we have to say is this:

'God's will for you and for your wife is that in Christ you will truly find one another, as full partners in life, sharing one another's joys and carrying one another's burdens. God has instituted marriage so that neither of you should be alone, so that in your home you will be able to share fully with each other everything that life means to both of you. In marriage you can find a unity that no other relationship can offer, not even the relationship between mother and child, or between a man and his mother's child, or between two friends. This is the relationship to which you are called, because God wants you to have this happiness.'

When the writer to the Ephesians wanted to find a relationship to which he could compare the relationship between Christ and His Church, it is not strange that he chose the relationship of marriage (Eph. 5.21–33), for no other human relationship is as close.

1. Thus our first message on the subject of marriage is a positive one. It is a joyous announcement of the new possibilities of marriage in Christ.

When we make this announcement, people will probably ask: Is such a relationship possible when a man divides his love between two or more women? Can there be such deep interpersonal unity when there are three partners to the unity? In answer, we can think of what Jesus said at another time: 'No one can serve two masters' (Matt. 6.24). The sort of devotion to another person, whether to God or to man, toward which Jesus always pointed His disciples, was the devotion of the single heart. It was the devotion of the undivided self, a relationship in which the one *gives* himself to the other. So people will ask: Can a man give himself to two different women?

The teaching of the Church to those who have not yet married, or to those who have only one wife or husband thus seems clear. We should seek in marriage nothing less than the total unity between persons which can only happen when each gives themself fully to the other. In doing so we shall discover the joys of complete, life-long togetherness in marriage in Christ.

But what attitude should the Church take to a man who already has more than one wife? Must it say: 'Forsake all but one of your wives so that you can then give yourself fully to that one and discover the joy of true Christian marriage'?

Some Christians think that the Church should say this. But it is difficult to reconcile such an attitude with the second 'rock' of New Testament teaching concerning human relationships: the Great Commandment to love one's neighbour as oneself.

2. The Church must not be concerned only with the man who may become a new member, who has two wives. And it must not be concerned only with the first of his wives. The Church must be concerned for the welfare of *all* of the persons involved in the polygamous marriage —the man, both of his wives, his family, the families of his wives, and the children.

In such a situation there are many questions which the Church needs to ask: What will happen to the second wife if she has to go away? Will anyone provide for her? Will anyone marry her? Will she become a prostitute? What will it mean for her children, whom God has given to her and her husband? Will they be deprived of the fatherly or motherly care they need? Will they be regarded as bastards?

Whether the second marriage was God's will or not, the fact is that it took place. It is recognized in the community to which the family belongs. Probably children were born out of it. Because it has taken place, it is clear that the man has the responsibility to provide for, and to love, both the children and their mother. Is the Church right to demand that the man can follow God's way in marriage, only by breaking God's commandment to love?

Or is the Church to say to the man: 'We will not baptize you or welcome you into our fellowship until you have sent away all your wives except the first?' It is difficult to reconcile such an attitude with the first 'rock' of New Testament teaching, i.e. that it is based on Gospel,

'I am responsible to all of them and to their children' (p. 53). In many tribes the accepted custom is for important men to have several wives, like this chief in northern Kenya.

If such a man truly wants to offer himself and all he has, including his polygamous marriage, to God, can the Church refuse to baptize him?

not on law. 'While we were yet sinners, Christ died for us,' Paul wrote (Rom. 5.8). God's love comes to man as he is, sinful, having fallen short of God's grace, having nothing of which to be proud. It comes to him before he changes his ways, without condition.

God does not say, '*If* you do such-and-such, *then* I will call you to be my own.' He says: '*Because* I love you, I *have* called you to be my own.' And in response to God's love, man repents of his foolish ways. He feels sorry because of what he has done which is not in accordance with God's will for mankind.

The man who has previously married more than one wife, hearing the good news of the Church concerning marriage, says to himself: 'I, too, ought to have known, but I didn't. Now I see that this door is closed to me. I cannot have this deep relationship with one woman that the Bible says is my God-given right and opportunity. My wives cannot enjoy complete unity with me either, for I am divided between them. However, I am responsible to all of them, and to their children.' And he will probably go on to say: 'I cannot send any of them away, for I must love them and not only think of my own happiness. I am sure that the God who has loved me so much has forgiven me. In many ways I can still try to let God reshape even my polygamous marriage, so that there is more love in it, even if it cannot be the full love God has desired for us. I will teach my sons to look for the full treasure, to marry only one wife, and I will not give my daughter to any man who will not give himself completely to her alone.'

Can the Church refuse baptism to such a man? If the Church preaches about the free, accepting love of God and yet does not freely accept all who come to it, in love and joy, by grace and not by law, does it not deny its own preaching? These are difficult questions, and at the present time not all Churches or all Christians would answer them in the same way.

THE CHURCH ACTS

From Chereponi we took these questions to our presbytery meeting in Southern Ghana, where the Church had refused baptism to polygamists for a hundred years past, though before that it had taken a more open attitude. We presented our views and the report of the All-Africa Seminar. We explained how whole communities were ready to come into the Church, but that they would probably not be so ready if we were to refuse to baptize the community's leaders.

The Southern pastors and elders considered the matter. They thought of the divided society of which they were a part, where there was often a 'pagan town' and a 'Christian town' within a single community. They thought of the difficult relationships between the two parts of each community. They wondered how far the Church's past strictness on the question of polygamy had been responsible for dividing those communities in such a tragic way. Could this be avoided in the North, they wondered?

They considered the polygamists whom they knew, many of whom were more dedicated Church members than the monogamists, but who could never be baptized or receive the Lord's Supper. They asked whether these people really were morally and socially free to send their other wives away. No one could think of a single polygamist who had done so.

They thought of the wives of polygamists who belonged to their congregations, and how two wives from the same household could only become members of the Church by joining two different Churches. Was this the will of Christ, they wondered?

At the end of their discussion they passed a resolution giving the pastors in the North permission to baptize any polygamist who wanted to become a Christian, during the first years of the work. (Some thought this might mean fifteen to twenty years, others thought perhaps ten years.) During this period a polygamist could be baptized with his wives and children. This permission was given *provided* that from the start: (1) the Church would give clear and consistent teaching on the Christian ideal of marriage, and (2) those so baptized would agree not to marry any additional wives.

Four years later this policy was extended to new evangelistic areas in Southern Ghana as well. One year after that, the Evangelism and Lay Training Committee of the Presbyterian Church of Ghana recommended a similar action in that Church 'for a trial period of ten years'. During this time 'the pastors in the North, under strict conditions, should be allowed to baptize polygamists, both the male polygamists and their wives.' Here too it was recommended that 'this allowance should be complemented with vigorous teaching of the meaning of Christian marriage.'

In the five years before I left Ghana, we had to deal in Chereponi District with five cases of baptized monogamous Christians who had taken second wives. When one Church leader asked whether this did not mean that our policy was a failure (implying that five cases out of about 300 adult baptized males was many), I enquired whether this was worse that the figures for any of the Southern districts, in which the 'strict' policy on polygamy had been followed for a century. Most of the pastors smiled an embarrassed smile. The Church did not reverse its policy. We were permitted to continue.

As a result of this policy, we were able to bring in the full, rich harvest of whole communities offering themselves to God. Several entire villages and whole sections of other villages became Christian.

In summary, then, in our ministry to God's people, we meet men and women who live in society and who have a history. We minister to them in this history and in this culture. We do not have to bring them out of their culture or society for them to hear the Gospel. When they respond to the Gospel, they will normally do so in the ways which their culture has provided. In many cases they will respond not just as individuals, but as individuals within groups. If we accept them as who they are, that is how they will come. And we can praise God that He is able to use these groups for the rapid communication of the good news, and the spread of His kingdom, praying for the day when 'the kingdoms of this world shall become the kingdom of our Lord and of His Christ' (Rev. 11.15).

STUDY SUGGESTIONS

REVIEW QUESTIONS

1. What three great principles about human relationships do we find in the teaching of the New Testament, which can help the Church to know what should be its position with regard to marriage?
2. How would you interpret Mark 10.5-9 to someone who asked what was Jesus's teaching about marriage?
3. What, if anything, do the New Testament writers say about polygamy?

DISCUSSION AND RESEARCH TOPICS

4. The All-Africa Seminar on Christian Home and Family Life described Christian marriage as 'life-long fellowship in which there is the fulfilment and completion of husband and wife, each in the other'. But monogamous marriage is the practice among many peoples of other religions than Christianity.
   (a) In what ways, if any, are such marriages different from Christian marriage?
   (b) Do you think such marriages can provide 'the deep interpersonal fellowship of "one flesh"' (p. 50)?
   Give examples to support your answers.
5. What are the different positions which the Church can take with regard to polygamy, and what are the likely results of each? (In discussing this question it will be helpful if those in the group who stand for one position explain the opposite position, to see whether they understand it.)
6. (a) Ought the Church to apply Christian teachings about marriage to people who, following the ways of their cultures, have already married several wives?
   (b) Are such polygamists sinners?
7. If a Church proclaims one message in its preaching, and seems to teach a different message in the rules it makes for accepting new members, what is likely to happen?

8. The sort of devotion to another person, whether God or man, toward which Jesus always pointed His disciples, was the devotion of the single heart, the undivided self (p. 51).

   (a) If a man or woman gives 'the devotion of the undivided self' to God, what sort of devotion can they give to their family and friends?

   (b) Can a person give 'the devotion of the single heart' to *each* of his friends?

9. What position has your own Church taken with regard to polygamy? If you can, give examples of the result which this has had in the society in which you live.

10. How do you yourself think the Church should answer questions (a), (b), and (c) on p. 49?

PART 3
THE MINISTRY OF PREACHING
THE WORD

10. Proclamation

We saw in Part 1 that our total work in the Church on behalf of our Lord can be described as ministry. We are called to be ministers, or servants, of God in Christ. We are called to minister to one another in order to build up the Church as the people of God; so that it may minister more effectively to God's people in the world, in the name of Christ.

In Part 2 we thought about those in the world to whom we minister. We saw that they are people who live in societies which have different cultures. And we saw that these societies and cultures are not fixed or unchanging, but have ongoing histories. In our ministry to God's people we become part of their history. We hope, that through our ministry to them, they will come to recognize that they are part of the ongoing history of the relationship of God to His people. We want them to become aware and committed members of the Church, who will give their lives to Christ so that He may re-create them as His people, and as members of His coming kingdom.

One of our ministries, the ministry of proclamation, is central to our ministry as a whole. By preaching or proclaiming God's Word, we express what is at the heart of all our ministries: God's call to mankind to be reconciled to Him. As Harry Boer has written, the proclamation of the Gospel is not just one activity among many in which the Church of the New Testament engages; it is the basic and essential activity. The *preaching* office is the *central* office in the Church.

In this Part, we give special attention to this ministry of preaching the word. We need to remember that preaching can be of many kinds, depending upon the hearers. We can preach to fellow Christians, as Church leaders do Sunday after Sunday. Or we can preach to people who have enrolled as hearers or catechumens, and have made a first commitment to the Gospel and to Christ. Or we can preach to people who are outside the Church, and perhaps belong to other religions.

Here we shall especially consider preaching to people who are not Church members or catechumens, people who may have no knowledge of the Gospel, and who may indeed not even have heard of Christ. These were the sort of people to whom we had to preach in Chereponi.

Many of them became Christians in the course of our ministry to them, and our style of preaching changed as they became members of the Church. We could then begin to speak of things which we could not speak of at first. We still were preaching to them, but we were preaching to them as brothers and sisters of the faith, and not as strangers any more. We knew that they had made a commitment to Jesus Christ, so we did not have to encourage them to do so again, but instead to renew and deepen their commitment.

But there is no better way to understand what Christian preaching really is, than to consider what is sometimes called 'primary evangelism': i.e. the proclamation of the Gospel to those who have never heard it. We can then apply to our preaching within the Church much of what we learned about this preaching of the Gospel to strangers.

THE MEANING OF CHRISTIAN PROCLAMATION

The Greek word which is translated 'preach' in English is the verb *kerussein*, which means to 'proclaim' or 'announce'. This verb comes from the noun *kerux*, which means a herald. A herald is one who either goes before a king or chief to announce that he is coming, or goes at the direction of a king or chief, to announce his will, or give his instructions, or his edict or laws.

Today, with the coming of radio and telegraph and telephone, heralds are no longer needed in many countries. However, there are some areas, in Africa and elsewhere, which still have them. In Ghana, for example, many chiefs have heralds who are called 'gong-gong beaters'. The chief sends them before him, beating the gong-gong to announce that he is coming; or else he commands them to go out to make important announcements on his behalf. They are not unlike radio announcers in what they do.

Our role as preachers, as proclaimers of the Word of God, is to be the 'gong-gong beaters' of Christ. We are heralds of the King, announcing His will and His coming. In other words, we go out, not to express our own opinions, beliefs, or understanding; or our culture, our ways, or even our religion. We go out to announce what the King has told us.

The message that we are to announce is the 'evangel'. This word comes from the Greek word *euangelion* (from *angelion*, meaning news, and *eu*, meaning good), and means the 'good news', i.e. the good news concerning Jesus Christ. By God's orders we, as preachers, are to tell all men what He has done in Jesus Christ, Through us His messengers all Chokosis, Yorubas, Papuans, Thais, Meos, Konds, are to learn that, in Jesus Christ, He has brought mankind back into union with Himself. 'God was making friends of all men through Christ,' we say, 'we beg you, let God change you from enemies into friends!' (2 Cor. 5.19–20).

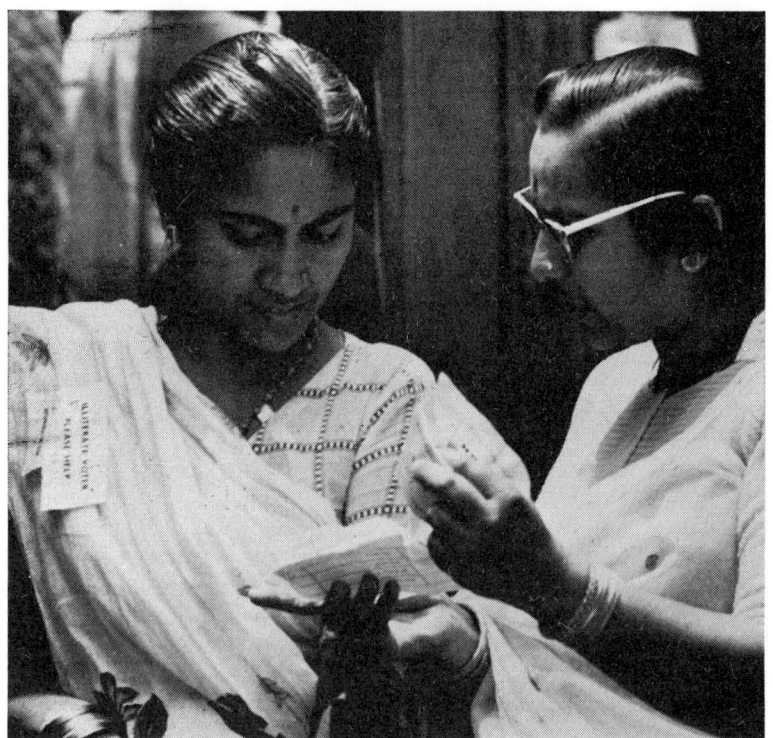

'The only difference between ourselves and those to whom we preach is that we already know what God has done for mankind in Christ, and they do not' (p. 60). Each of these two Indian women in Fiji has an equal right to vote in the election, and each must decide for herself which candidate to vote for. But one of them cannot read, so the other is explaining to her what the different parties promise, and what she needs to do in order to register her vote.

List some of the ways in which preaching is like canvassing for a political party, and some ways in which it is *un*like.

This message that we have is not one that should make us feel superior to those to whom we preach. It makes us feel our oneness with them. We are not better than they. On the contrary, we know how far we are from what God wills us to be. Jesus Christ, we announce, took on human nature in order to redeem all men, whoever they are.

The only difference between us and those to whom we preach is that we already know what God has done for mankind in Christ, while they do not yet know. We have accepted Christ as Lord and Saviour, and have 'tasted and seen that He is good', whereas they have not yet given Him their trust, and do not yet know how gracious a Lord He is. We are, as D. T. Niles of Ceylon used to say like 'one beggar telling another beggar where to find food'. We have nothing of our own to proclaim, but only what He has given us by His grace, not because of our efforts.

We do wrong, therefore, if in our preaching we seem to say, 'Look at us!' and not 'Look to Him!' Once we Christians also were what the writer of 1 Peter, following Hosea, called 'No people'. Once we 'had not received mercy', but now we are God's people, now we have received mercy. Our task, therefore, is not to preach our own ideas, but 'to proclaim the wonderful acts of God' who calls us 'from the darkness into his own marvellous light' (1 Pet. 2.9–10). We announce what God has done, and hope that our announcement will call forth from those to whom we preach the response of repentance, and of turning to Christ in faith.

Like heralds, or gong-gong beaters, we do not act on our own authority. The authority is Christ's. At His resurrection He told His disciples that God had given Him 'all authority in heaven and on earth' (Matt. 28.18), and it was on that basis that He commissioned the disciples, saying 'Go then to all peoples everywhere and make them my disciples' (v. 19). We act on the same authority as the apostles did: the authority of Christ. And we depend on the apostles' eye-witness testimony concerning Christ, and the New Testament records of Him.

The apostles' testimony to Christ centred on His resurrection. To them, the fact that God had raised Christ from the dead was proof that He was Lord. Our preaching too must centre on Christ's resurrection. This is the central doctrine of the Christian faith. The Scottish theologian H. R. Mackintosh used to tell his students, 'Every sermon you preach ought to be an Easter sermon.' We go out to announce Christ's resurrection, to proclaim that He is alive and that God has made Him Lord.

Now this announcement is quite exciting if we understand it correctly. We do not go out just to tell people that Christ is *our* Lord. We do say that; but we also say much more. We say that He is Lord of heaven and earth, that He is the Lord of all mankind, of those who know Him and of those who do not know Him, of those who have trusted in Him and of those who have not, of those who are His disciples and of those who are not. We announce the fact of His Lordship, and we witness to its truth. And we call people to acknowledge this fact by giving their lives to His service, and we tell them that they will find new life in Him.

Our message is thus a joyous and positive one. It is both authoritative and universal. We are not 'selling' a religion or a set of opinions; we are presenting the King of all the universe to His people. Our goal is to be instruments of God's plan as described in Ephesians, that all creation, everything in heaven and on earth, should be brought together with Christ as head (Eph. 1.10). We are not carrying out our own 'Church expansion scheme'. Rather, we believe that through our preaching God is fulfilling His own plan.

STUDY SUGGESTIONS

WORD STUDY

1. (a) Explain the meaning of the Greek verb which is translated 'preach'.
   (b) Complete this sentence in your own words: 'Preaching is . . .'

REVIEW QUESTIONS

2. What can a preacher assume when he preaches the Gospel:
   (a) in a Church service where all who are present are baptized and confirmed Christians?
   (b) in an open-air meeting in a mainly non-Christian area in a town where the Church has been present and working for 80 years?
   (c) in a first meeting with people who do not know who Jesus is or what the word *Church* means?
3. What is the central content, or 'evangel', of the message we preach?
4. Read Acts 13.13–43; Acts 14.8–18; and Acts 17.16–34.
   (a) Compare Paul's sermons in the Jewish synagogue in Antioch of Pisidia, with those he preached in the pagan town of Lystra and in the Greek cultural centre of Athens. Describe the sort of approach he used in each.
   (b) What scriptural texts did Paul use in Antioch? Did he use scriptural texts in Lystra and Athens? If not, on what did he base his sermon?
5. (a) On whose authority do we preach?
   (b) How do we know that it is a valid authority?
   (c) Over whom does that authority extend?
6. 'The message that we have is not one that should make us feel superior to those to whom we preach' (p. 60). Explain this statement.

DISCUSSION AND RESEARCH TOPICS

7. Education has been defined as 'bringing people from the known to the unknown.'

    (a) In what ways can this definition be applied also to preaching?

    (b) What is the 'known' for those people in your society to whom the Gospel is 'unknown'?

8. What is your opinion of the following imaginary sermon? Is it the sort of preaching so far described in the chapter? Would it be a good sermon to preach to those who know nothing about the Gospel? What do you think its effect would be on those who hear it? Give reasons to support your answers.

    'Chief, I have asked you to call your elders and people together today to hear the Gospel of our Lord Jesus Christ. I know you will be happy to hear it, although, in your uncivilized state, you have never even heard the name of Jesus before. I am confident that you will hear it and repent and receive baptism and become members of our Church, and be saved on the day of judgement.

    'Before I came here I thought for a long time about the words I should bring to you. I know that one thing troubles you greatly— what will happen to your souls when your bodies die? I know that you worry about this, and that you go to the fetishes to make sure that your souls will gain immortality. You also go to juju men to find out which ghosts are troubling you, but you have no peace. Happiness escapes you. You are afraid of witches, because many of you have seen witches performing black magic.

    'I therefore come with the news that you should turn from these evil ways—they are the ways of Satan—and turn to the one true God. You must leave all gods and worship God, the Father of our Lord Jesus Christ, and He will give your souls immortality.

    'Does wood speak? Look! I can beat this tree (he beats it). It cannot complain. I can throw this stone on the ground (he throws it): Look, it does not protest! Why do you worship wood and stone? Why do you not worship God? The white man worships God alone. That is why he is so rich and powerful. You see him flying overhead in aircraft all the time. Can any of your fetishes do that?

    'Repent! The patience of God is coming to an end. Be baptized. Send your children to school. See that your women dress properly. Stop practising witchcraft. God will give you life without end. Amen.'

11. Preaching to People where they are

Some readers may ask: What use can we make in our preaching of our studies in Part 2? What about our efforts to understand the society, culture, and history of the people to whom we go? If there is only *one* message, can we not simply proclaim that message everywhere? Need we do more than just translate it into the local language, so that people will understand it?

The answer is that preaching is not just delivering a message to another person, as if it were a parcel. Preaching is witness. And the person who witnesses, as well as the person to whom he witnesses, is himself an important part of the proclamation, and of the whole process of preaching. That is why Jesus said, 'You shall receive power when the Holy Spirit comes upon you, and you shall be my witnesses . . . to the ends of the earth' (Acts 1.8). Without such power, no one can witness, and without the presence of the Holy Spirit to open the minds and hearts of the hearers, the hearers cannot truly hear the Gospel and respond. Ever since the Tower of Babel (Gen. 11), communication has been a problem for mankind. And it is only the Spirit of Pentecost who breaks down the barriers which keep people from communicating fully with one another. He gives us the ability to understand one another.

But the Gospel is not easily understood by people of other religions. Our task in preaching is to make it understandable and accessible. We are the bridges which people will use to come to understand what Paul called 'God's wisdom' (1 Cor. 2.6–16). But where people have not understood it, few of them will make the effort to come to do so. So, it is we, who have to initiate the process of communication when we want to preach, who also are responsible to make the message acceptable to them.

The first responsibility of making God's message understood is therefore the preacher's. We must first understand the people to whom we wish to communicate it, and then express our message in such a way that they can hear it speaking to them within their own culture and history. We must not expect them to come to us before they can hear the Word. It is we whom Christ sends to them. We are commissioned to go to them, to study them, and to understand the world they live in.

For this we need sympathetic understanding. We have to be able to see and feel as if we ourselves were the people to whom we go. We have to be able to hear the Gospel as it sounds to someone who is hearing it for the first time. We have to guess the questions he will want to ask, the new ideas and feelings he will have, the joys he will experience.

EMPATHY

But we cannot share another person's experience if we don't understand what his world is like. We have to become so involved in his world that we ourselves become two persons! We have to *become* a Mossi or a Kond or a Papuan or a Galla, even while we remain ourselves. This ability to feel one's way into another person's soul is the gift called *empathy*. As John V. Taylor writes of the Christian evangelist:

> His desire and longing . . . must be to enter, sensitively and appreciatively, into that other man's world, not, first, in order to *talk* more effectively about his Lord, but in order to *see* what the Lord of that world is like.

Christ is one, but you and I are different. And so the knowledge I have of Him as my Lord is different from the knowledge you have of of Him as yours. The Dagaba know His Lordship in one way. The Akan know it in another. The Akan who wishes to witness to the Dagaba must know what Christ as Lord will look like to a Dagaba. Taylor also says:

> Those who have not shared the terrors of a half-sinking ship at the height of a storm can never see the glory that comes walking on the waves at midnight. Only from within the nightmare world of the possessed can one know what he who casts out demons looks like, only from within the tomb can one hear the voice that summoned Lazarus, only from a cross see the dying robber's king.

If we want to understand a person, we can only do so by placing ourselves 'empathetically' in that person's place. To do this, we need to know about his society, his culture, his people's understanding of God and the spirit-world and the values of life. We need to know what he fears, what he cherishes, what he hopes for, what he suffers from.

An Ewe pastor, shortly after he came home to Africa from studying overseas, preached a sermon in the secondary school in Ghana where I was chaplain. He based it on the story of Jesus casting out the unclean spirits from the man who called himself 'Legion' (Mark 5.1–20). He began like this:

'Now what are we to make of such a story? Of course we cannot take it at its face-value! None of us believes in evil spirits of that sort any more. Yet the story must have some meaning to us. What meaning can we find in it?'

And he then went on to interpret the story to the rural schoolboys in the way in which he would have interpreted it to a university congregation in Scotland ten months before. Yet in that same secondary school,

I had just had the task of escorting to his home town a boy who was sure that he had been the object of sorcery on the part of his classmates, and who had himself been trying to use magic to get a higher place than they in the end-of-term reports.

We often assume that we already know what other people are like. And we preach to them as if we were preaching to ourselves.

If we are too lazy to undertake the difficult work of understanding another person's world, we shall probably assume that he is just like ourselves. Then when we speak to him we miss things which are important to him, and we needlessly spend time on problems which are ours but not his. If, on the other hand, after trying to share his feelings and to understand his world, we turn back to the Bible, all of a sudden we find that we understand things standing out which had never struck us before. All of a sudden certain things seem obvious which before we found difficult, and other things seem strange which before we found obvious. This is because we hear the word of God as it comes to the other person and to his people, bringing them exciting news which we never thought of.

When this happens, we are better fitted to be ambassadors for Christ. The first requirement for a successful ambassador is that he should be able to speak the language of the people to whom he goes. And language includes much more than words. It includes ways of thinking, an understanding of local customs, all that makes a Tiriki a Tiriki, and a Zulu a Zulu. These things are much more difficult to understand than the language of words. It is possible to speak a language fluently and still not understand the people who use it.

STUDYING THE PEOPLE'S RELIGION

In preaching, one of the most important things we have to understand—but not the only important thing—is the people's religious belief and practice. This will take considerable study on our part. (Appendix 1 p. 194 shows how such a study can be undertaken.) If we do not take the time to do it well, we are likely to use words which mean one thing to us and another to our hearers. Even some of the Bible translations now being used in different parts of the world are a hindrance rather than a help to good understanding, because the translators did not take the trouble to find the right word, or words, to express an idea previously unknown to the people.

Too often Christian preachers condemn the religion of the peoples to whom they go as 'superstition and ignorance'.

'What are the people with whom you work like?' I once asked an American missionary working in Ivory Coast.

'They're devil-worshippers,' he replied, his eyes glistening.

65

I was taken aback. I'd never heard of any 'devil-worshippers' since I came to Africa eight years before. My curiosity was excited. 'Do they themselves call their religion devil-worship?' I asked. 'Or is that the way you describe it?'

'I don't know what they call their religion,' he replied, scratching his head.

'Then how is it that you call it devil-worship?' I demanded.

'Well, it sure isn't the worship of God!' he replied, somewhat annoyed by my questions.

If we fail to understand the people to whom we go, we are likely to reach the kind of wrong conclusions that missionary made, and we shall not succeed in communicating anything to anyone.

Our job is to help the encounter between Christ and the people to get started. We do this by ourselves beginning to experience for them what the Gospel might mean to them. Once they have heard the Lord really speaking to them through our witness, they will want to hear more for themselves. Then our first job is over. We have led them to the side of the market from which they may find their own path home.

Here is an example. In Chokosi society there were two groups of Muslims. One group are 'real Muslims', and the other are considered only semi-Muslims. Once, I was preaching in a small village of the semi-Muslims, and I wondered what God was calling me to preach about. It was during the fasting month of Ramadan, and I knew that they kept the fast, although they did not follow many of the Muslim religious practices. They considered themselves Muslims, but they knew that they were not as 'good' Muslims as the other group, and that the real Muslims looked down upon them. Understanding this, I could in a certain way feel what they felt.

It struck me that the way they felt was very much the way that the 'people of the earth'—the ordinary Jews—felt in Jesus's time. They tried to be good Jews in their simple way, but the Pharisees, who tried to follow every commandment of the Jewish law, made them feel inferior.

But it was not the Pharisees whom Jesus befriended, it was the 'people of the earth', the humble poor. There was no doubt in my mind as to which of the two Chokosi groups Jesus would have befriended. He would have stood with the semi-Muslims, the kind of people who found 'religion' difficult, but still loved God. I could feel how happy it would make them to learn of Jesus' love for people like them, and of His impatience with the Pharisees' pride.

I read the first half of Matthew 6 to them, slowly and deliberately. Everyone was solemn, but suddenly they started laughing. At first they laughed quietly, at the mention of those who sounded trumpets before them as they give alms, and then uproariously, at the mention of those who showed off in the synagogues, made long prayers to impress people, and went around with a hungry look to let people know they were fasting.

These were the 'real Muslims', they recognized. How did Jesus know about the Muslims, they wondered? And as for praying privately, with few words, in sincerity of heart, that was what they themselves had been trying to do, but everyone laughed at them and said they weren't 'good Muslims'.

That night the people felt a warmth of attachment to the person of Jesus which I never saw them lose in all our visits which followed. My job was to lead them to personal encounter with Jesus, but to do that I had to know where they were, and to be able to understand where Jesus could meet them, and how they would feel about Jesus.

'I am the way, I am truth, and I am life,' Jesus said (John 14.6). When a man comes to know Jesus Christ, he knows the truth. But the truth of Jesus Christ is not something which we can possess; it is not an object which we can simply hand on to other people. Truth arises out of the meeting of every man and every society with Jesus Christ. Europeans experience the truth of Christ in one way: the Africans to whom they witness experience Christ in the way in which Christ speaks to them, as Africans. Those Africans in turn witness to the Christ they have known, but the other peoples who hear their witness will not simply receive something which the Christian Africans hand over to them. They will themselves meet Jesus Christ in faith.

Jesus's meeting with the Samaritan woman at the well (John 4.1–42) is a good example of how truth rises out of the meeting of people with Christ. The Samaritan woman was amazed at Jesus. 'He told me everything I have ever done,' she told her friends. 'Could this be the Messiah?'

Because of what she said, her fellow villagers believed, and they went out to see Jesus. But then they invited Him to come and stay a couple of days in their village. When the time was over they told the woman, 'We believe now, not because of what you said, but because we ourselves have heard Him, and we know that He really is the Saviour of the world.'

MONOLOGUE OR DIALOGUE?

The story of the Samaritan woman is an example of evangelism, i.e. of mission. It shows what happens when one person testifies to another what he has believed and experienced of Christ. But this is only the beginning of the process. When the other person believes, then his meeting with Christ begins. The exciting thing happens when that person himself actually experiences Christ. Then he comes really to know the truth, and in that process he becomes free (John 8.32). *The life-giving truth of the Gospel makes itself known in the 'dialogue' between the two people.*

The Gospel flourishes in *dialogue*, i.e. when there is conversation back and forth between the person who brings the message and the one who receives it. In dialogue our hearers become more than simply receivers of a message, or targets toward which we aim our proclamation. In a dialogue, they also contribute to what is happening. They reveal themselves—their hopes, their fears, their joys, their sorrows, their needs, their experiences. When they do that, the good news comes to them in a way they can understand. It comes to them as Jesus Himself would have spoken it to them, if He had met them at the well.

That is why a *monologue*, in which only one person speaks and all the other can do is listen, is not an adequate way of proclaiming the Gospel.

John Taylor describes evangelism as a 'meeting of three': the witness who proclaims Christ, the other person who does not yet know Christ's name, and Christ Himself. As Paul said to the crowd at Lystra, God has nowhere left Himself without witness (Acts 14.17 RSV). God has already been speaking to our hearers before we come to them, and in our dialogue we not only discover each other, we also discover God as our hearers have known Him.

One of the most important things for us to remember as we try to be sensitive and appreciative of other people's understanding, is that we must be careful 'never to call another person's light darkness'. The people to whom we go have their own ways of distinguishing between what is good and what is evil, between darkness and light. If we call their light darkness, then we are accusing them of wilful evil. We ought to be careful about this, for they themselves may be sure that they have been faithful to the truest insights of their religion and culture.

If we try to bully people into agreeing that their 'right' was wrong, and that they have been serving the devil, we may make them fear God's punishment, and this may lead them to accept our message. But are they accepting it because their conscience convicts them, or because we have forced them into it? *We* tell them what they are guilty of. *We* tell them they ought to feel guilty. We may succeed in making them feel guilty. But, as Taylor comments:

A Christ who releases me from guilt that has been induced, and forgives sins of which the Church but not my conscience has accused me, will not be the Saviour of *my* world. The true Christ of the Gospels works more fundamentally. Starting with the question, What wilt thou that I should do unto thee? He is prepared to be present to the other man with an infinite patience until he himself recognizes and points out the shape of evil in his own world.

START WITH CHRIST

In our preaching, therefore, we should not start by talking about sin and guilt. We should start with Christ. In the light of Christ's presence, those to whom we go will come to know their own deepest need:

> The evangelism that proceeds by listening and learning, entering into another man's vision in order to see Christ in it, does not start with assertions about sin, but waits to be told about it. And usually the truth about sin is almost the last truth to be told.

In every culture people have questions which they ask about life. They have problems which trouble them, and which they have not been able to solve. In dialogue, we shall soon discover what some of these questions are. Many of them are questions about God, and not about a God far off in the sky, but about God as He moves among men.

When I was learning the Chokosi language, I asked my teacher to dictate proverbs to me. Part of one proverb went: 'There is no medicine against hatred.' This puzzled me. I asked many people questions about it. I began to see that the word 'hatred' was a disguised way of speaking about witchcraft, so that the proverb meant, 'There is nothing you can do to keep people from practising witchcraft against you.' This was the first time I had come to see that witchcraft was one of the great unsolved problems of Chokosi society.

Medicine, the people believed, came from God. God had given man medicines which are effective against many troubles and diseases. But there was this one problem which God seemed to have provided no effective safeguard against. Another proverb was: 'If you erect a barrier here and you watch there, there is no way for the hyena to surprise you.' No matter how many precautions a person takes, there will always be a need for watchfulness, the people were saying. But if a person watches, he can perhaps avoid the danger.

The real question which the Chokosis were asking was, 'How can we be safe? How can we be protected from the evil which seeks to destroy us?' This worry was what kept people from sleeping soundly at night. 'Night falls, and all of a sudden there's trouble,' was another proverb. When the day is over, everyone should be in his compound eating peacefully and chatting quietly for a while before going to sleep. No one should have to confront any more serious problems before daybreak. But just at that time—when people let down their defences—that is when trouble is likely to arise.

THE SEARCH FOR PROTECTION

The people's question was, how to find protection against the trouble that might suddenly appear and bring to nothing all that one had worked for. The many medicine pots and talismans and amulets and protective 'medicines' which people kept outside their houses, in doorways, and inside their huts, all showed their fear very clearly. And yet, the people found, not even all these devices worked. Where is a man to look for protection, they wondered.

Another proverb said: 'If you throw your club at the monkey and it misses him and remains in the branches, will the monkey's friend give it back to you?' Here was a pointer to the answer. If a person could have a friend who would defend him and protect him against his enemies, all would be well. That person could be safe. But where was such a friend to be found?

The Chokosis' question was a question about God. It was a question which the people themselves were asking about God, not one which I or any stranger asked. The word 'God' was not found in the question, but it was a question about the deepest problem of life: Where can we look for protection? It was the same question which the Psalmist asked:

I lift up my eyes to the hills.
From whence does my help come?

It was a question the Chokosis asked, and the answer which the Psalmist received turned out to be an answer which meant a lot to them:

My help comes from the Lord,
Who made heaven and earth.
He will not let your foot be moved,
He who keeps you will not slumber.
Behold, He who keeps Israel will neither slumber nor sleep.
The Lord is your keeper;
The Lord is your shade on your right hand.
The sun shall not smite you by day,
Nor the moon by night.
The Lord will keep you from all evil;
He will keep your life.
The Lord will keep
Your going out and your coming in
From this time forth and for evermore. (Ps. 121)

When we talked about this, we talked about something which spoke to the needs of the Chokosis. For too long, Paul Tillich said, we have been answering questions which people are not asking, and failing to answer

'In every culture people have problems which trouble them . . . many are questions about God' (p. 69).

In Ghana a man goes to the medicine man for protective 'medicine' against disease, or perhaps against misfortune or witchcraft. In Japan a priest sells 'prophecies' at the entrance to a temple.

What problems chiefly trouble your own people today, and where do they go to find solutions?

the questions which they are asking. Taylor agrees: 'Christ has been presented as the answer to the question a white man would ask, the solution to the needs that Western men would feel, the Saviour of the world of the European world-view.'

There is an English proverb: 'One man's meat is another man's poison.' If this is true, Africans and Indians and Indonesians cannot simply adopt a European form of Christianity. When they hear Christ speaking to their own needs, they will know how to reply. That will be an African Christian faith, an Indian Christian faith, an Indonesian Christian faith. The names of God which the Chokosi Christians came to use most often were 'Guardian', 'Protector', 'Defender', 'Restorer'. And they had a lot to tell me about that God, from which I learned much.

The truth of the Gospel arises out of the dialogue between the ambassador of Christ and the people to whom he witnesses. When that dialogue is free and open, something wonderful happens: Christ reveals Himself. 'No more do we believe,' the hearers then tell the ambassadors, 'because of your word, for we ourselves have heard Him, and we know that He is really the Saviour of the world.'

STUDY SUGGESTIONS

WORD STUDY

1. What is 'empathy'?
2. Give examples from everyday life to show the difference in meaning between 'dialogue' and 'monologue'.

REVIEW QUESTIONS

3. What are some of the qualities needed for a successful ambassador in international relations? Which, if any, of those qualities do we, as ambassadors of Christ, also need? What other qualities, if any, do we need as well?
4. 'We must be careful never to call another's light darkness' (pp. 68, 69). What is meant by this statement? What happens when we do call another person's light darkness?
5. It has been said that evangelism is a 'meeting of three'. Who are those three?

DISCUSSION TOPICS

6. How would you reply to someone who said: 'Jesus Christ is one. Therefore all peoples must experience Him in the same way'?
7. Give examples of any proverbs you know which express unsolved problems of life in your country.
8. What are some of the deepest questions which your own people ask

about life? In what ways does the Gospel help to answer these questions?

9. What things do you yourself most fear? Where do you find protection against them, and in what way?

10. Give three examples of things which Christian evangelists can do, which will help them to understand the people to whom they preach.

11. Read again the imaginary sermon on p. 62. What is wrong with it? What did the preacher fail to do before he preached? What is his basic attitude toward the people to whom he is preaching? Is his message likely to be good news to them?

12. Do you think that the Church is ever in danger of behaving like the 'real Muslims' described on pp. 66 and 67? Give examples to support your answer.

12. Ready for the Gospel?

In the preceding section we assumed that anyone from any culture can meet Jesus Christ in the same way as people who are members of the Church and come from Christianized cultures.

Some Christians find this assumption difficult to accept. There is a great difference, such Christians say, between preaching Christ to people who live in a Christianized society, and preaching Him to people in a society which has never been influenced by Christianity. They believe that people who have been prepared for the Gospel by membership in a Christianized society are ready for evangelization, but that those who have had no contact with the Gospel must first be 'pre-evangelized'.

Christians who take this view point out that many of those to whom the apostles preached were Jews or 'God-fearers', i.e. Greeks or Romans who had attached themselves to the Jewish synagogues. They had been 'prepared' for the Gospel. They already believed in one God and worshipped Him. They had turned away from crude, materialistic forms of worship, and no longer practised idolatry. They knew the basic moral demands of the Old Testament Law and tried to follow them. But in our preaching situation today, such Christians say, we often encounter people who either don't believe in one Supreme God or who worship Him along with a whole company of other gods. Their religion includes idolatry and superstition; they practise magic; and they have no real idea of what is right or wrong, only of what is or is not 'customary'.

Therefore, these Christians say, before we can begin to evangelize such people we need to purify their ideas of God. We must turn them from idolatry, and make them understand the natural law of right and wrong. Only when this has been done, shall we be able to present Christ to them and they be able to receive Him. Until that time, Christ can make no sense to them; they need to be properly prepared before they can understand and believe in Him.

This view of the need for 'pre-evangelization' does not, however, seem to be supported by Scripture. Paul's letter to the Romans does not seem to suggest that the Jews' possession of the law and their knowledge of God's revelation helped them to achieve salvation. It does not seem that the Jews in fact (not in theory) had any advantage over the Gentiles. It does not seem that salvation is easier for those who have lived under the Old Testament Law, or natural law, than it is for those who have not. Mankind is not saved by the law, but by God's grace in Christ.

Christians who say that people need to be prepared in advance for the Gospel seem to be saying, in a modified way, what the Jewish Christians from Jerusalem claimed in Antioch (Acts 15): that Gentiles could not be saved unless they became Jews, and the only way to become a Christian was to become a Jewish Christian. But this claim was firmly rejected by the Church then, and even in its modified form it ought to be rejected by the Church today.

A man is put right with God only through faith and not by doing what the Law commands, or is God only the God of the Jews? Is He not the God of the Gentiles also? Of course He is. God is one, and He will put the Jews right with Himself on the basis of their faith, and the Gentiles right through their faith' (Rom. 3.28–30).

Thus there is no need for pre-evangelization, but only for the sort of evangelization which speaks to people where they are, whatever their personal, social, cultural, and religious background. This sort of evangelization presents Jesus Christ as the Lord of all peoples, as the One who can speak to the Jew under the law and to the Gentile in a world influenced by Judaism or Christianity, as well as to the Gentile who lives in a world which has not known the traditions of a synagogue or Church.

As preachers, we must be sensitive to the different understandings of the world which our hearers may have. But, to say that there is a basic difference between those who are ready to be evangelized and those who need 'pre-evangelization', is to be like the racists who say that there are 'superior' and 'inferior' peoples, 'higher' and 'lower' religions, 'civilized men' and 'savages'.

As preachers of the good news of the grace of God in Christ, we know that that good news is sufficient for all sorts and conditions of men. We need not withhold the Gospel from people until they are 'ready'.

On the contrary, it is our task to discover the place where it will meet them now. We believe that Jesus Christ is Lord of all, and so He can meet His people whenever and wherever He wills. As bridges for His meeting with men, all we have to do is to try and find the proper place for it.

THE WITNESS OF THE SPIRIT

We shall be helped in this task by our belief in the Holy Spirit, if we remember that He has been working in the hearts and minds of the people to whom we go, even before we arrive. As we saw above, He has not left them 'without witness' (Acts 14.17; Romans 1.20). This means that we can link our witness to the people about God's acts in Christ, to the Holy Spirit's witness to them. But we shall never be able to do this if we start by arguing that everything in the people's existing religion and culture is 'pagan', and that God has never before revealed Himself to them. Unfortunately the Church did in many places start by arguing that people's existing beliefs were wrong and wicked. But most Christians today recognize that the Church itself was wrong to do so.

We are not sent to argue, but to bring good news which has the power to wash away everything that is not worthy of it. We don't need *first* to destroy in order *then* to build up. By bringing in God's revelation we are bringing in a bright light which itself dispels the darkness. But the light must shine into the very house in which the people now live, and no other.

Here is an example. Many of the people to whom we preach believe in many divine beings and in many different spirits. It is not our task to argue with them and say that these divine beings and spirits do not exist. We have to witness to these people in terms of what they already believe. We find a clue to the relation between Christ and such unseen powers in Colossians 1.16: 'By Him God created everything in heaven and on earth, the seen and the unseen things, including spiritual powers, lords, rulers, and authorities. God created the whole universe through Him and for Him.'

This shows us where to start. If we preach that Christ is the head of all things—including the 'unseen' powers in which people already believe—and that all divine power dwells in Him (Col. 1.19), then people will be able to understand us, and will relate our new preaching to their previous beliefs.

THE CAUSE OF SYNCRETISM

If we ignore people's beliefs in spirits and gods, we shall only be adding a belief in Christ to their previous beliefs. We shall not be changing their beliefs into a belief in a Christ who is Lord over the spirits and gods. They will say, 'It's all right for Christians to worship only God in Christ, but we, who have many other gods, will need to continue worshipping them as well as God in Christ.'

This adding of one belief to another is called *syncretism*. When it happens, people become divided in their loyalties. They fail to see how the different beliefs are related, and they become confused and dissatisfied. They feel like the man who told Jesus, 'my name is Legion, for there are many of us' (Mark 5.9). But our task is to show people how to relate what they have previously believed to what we now have to tell them about Christ.

Another example is the belief which many peoples hold, in a kind of life after death for the departed members of their clan or family. If we take no notice of such a belief, and say that the dead are dead, and go on to talk only about the living, the people will not know what to do with their previous belief in what John Mbiti of Kenya calls the 'living dead'. They will want to go on to make sacrifices and libations to their ancestors. So instead, we should preach sensitively, and show that there are many passages in the New Testament which refer to the dead, and to Christ's relation to them (e.g. Eph. 4.8–10; Acts 14.16; 17.30; 1 Pet. 3.9–10, 4.6). Then people will be comforted to hear that the message we proclaim concerns not only them but their beloved ancestors as well. In this way we can avoid the danger of syncretism, for we shall show that God is speaking to them in what they already know.

It is probably true to say that when Christians in Africa or Melanesia or wherever it may be continue in pre-Christian religious practices after their baptism, they do so for the same reason that the Israelites turned to the Baalim. They do so because they think that the God whom Christians proclaim does not have power in certain areas of life. The Israelities first experienced Yahweh as a desert God and a God of war, who led them to victory in battle. When they came to live a settled existence in Canaan they found it difficult to think of Him as a God who was involved in agricultural life, and therefore they turned to the fertility cult of Canaan: Baal-worship.

In the same way, Ghanaian Christians whom I knew often forsook Christian practices in order to perform pagan rites in connection with such things as fertility, their relation to the dead, and their fear of witchcraft. In at least the last two of these, I believe the Church may have been to blame, for it chose to ignore or belittle the people's beliefs in these matters. It failed to give people a new Christian understanding, starting from where the people were, of death and witchcraft and of the relation between spirits and sickness and death.

If we listen carefully to what people are saying as we preach, and to the kinds of responses they make, and not expect them to listen in silence, then we shall see the kinds of questions which are on their minds. Then we shall know what direction to take in answering them. We must not be guided only by what we want to preach about, but also by what the people themselves need to hear.

STUDY SUGGESTIONS

Word Study

1. (a) What is the meaning of the word 'syncretism'?
   (b) Give an example to show how syncretism is often caused.

Review Questions

2. For what reasons do some Christians claim that 'pre-evangelization' is needed for people who have no previous experience of Christianity?
3. What reasons have been given in this Guide for saying that 'pre-evangelization' is not needed?
4. What sort of preaching is necessary when we are speaking to people who have no previous experience of Christianity?

Discussion Topics

5. A pastor counselling a new catechumen who feared that he was being bewitched, said to him, 'There is no such thing as witchcraft—just believe in God.' What do you think would be the result of such counselling?
6. Read again the imaginary sermon on p. 62. What attitude towards the people did the preacher convey? How much understanding and sympathy did he show? Do you think he embodied a witness of love? Was his message a message of grace?
7. The following are questions which people might have asked the preacher, or comments which they might have made, after he had given that sermon.
   Say in each case how the preacher might have avoided misunderstanding the people, and how he might have related the Gospel to what they believed, instead of trying to tear down their beliefs
   What things did the preacher assume that these people knew about Christianity, which in fact they did not know?
   (a) But we do worship God! We believe that He has given us these things, so that when we worship them we are worshipping God!
   (b) There is only one God—any child knows that! Those things which we may call 'gods' are all one with God; we never say we worship 'gods' without adding 'our'. It is through these 'gods' that God has made Himself known to us. God himself is one.
   (c) Witchcraft is troublesome to us indeed, but it is troublesome because we believe that it is in sleep that the witchcraft goes out of a person and brings about destruction. Many of us not only

fear the witchcraft of others, we fear that *we* ourselves may be witches. Witchcraft is very different from black magic, which people perform when they are awake—we don't want any of that in our town!

(d) Juju men, as you call them, are our doctors. To find out what our fathers and mothers want, we do not go to juju men, but to diviners. Notice also that we speak of 'our fathers and mothers'; we don't call them ghosts. What you call ghosts are to us evil, nameless spirits, against whom we may go to the medicine men to get protection.

(e) We believe that when a man dies he goes to the place of the departed. We don't know what you mean by 'the immortality of the soul,' but we do believe that all who die go to the place where they meet their ancestors. Did you say we are made of body and soul? Why do you not distinguish between the different kinds of soul?

(f) We do not worship wood and stone. That tree in the centre of our village is the place where, it was revealed to us, divine power dwells in our village. We worship the power of God which is there, not the tree itself.

(g) We don't know why you call us 'uncivilized'. We feel that it is Europeanized people who behave in uncivilized ways; for you have forsaken the paths of culture which our fathers taught us.

(h) The white man is full of surprises, but we're not sure we want to be like him. Why should we want to fly in aircraft? Are we birds? Where do we have to go so quickly that we can't walk or go by bicycle or lorry?

(i) We don't send our children to school because we have seen that those children who go to school cease to obey their parents. We don't want to sacrifice our children to the Europeans.

(j) Why do you say our women don't dress properly? They are modest, and they do not try to seduce men with suggestive clothing and perfumes, the way your 'civilized' women do.

13. Selective Preaching and Selective Hearing

Most preachers would admit that they do *select* certain things which they wish to preach about, and that no one in his preaching ever succeeds in preaching *all* the Gospel. But it is important to try to preach on as many aspects of the Gospel as possible, and not just on our 'favourite doctrines'.

In order to do this we may find it helpful to use a lectionary, or almanac of Scripture readings based on the whole Bible. Such lectionaries are planned to include all the main teachings of the Christian faith, and present the whole Gospel better than we are likely to do by making our own choice of passages to preach from. But nearly every lectionary is planned to suit the needs of a particular group of readers, and some lectionaries are better than others for use with new hearers. Before you start to use one it is helpful to examine carefully the passages set, and see whether you think they will serve well for your particular purpose. For example, I found the lectionary of the Church of South India better for use in preaching to new Christians and hearers than the lectionary of our own Church in Ghana.

Even so, the fact that a passage is included in a particular lectionary does not mean that all preachers will interpret it in the same way, or emphasize the same aspect of it. We all select 'what speaks to us', and try to communicate that; just as we tend to reject, or not to notice, those aspects of Biblical teaching which don't fit easily into our previous understanding of the faith.

Because each preacher is himself an individual, this variation is unavoidable, and is not necessarily a bad thing. We are who we are, and we cannot pretend to be someone else. God, knowing this, has nevertheless called us, and He will use us in His own way for His purpose of communicating the Good News to those to whom He sends us. He can make up for our failings, and within the total Christian fellowship it is likely that what one preacher neglects another may express, so that in the end, the whole Gospel may be communicated.

But we must also recognize that selective preaching is only one side of the process of communication. Selective hearing is another. In communication, the one who gives the message and the one who receives it both take part. The receivers are active not only in accepting or rejecting the message, but by accepting or rejecting certain parts of it. Each will hear some things and not hear others. Each will reinterpret some things to fit better with his previous understandings, and will thus give new meaning to what he hears. Whether a preacher intends it or not, people will select some parts of our preaching and reject others. They may not do this consciously. It is an almost unconscious process of selective hearing which takes place. People will hear what they understand, or what seems important to them to try to understand. They will not hear what seems not to concern them, nor what seems impossible for them to understand. They will not hear what seems to them to be the answer to a question they have never asked.

This is different from saying that they will hear what is easy, and reject what is difficult. That is not true at all. Often what is difficult will stand out most clearly. The things which people refuse to hear are not the things that are difficult, but important; they refuse to hear the things which are unimportant, and irrelevant, i.e. the ones they cannot see why they should bother to try to understand.

But we need not be nervous. God uses this process of selective hearing. We can relax, for in the end God knows His people better than we do, and He can communicate to their hearts even through our poor messages. He may choose to use only our love and concern for the people, and not our message. Perhaps *who we are* will speak louder than *what we say*. We cannot know for sure. All we have is His assurance that 'My word shall not return to me empty.' But that assurance is enough!

AN EXAMPLE

I saw this happen with the Chokosis in an exciting way. In listening to them, I often heard them using words which could be translated as 'those who improve the town' and 'those who destroy the town'. 'There are two sorts of people in the world,' they said. 'The "improvers" are the ones who make the town a better place, and the "destroyers" are the ones who destroy the town.'

The 'improver' is a person who co-operates with others, tells the truth, helps other people, is not greedy but generous, and seeks the good of the whole community. The 'destroyer' is a person who lies and speaks evil, gossips, abuses others, brings about trouble between other people, refuses to co-operate, is greedy, seeks his own benefit in everything, and refuses to work for the good of the community.

Later on I learned that the Chokosis also used the word 'destroyer' for people whom they suspected of practising withcraft. These were the people they feared the most. They went to buy medicines and charms to protect themselves against them, and many people left their own villages to settle elsewhere when they thought they were being bewitched.

I talked with them about their fears, and about what they believed it was which caused a man or woman to hate others so much that he would seek to destroy their lives. I sought to understand precisely how they thought. They knew that I had heard what they were saying, and that I didn't belittle it. This was important. They let me into the innermost chambers of their souls. I seemed, they felt, to understand what they feared and why they feared it. I knew what the world looked like to them.

I did not preach much about witchcraft—perhaps only a mention from time to time. But I did preach about Christ and about His omnipotence, His power in every area of life, His power over all beings. I described how He had healed sick people and people possessed with demons.

From time to time I heard them apply the word 'improver' to Christ.

I had called Him Redeemer, Master, Lord, and Saviour, but never Improver or Restorer. The Chokosis had an old proverb: 'When the redeemer has come, then we will all rest,' and they said that Christ was such a redeemer. He had helped so many people and brought new hope to them. He must be the redeemer for whom they had been waiting, the one who would restore to the world its proper order and unity. One by one, they started to trust Christ. In this trust they also came more closely together to one another.

New things started to happen in the communities where we were preaching. People started to work together to make roads and dams and latrines, to make their villages, as they said, 'a better place'. It had been many years since such community action had been seen. And they sang praises to Christ for it. In the words of an old Chokosi song (about a chief who had shown them a way when an enemy chief had said there was no way), they sang, 'Jesus says there is a way!' 'We have a restorer!' they announced, 'We have a redeemer.'

We had preached the Gospel. The people had heard it, and they had responded to it in their own way, in terms of their own traditional ideas. I could not have predicted beforehand how they would respond, or what it would be in our preaching which would strike a responsive note. I selected, as faithfully as I could, in faithfulness to the Word and in faithfulness to my understanding of the Chokosi people, what I would preach about, and they selected what they were going to hear and what they were not. I believe that God was active in all this, making sure that His Word would not return to Him empty.

EXEGESIS AND EXPOSITION

In this chapter on preaching we have not so far considered many of the subjects that usually come into a seminary course in 'homiletics'. There are many books available which give practical guidance in planning and writing sermons. Instead, we have given attention to what happens when people communicate with each other. There are many people who can construct a well organized sermon, but who cannot preach successfully because they do not understand what Christian communication involves. They don't understand who they are in relation to those to whom they preach. They do not understand their hearers, nor what the situation is in which they are preaching.

But in all Christian preaching there are two things which have to be done if we are to be faithful carriers of God's Word as handed down to us in the Bible. All that we have considered about understanding our hearers and their situation is the background to these two essential tasks. In formal courses on homiletics these tasks are called 'exegesis' and 'exposition'.

1. *Exegesis* is making sure that we understand exactly what the original setting of a chapter, book, or verse of the Bible was, and what its meaning was in that setting. We have to ask such questions as: To whom was it spoken or written? By whom? On what occasion? Why?

In other words, we have to forget for the moment what the verse has meant to us in the past, and to our society and culture, and to our Church. We have to get back to what the verse meant in the first place, in its original context.

2. *Exposition* is what follows exegesis. Once we have found out the original context of a passage, we shall know better how to interpret its meaning for our own time, and to ask ourselves what it can mean to the people to whom we are preaching. 'Exposition' means showing how the message applies to us and our hearers today.

In exegesis we are concerned only with the Word itself. In exposition we are concerned primarily with those to whom we are preaching, and our task is to find ways to communicate the Word we have exegeted to those people in their particular situation.

Here is an example of the exegesis and exposition of Matthew 10.8:

This verse was often used in the Church I attended while in college as a reading before the offering, and in the version used there read: 'Freely ye have received, freely give.' Used in that context, we interpreted it to mean: 'God has blessed you with much; give much.'

If we study that verse in its context, however, i.e. doing exegesis, we see that Jesus was speaking to His disciples, not to everyone. He was giving them instructions for their missionary journeys, for their preaching and healing ministries. One of the disciples must have asked Him: 'Can we take any money when we heal the sick?' or 'how much should we make them pay?'—as other 'healers' of the time did and as most doctors do today. Jesus replied: (TEV translation) 'You have received without paying, give without being paid' (TEV); or, in the NEB version: 'You have received without cost, give without charge.' So we see that what the verse really means is: 'As God has blessed you with spiritual gifts without your having to pay anything, do not charge others for the use of these gifts.'

Now that is *exegesis*, understanding the original meaning of a verse. The preacher should do it at home, in his room, and not before the congregation. It is what you and I must do as our homework before we can go on to share the Word with others. We must understand the Word in its context.

The next step is *exposition*. In exposition we take the passage or verse or theme and *expose its meaning to those particular people to whom we are preaching.*

This step has two parts: what we do at home and what we do before the people. Not all verses and passages when exegeted will appear useful in preaching to new hearers. Mathew 10.8 would not ordinarily be suitable in such a situation. But there might be an occasion when it could be helpful.

Here is an example of such a situation. Imagine that you have been going to a village three or four times, and each time you go, the village, or different individuals in it, give you gifts. At first you are thankful, but after a while you realize—they are not shy about it—that they are actually hoping for something in return. They want your help in getting them a well; they want you to send someone to teach them English; they want you to use your good offices to get them food or clothing.

In other words, they feel they must give you something in order to get you to do something for them.

Now you think about that, and you recognize that the local health centre nurses expect bribes before they will treat people after hours. The local politicians expect 'dashes' before they campaign for new amenities for any village, and the chief expects a gift before he goes with a man's son to the court. In that village the diviner is paid, the medicine man is paid; even people who come to communal labour projects on individuals' farms expect to be 'paid' well with food and drinks.

And you think about Jesus Christ and about what He did. You remember how He was in the form of God but emptied Himself and accepted human form, the form of a servant (Phil. 2.6–11), and how He said, 'The Son of man came not to be served, but to serve, and to give His life as a ransom for many' (Mark 10.45).

And you think of Naya, a man you know in a nearby village, whose rice was eaten by birds last month because he went on a two-week journey just before harvest time. You remember how he went on the journey to help a neighbour, Kwaku, search for his missing son. You remember how, when he got back and saw the rice, he simply said, 'It doesn't matter. If I'd stayed here to watch it, Kwaku would have had to go alone.' And you knew that Kwaku could not pay him anything.

And you relate these things together and you prepare your sermon. You will start to talk with the people about the nurses and officials and the ways in which they expect 'dashes', and about how Jesus's disciples wondered whether they should also expect payment. You will tell them about how Jesus was different. You will talk about how Naya, the man in the neighbouring village, was to Kwaku. Then you will talk about how you are called to be like your Master was. You will say that you are interested in helping the people in any way which you can, but they should not feel they need to 'grease your palm' before your hand will move on their behalf.

'The ambassadors of Christ have a responsibility to understand the people to whom they go' (p. 85).

When a large rice-growing scheme was launched to provide against famine in the Sudan, a careful survey of the land was first made so as to know how to plan the scheme to suit the local conditions.

What are the Pastor's instruments for 'surveying' the needs of his congregation and of the rest of the community?

This is the basis for a sermon. But we must remember that the purpose of any good sermon is to witness to Jesus Christ. You are not called to preach about yourself, but about Christ, so your exposition must serve that purpose. The theme of your sermon might be: 'Jesus Christ—the one who gives without charge.' Or you might be able to develop the theme in some other way.

In any case, what you are doing is sharing the word of Matthew 10.8 with your hearers in the context of:

(a) your relationship to them, and

(b) the ways of the world in which they live, into which the Gospel comes as the new message of God's grace. You witness to Jesus Christ, not as an abstract idea, but as directly related to the actual real-life situations in which you and they are involved.

In the process of communication, we must believe that Jesus Christ will come to meet our hearers with love and a call for response, and we must hope that they will respond to Jesus with commitment and faith.

SUMMARY

There are thus four steps involved in this kind of preaching:

1. Our own understanding of the faith,
2. Our understanding of the culture of the people to whom we go, and their actual life-situation,
3. Our faithful exegetical study of the Word; and
4. Our exposition of that Word to the people as it would apply in their situation, so that they may hear the Lord speaking His Word to them in their lives.

In summary, then, the Gospel is proclaimed to peoples who belong to societies with their own cultures and religions. The ambassadors of Christ who take part in the ministry of preaching have a responsibility to understand the people to whom they go, so that they can engage in full dialogue with them. Three parties are involved in the dialogue: the preacher, those to whom he goes, and Christ.

STUDY SUGGESTIONS

WORD STUDY

1. (a) Give examples to show the difference in meaning between the words 'exegesis' and 'exposition'.

    (b) Which of the following words are nearest in meaning to 'exegesis' and which to 'exposition'?

> exploration   explanation   expression
> excavation   examination   expounding

REVIEW QUESTIONS

2. What is a lectionary? Is it customary in your Church to use one and, if so, in what way is it used? Why is it a good thing to use one? Are all lectionaries compiled for the same type of audience?
3. (a) Who are the active parties in the process of communicating? In what ways is each active?
   (b) In what ways is communicating the Gospel different from any other sort of communication?

DISCUSSION AND RESEARCH TOPICS

4. Is it always wrong for people to reinterpret what a preacher says, and apply it to something else? Give reasons for your answer.
5. Use the following passages as a basis for practice in exegesis and exposition. The questions will help you to plan sermons addressed to particular congregations which will take account of their culture and life-situation.
   (a) *Hebrews 11*—faith—how would you relate this to a people who don't know of Abraham, Gideon, Barak, etc.? Can you think of examples of this type of faith of which your people know?
   (b) *John 15.1–10*—the relationship of the believer to Christ—why does Jesus use the image of a vine? How, if you are working with people who do not know vines and vineyards and wine, could you express the same idea of the unity of the believer with Christ through images with which they are familiar?
   (c) *Luke 22.20*—Jesus describes His blood (His death) in terms of a cup of wine by which a covenant is made. What kind of covenants or agreements or alliances are customary to your people? Do they have any religious customs which involve eating or drinking together? Can these customs be used, *without leading to misunderstanding*, as examples to explain the relationship between Jesus's death and our relationship with God?

PART 4
THE MINISTRY OF MAKING
AND EQUIPPING DISCIPLES

---

14. The Call to Enlist

So we go out and preach the Gospel. We may preach once or twice or
we may preach many times over. No matter how many times we preach,
we always expect to see something happen, or else we wouldn't go.

What do we expect to see happen when we preach? One catechist I
met told me: 'I went to a certain place to preach for the first time just
last Sunday. Many people repented. I am now preparing them for
baptism.' He expected an immediate and total response.

A priest I knew was quite different. He had been preaching in several
villages for a number of years. I asked him whether he felt the people
were ready to become Christians. 'Oh no' he replied. 'I don't suppose
they ever will. We just go out to let them know what the Christian
faith is all about. Maybe some of their children who go to school will
become Christian, but we don't really expect we can convert the fathers.'

The one expected everything and immediately. The other expected
no definite results, even in the distant future!

HOW MUCH CAN WE PLAN?

Usually we plan our work according to our expectations of what is
going to happen. Therefore it is important to ask: how do we see the
process of mission? What do we expect to see happen when we preach?
Do we expect an immediate response? A gradual response? Little
response? Do we expect that our preaching will lead people to become
angry with us? To understand us better? To repent? To be converted?
Do we preach and then, when there is a response, immediately baptize
the people into full membership in the Church? Or must people go
through a stage or several stages between preaching and baptism? Have
we really planned how the work will be carried out? Before we answer
these questions we must remember that the Holy Spirit is the power
behind Christian mission. As we saw in chapter 1, He builds up the
Church so that it may take part in mission. The Church must be
responsive to His working and His leading. Although there is no one
plan for mission everywhere and at all times, there is one Spirit who

enables men to take part in mission at all times and in each place. This means that we cannot plan, from start to finish, what will happen. If we do, we are trying to box the Holy Spirit in. Our ideas of what may happen must be open to possible new happenings which the Spirit will bring about.

Secondly, our preaching cannot bring people to repent. *We* cannot convert anyone. Repentance and conversion are the work of the Spirit. He may use us as His instruments to move people's minds and hearts to give themselves to Christ, but we cannot control Him, or *make* other people Christians.

Therefore, all work in mission should be carried on only with continual intercessory prayer. We work, but we also expect to see God working. And He will be working even without us—before we get to a place to preach for the first time, between our visits, while we are on leave, at all times.

A university student who visited our work in Chereponi early on, wrote me after his return to the university: 'I shall be praying for your work every Tuesday.' It was amazing to me to see how the work we were doing on Tuesdays progressed faster than our other work! I began to think: 'What if we were to gather together every day and pray for the work we are going to do that day, actually naming the villages we are working in, and asking God's blessing on our work? Would all the work be like the Tuesday work?'

We tried it. Every morning a group of four to eight of us gathered together at dawn for Bible reading and prayer. I date the real progress of our work from that date. 'Ask and you shall be given; seek and you shall find; knock and it shall be opened to you.' That was how Jesus advised His disciples (Matt. 7.7). We found it was absolutely true, not as a kind of 'magic', but as an opening of ourselves and our work to the blessing of God.

Some people are afraid of making particular requests in their prayers. They think it is wrong, or else they are too shy, to name actual people and places in their requests, or to refer to specific problems. But this is the kind of prayer which Jesus taught to His disciples, and Paul reminded the Philippians what he had learned of the Master's teaching: 'Have no anxiety; the Lord is near; in everything make your requests known to God in prayer and petition with thanksgiving' (Phil. 4.6). We need not be shy of asking God to do His work!

We must also remember, however, that we are called to be responsible participants in mission. God will not give us day-by-day instructions for what what we are to do. He expects us to use our heads and to plan our work. And as long as we have asked, and continue to ask, the Spirit's guidance in all our thinking and planning, it is rather irresponsible of us not to do so.

DISCIPLING: A PROCESS

If we are to plan our part in mission responsibly, we must have a clear idea in our minds of what the relation is between (1) preaching, (2) baptismal instruction (or 'catechesis'), (3) baptism, (4) Church membership, and (5) Christian nurture (the regular, ongoing education and equipping of the members of the Church). These are all parts of one work: the making of disciples.

In this chapter we are concerned with what the New Testament writers call 'discipling' (from the Greek verb *matheteuein*, meaning 'to make disciples'). This one work has several different parts, and there are many different ways of seeing the relationship between them. Some people see a series of separate stages, others a sudden change, still others see a gradual growth. The diagrams below may help us see the difference.

1. One way of describing the process of discipling is to say that a person who hears the Gospel goes through several stages until he becomes a full member of the Church, as in diagram 1.

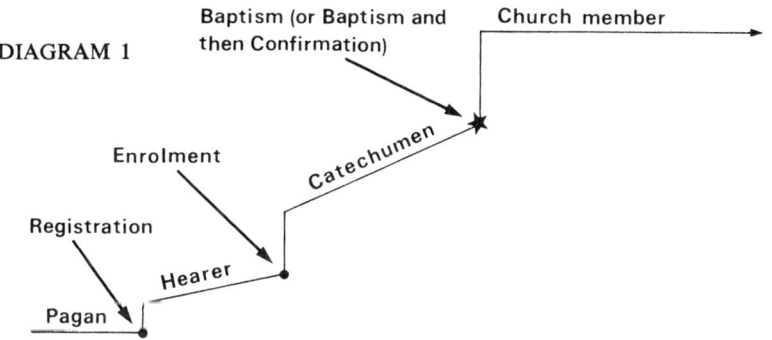

DIAGRAM 1

2. Another way of describing the process is to say that it means a sudden change from one state to another, as in diagram 2.

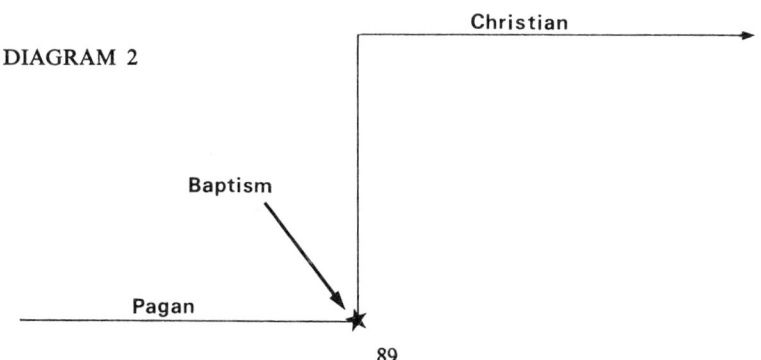

DIAGRAM 2

3. A third way of describing the process is to say that it is a progress, or period of continual growth, marked by no sudden changes of status. There will be a baptism, and the names of catechumens may at some time be written down, but these events are not strongly emphasized, as in diagram 3.

DIAGRAM 3

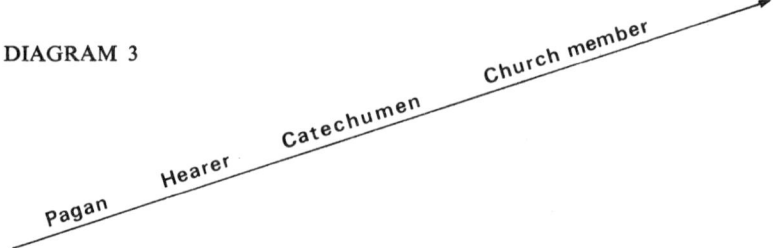

But none of these diagrams fully illustrates the process. The first diagram suggests that all growth stops when the person becomes a Church member. There is a long process before being admitted to the status of member of the Church, and the whole of a person's pre-baptismal life seems to be a preparation for Church membership. Once a person is baptized he can consider himself to have 'passed out' or 'graduated'—he need no longer struggle or strain. But many people find this very difficult to accept. (Compare Phil. 3.13f.)

In the second diagram the same thing is true of the state of the Christian, once he is baptized as a member of the Church. And according to this diagram there seems to be no possibility of growth towards life in Christ before a person is baptized. One is either 'in' or 'out'.

In the third diagram growth is going on all the time. It assumes that pagans are already growing in their knowledge of God. They continue to grow as they hear the Gospel, receive instruction, and enter the Church, and the same sort of growth seems to continue after they have come into the Church. Christian nurture is thus an extension of pre-baptismal instruction.

Many Christians would agree with this third diagram, but find it difficult to read passages like Romans 6 and letters like 1 Peter without believing that at some point in becoming a Christian one's life is changed in a dramatic way. Such people would find it difficult to call a non-Christian their 'brother in the faith', or to believe that hearers or 'inquirers' have the same commitment to the Lord as they themselves have. Even though full Church members should regard themselves still as learners (the word *disciple* means learner), they are learners in a different way from catechumens.

It seems clear that certain things happen along the way which make the people at each of these given stages—i.e. (1) member of another religion or pagan, (2) inquirer or hearer, (3) catechumen, (4) Church member—different from what they are at the others. 'Expression of interest' puts a man as a hearer or inquirer in a different group from the great mass of people of other religions. 'Intention to enlist' distinguishes him as a catechumen from mere inquirers. When he shows his 'decision and commitment' by being baptized, he is no longer a catechumen. But even as a full Church member he is still one who learns from the Master. His progress is still upward. He has not 'passed out', nor will he ever, even when he reaches the Kingdom.

In trying to show the process by which mission proceeds, we must therefore indicate the changes which take place, while still showing that growth never stops. It seems clear, however, that, by our Lord's command, the change which takes place at baptism is always the greatest. Each of the three diagrams thus shows part of the truth, but an accurate model would have to be a combination of all three. It would have to show the truth that there is in each of them, while at the same time correcting the errors resulting from their oversimplification.

Perhaps it would be something like diagram 4.

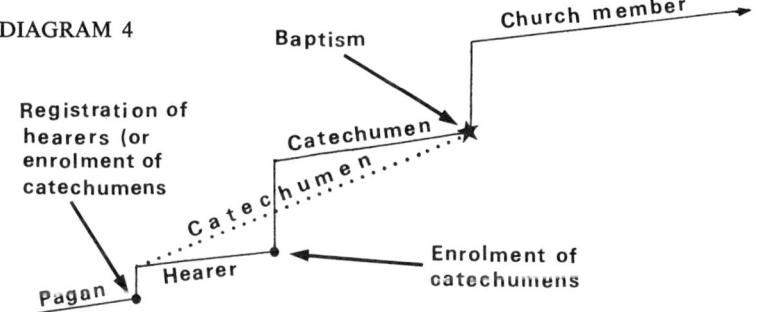

DIAGRAM 4

Some Churches add confirmation as a separate rite after baptism, and limit full Church membership and reception of the Lord's Supper to those who have been confirmed. But others find it difficult to see any biblical authority for the idea that a person who is baptized as a responsible adult needs to be confirmed afterwards. They believe that the baptism and the prayer for the Holy Spirit's confirmation should be one rite.

REGISTERING HEARERS

Notice in diagram 4 how two alternative patterns are found in the early stages. In one, hearers or inquirers are registered; in the other, they are not, but catechumens are enrolled directly from the general mass of those who have been hearing the Word. There may be a good reason for following each practice, and each may be helpful in different situations. In Chereponi we did not try to register hearers where there was a general positive response from a whole village. We felt that to ask a question about future intentions at that stage would not be constructive. It might cause some people to be afraid at a time when they were not yet ready to make a decision. Since they were willing to come and hear, we did not feel we needed to register them as 'hearers'.

But in a couple of villages where the general response was lukewarm, and it appeared highly unlikely that the whole village would, within a reasonable time, decide to become Christian, we found that to ask hearers to register helped to stimulate those who were interested.

The important thing in all situations is to be extremely careful at such an early stage, not to turn people against continuing to consider the possibility of becoming Christian. The guiding questions should be: Will it help in any way if we register some people as hearers? Will this bring them to a new seriousness about the faith? Or will it turn away from the faith those who are not willing to be registered?

HOW LONG DOES IT TAKE?

Though diagram 4 shows the stages one goes through in becoming a Christian, it does not show the length of such stages, or the rate at which religion growth takes place. Nor does it indicate the amount of change which occurs.

What *does* happen? Was the catechist right to expect a total change almost overnight. Or was the priest right who didn't believe the leopard could ever change his spots? Can we expect that every hearer will 'experience a conversion? If so, what kind of a conversion will it be, sudden conversion or a gradual one? Will it be a complete change of life, or just a change in some aspects of life?

We can find some of the answers to these questions in 1 Peter, much of which was addressed to newly-baptized Christians. It tells us a lot about what baptism and the Christian life should mean: The Christian life is 'new life' (1 Pet. 1.3). It involves 'new birth' (1 Pet. 1.2), a complete change of ways (1 Pet. 2.1, 12, 3.8–9), and a 'coming to the Lord' to be 'used by Him' (1 Pet. 2.4–5). It means being 'chosen' to be 'God's people' and to 'receive mercy' (1 Pet. 2.9–10), a complete submission to God's will (1 Pet. 1.22; 4.2), a turning away from the evil of the past (1 Pet. 4.2–3), and a readiness to suffer if necessary. Thus the change from pagan to Christian is like the change from night to day.

But we may notice two things:

1. Nothing is said about how long it takes for this change to take place.

2. The Christians addressed in the letter have to be told not to give

in to the evil one, or to behave like unredeemed men, but to be strong and firm in the new life, i.e. they are still subject to temptation.

What then is central to this change? What is the truly important difference between the old life and the new? If we read the New Testament carefully, we shall come to see that central to the change is a change of allegiance, a change of loyalty. *In becoming Christians the chief thing that happens is that we make a commitment of ourselves to Jesus Christ as Lord: we become His disciples and He takes us into His service.*

That is to say, we do not overnight become personally righteous. We do not become all-knowing, we do not change from utterly faithless beings to completely faithful ones. What does happen is that we no longer belong to ourselves, we no longer belong to any other, we now belong wholly to Jesus Christ. As one Chokosi woman expressed it, 'Before we heard and accepted the Gospel, our hearts were divided; now that we have accepted it, we have a single heart.' A heart is single when its loyalty is to one alone.

The chief meaning, then, of the decision to become Christian in baptism, is a coming into *discipleship*. Conversion means to be converted from loyalty to other lords—including the lordship of self—to the lordship of Christ. We become His disciples.

DISCIPLING AND BAPTISM

This change of loyalty is why our Lord's command to baptize as recorded in Matthew 28.18–20 is so closely connected with the verb *matheteuein*, to 'make disciples'. 'All power has been given to me' the risen Christ said, 'in heaven and on earth. Go, therefore, and make disciples of all nations, baptizing them in the name of the Father, the Son, and the Holy Spirit, teaching them to observe all things which I have commanded you.' In baptism a believer thus shows that he has heard the message, that he believes that Jesus Christ is the Lord of heaven and earth, and that he wants to be His disciple. By baptizing him the Christian community shows that it has preached the Gospel to him, that he has believed that its Lord must also be his Lord, and that it is accepting him in the name of the Lord as a fellow disciple.

Thus, whatever other meanings it may have, baptism is Christian enlistment. It is the rite by which men are enlisted as servants of the King, as disciples of Christ.

Once we understand baptism in this way we can see what must come before it. We can judge what length of time must be spent as a hearer and a catechumen, and what comes after. Just as a soldier does not receive his military training before he enlists, but after, so it cannot be expected that those who enlist in the army of Christ will complete their training before enlistment.

'Baptism is Christian enlistment . . . liberation from the service of other lords for the service of Christian discipleship' (p. 93).
Villagers in the Near East receive arms and equipment as they volunteer for service against invaders.
What sort of 'equipment' do most Christians receive when they 'enlist' for service as members of the Church?

But a man who wants to enlist in the army needs to know something of what life in the army is like before he enlists, or else he may enlist for false reasons. He must know that an army fights, and that as a soldier he will have to fight. He must know that an army follows orders, and that he will be expected to obey orders, and can no longer behave as an independent individual. He must know the terms of service.

So also a man who wants to become a Christian must know what the Gospel is about, and what the Church is, in which he will be a servant of the Gospel. He must know who Jesus Christ is, and what His Lordship over him will mean. He must know all he needs to know in order to make a responsible decision whether to become a Christian or not. And the Church must be sure that his decision is an informed and responsible one.

This does not mean that a person must pass an examination in religious knowledge before he can be baptized, or that he has to be certified for perfect moral character before he can become a disciple. 'Make disciples, baptize, and teach,' Jesus commanded, in that order. He did not say, 'Teach, make disciples, and baptize.' If the Church, and not just the catechumens' class, is a learning community, then most of the teaching and training will take place in the regular, ongoing life of the Church, after the believer has been baptized, not before. 'Every member a learner' is a good motto for the Church.

One Church in America put a sign in front of its chapel saying: 'This organization is a training institute for service in the world.' That is what the Church ought to be (and how sad it is that so few of our Churches are). If that is what the Church is, then the important thing for a catechumen is that he should be fully ready, by the end of his catechumenate, to belong to such a Church.

BAPTISM AND MISSION

It was noticeable in our mission in Northern Ghana that those who were baptized always seemed to invite their as yet unevangelized kinsmen and neighbours to witness their baptism. No doubt this was partly because of the close ties which bound together the members of each family or clan or village. As shown in Part 2 we tried always to speak to people *within* the groups to which they belonged, not to detach them from those groups. So it was natural for them to want to have their families and friends share in the important occasion of their baptism.

At the same time, those who were baptized seem to have understood, without being told, that the decision which they had made for themselves involved them in the work of mission. Those who were liberated from the service of other lords for the service of the Lord Jesus wanted others also to be freed as they had been. After all, what is salvation for? For whose sake are we being saved? As we saw in Part 1 the whole purpose of ministry is for the fulfilment of God's plan of salvation for the world. When we go out in ministry we must hope that when we preach the Gospel men will become freed to participate in God's mission.

At our district conferences in Chereponi we noted that the newer congregations, in giving their reports, told of how they were witnessing to other villages and to the as yet unbaptized members of their own villages. The older congregations, however, tended to report more on internal affairs of the congregations—chapel building, Church attendance, and finance. They were in danger of losing the precious insight that they had when the faith was new to them.

So we suggested a slight change in the agenda for the meetings. Each congregation was asked, before it reported on its own life, to report on its outreach in mission to people who were not yet baptized. This served as a useful reminder.

If we are to be faithful to the Lord who had 'nowhere to lay His head' (Matt. 8.20), we must never become settled or turned in on ourselves and our own needs. Instead we must say, as He did, 'I am among you as one who serves' (Luke 22.27). Our goal is not just to win the prize for ourselves, but by word and example to bring all men to the prize of life with God in Christ.

STUDY SUGGESTIONS

REVIEW QUESTIONS

1. 'We need not be shy of asking God to do His work' (p. 88). What is meant by this statement?
2. Which of the diagrams on pp. 89, 90 and 91 do you think best illustrates the process of making disciples? Give reasons for your answer.
3. In what ways is it true to say that baptism is 'Christian enlistment in the service of the Lord Jesus'? (p. 93).
4. What do most Churches require of a person before he can be enrolled as a 'hearer' or 'inquirer'?
5. What do most Churches require of a person before he can be enrolled as a catechumen?

DISCUSSION AND RESEARCH TOPICS

6. What do you understand by the motto 'Every member a learner'?
7. (a) What practices with regard to making disciples have the Churches in your area followed? Describe the differences, if any, between the practices of different denominations.

(b) Why did the Churches adopt different practices? Because they had different expectations of what it means to be a Church member? Or different estimates of what people could be expected to do? Different practices in their home countries? Or for some other reason?

8. The word used to translate 'conversion' in one of the languages of East Africa means 'to enter the territory of another chief than your own'. In what way does this help to explain what happens in baptism?

9. How would you explain the phrase 'the Church inside out'?

---

15. Preparing for Baptism

One thing which a believer has to do before he is free to serve Christ is to give up all allegiances which might conflict with his allegiance to Christ. It is just like what happens in many African tribes before a girl is married. Her father informs her that she will be going to her husband to be married on a certain date. Before that date she pays one last visit to her boyfriend to bid him farewell, for everyone understands that to have a husband and a boyfriend at the same time is to have conflicting allegiances. Similarly one cannot serve Christ if one is not prepared to abandon all other lords. The Church must expect this of all new members when it baptizes them.

CONVERSION AND 'WORKS OF THE DEVIL'

But this change of allegiance raises a difficult question. What are we to say about the convert's past religious observances? Are we to call them 'idolatry'? What is idolatry? Is it not the worship of another god or an object *in the place of God*? God told the Israelites 'You shall have no other god to set against me' (Ex. 20.3 NEB). But if a convert has been worshipping a divinity or an object *which he believes that God gave to his people*, is that idolatry? Is that a conflicting allegiance? If he pours libation or makes animal or food sacrifices to his grandfathers, whom he believes are his fathers in God, is that idolatry? Does such an allegiance conflict with his allegiance to Christ? Are these 'works of the devil'? Does he have to say that they are 'deceptions' and 'lies' and 'works of darkness and ignorance'? Must he vow to forsake these when he becomes a Christian?

To the question 'Are these things idolatry?' we may perhaps say 'no' or 'not necessarily', though there are many Christians who would say 'yes' in all cases. But to the question 'Ought he to forsake them?' our answer must be a very definite 'yes'.

This double answer may seem difficult to understand. It rests on the opinion that *the Church has in the past often been asking the new convert to do the right thing for the wrong reason.* It has been right to insist that he should abandon the worship of all save God alone. But it has perhaps been wrong in demanding that he should call *all* pre-Christian forms of religions 'works of the devil'.

Some of these pre-Christian ceremonies undoubtedly were and are idolatrous. But the vast majority of them did not in any way involve worshipping the thing *instead of God.* And the real answer is simply that they are *no longer necessary* for anyone once he has learned of Christ. 'All power in heaven and on earth has been given me,' Jesus said (Matt. 28.18). 'There is one God, and one who brings God and men together,' Paul wrote to Timothy, 'the man Christ Jesus.' (1 Tim. 2.5.) 'For it was by God's own decision 'that the Son has in Himself the full nature of God.' (Col. 1.19.) 'I am the way, I am the truth, and I am life,' Jesus said, 'no one goes to the Father except by me' (John 14.6).

A man who has heard this message knows that he has no need to worship any being but God, as revealed perfectly in Jesus Christ. God is not far, but near, He is not unknown, but known. He is not unapproachable, but has Himself approached men. 'God was in Christ, reconciling the world to Himself' (2 Cor. 5.19). If a Christian continues to seek divine power anywhere but in God's self-revelation in Christ, he is denying Christ's sufficiency for all things. The fact is that something has happened, and as a result, man's situation has changed. He need no longer look for other ways of approaching God and gaining life. 'I am life,' Jesus said. The pagan who has been searching for life need go no further. To continue to search in other places for life is to deny that Christ is life.

'But,' the new convert asks, 'How can I thus cut myself off from my fathers, from the chain of life that has brought me forth, from the ancestors of my clan, our living dead?'

In answering, we must not shirk from giving him the whole message, the whole good news which the Gospel is, that Christ 'existed before all things', and that it is in Him that 'all things have their proper place' (Col. 1.17). 'Through the Son God decided to bring the whole universe back to Himself. God made peace through His Son's death on the cross, and so brought back to Himself all things, both on earth and in heaven' (Col. 1.20).

'Christ's work concerns your fathers and ancestors, even though they did not know Him during their lifetime here', we must say. 'His death was not only for you but also for them. God is God of the dead as well as of the living. Those who are dead to us are alive to God (see Matt. 22.23–33). You do not know what your fathers and ancestors now know. They may even have come to know of God's grace in Christ before you. By becoming one with Christ you can therefore become more fully united with them than you have ever been. Have no fear.'

Thus we can confidently ask the new convert to abandon all pre-Christian ways of worship. We need not waste time deciding whether to describe them as 'idol-worship' or as 'innocent pre-Christian rites'. The important thing is to show him the glory of what he is entering upon, its fullness and sufficiency, its power to meet his total needs both at the time of his baptism and always.

THE CATECHUMENATE: PREPARATION FOR BAPTISM

We found in Chereponi that we had to preach in a village once a week for at least six months before we saw signs that the people were even ready to be asked about baptism. Sometimes even after a year we could see no signs of a positive response, but we waited for such signs before we raised the subject of baptism. Once the response of the people was positive, we explained that the way for them to signify their acceptance of the Gospel and their wish to become united with Christ was through baptism. Then, if they were interested, we began to prepare them for baptism.

The lessons generally took place twice a week, and it took about three months to go through a specially written catechism, discussing the questions and answers in dialogue with the people. At the same time they were memorizing things they had to know in order to take part meaningfully in the liturgy of the Church: the Lord's Prayer, the Apostles' Creed, the Great Commandment or sometimes the Ten Commandments, and the 'Thrice Holy' from the Communion Service.

At first we simply translated the Ewe language catechism from Southern Ghana, which was itself a translation from a German catechism. But we soon found that it meant little to the people. Its questions were not *their* questions about faith, but someone else's. It failed to ask the questions which were really theirs. So we abandoned it, and began instead to write down the questions we heard the people ask over and over again, and to formulate answers to them. We arranged them in a logical order and we added questions on subjects about which the catechumens had not asked, but which those who had become Christian before them felt were important, asked in the way in which the people themselves might ask them. We put these together and this became our catechism. (See Appendix 2, p. 196.)

99

At first we required people to memorize all the answers, but we found that (a) this was very difficult for old people, and (b) it made the catechumenate sometimes take a year or more, and people became impatient. The district session therefore decided that catechumens should memorize only the answers to the most important questions. They would discuss the others fully, but not learn them by heart. Thus it was possible for baptism to take place within three to six months of the start of the catechumenate.

This decision was important, not only because it kept the period of preparation for baptism short, so that the spirits of the catechumens remained high. It also kept us and the catechumens from regarding their preparation for baptism as an educational affair, a matter of knowing things rather than of committing selves. True, it was our responsibility to teach the catechumens things which they ought to know: but we had an even more important responsibility: to prepare them emotionally and spiritually to give their lives to Christ. (See Appendix 3, p. 198.)

The Christian faith is, after all, not just an intellectual system, a set of ideas and statements about God and man. Nor is it just a cult, a set of religious practices and observances. The Christian faith concerns the kingdom of God, and the kingdom of God is God's reign over the lives of men, His sovereignty over mankind. A person who becomes a Christian is thus saying: 'God is King. I am His subject. I must give my whole self—every aspect of my life and personality, every hour of my life—to Him, so that He may reign over me and my life may give glory to Him.'

It is not only our minds, or our times of religious observance, that we give to God, but our bodies and the whole of our activity as well, in the fields and in the marketplace, at work and at rest, at home and and away, in our earning of money and in our use of it, in our relations with other people, in our families and in our communities. All the relationships which (as we saw in Part 2) each individual has, all of those relationships come under the sovereignty of God. We do not give just a section or slice of ourselves to God, we give *all*.

THE DANGER OF 'NOMINAL' CONVERSION

The Church has not always lived up to this. It has asked from its members and has received from them, far less. In many places it has been content with people who are Christians in name and form only, whose lives have just been painted over with a thin coat of Christianity. This is true in America and Europe, and it is already partly true in Africa. Walter Sangree gives an example in his study of the Tiriki people of Kenya:

The religious and magical revolution caused by the coming of Christianity is neither so profound nor so far-reaching as it might appear to be. The Christian Church and Christian beliefs are in effect a new method, perhaps as effective as the ancestor cult, for obtaining solace and aid in standing up to the dangers of a world full of uncertainties which the Tiriki still ascribe to sorcery, witchcraft, and bad luck. Christians generally view both prayer and hymn-singing as magic that will bring God's grace and good luck, and also as powerful deterrents to haunting ghosts and to many forms of sorcery. Traditional magical and religious rituals have in many cases been displaced or discarded since the coming of the Europeans. In very few instances, however, have the underlying magical and religious belief systems been discarded. Instead they have generally been reorganized, and sometimes augmented, by the coming of Christianity. In matters connected with individual and family fortune, birth, death, and disease, most of the traditional religious attitudes persist, though now largely clothed in Christian dogma and ritual.

A person may thus become a Christian in name only, without really being converted, without his life being Christianized. A whole village can become nominally Christian without being Christianized in any depth. A real conversion might not ever take place. And the danger of this may even increase where there is a strong emphasis on an emotional 'conversion experience'.

WHAT IS CONVERSION FOR?

What then are we to look for in real conversion? How will people come to real new birth? Will it be a once-and-for-all experience? John Taylor thinks not. He believes that the process of conversion will be gradual, and will remain hidden within the fabric of the community.

Change should be like a ferment working through the social organism. It will be seen in a multitude of tiny responses, imperceptible choices, moral and spiritual battles concerning innumerable issues. A person does not become a Christian through one rite or one experience, but is made a member of Christ through a long series of initiations and decisions within the Body of Christ. Baptism is thus not only the single event of new birth. It is the doorway to a continual process of death and rebirth, and so becomes a model for the whole of the Christian life. Martin Luther, when suffering temptation, used to write in Latin the words: 'I have been baptized' to comfort himself, and to recall himself to his vocation in Christ. In the same way baptism, which takes place once and for all, becomes the model for a decision which must be re-expressed and re-taken over and over again.

In 1968, when we already had many baptisms to report, and when the whole of our Church in Northern Ghana was looking toward our district as an example of successful evangelism, I had to make my annual report to the district and the presbytery. I recounted the impressive numbers, but I began to ask myself about all these baptisms: what are they for? That part of my report read as follows:

> When one has baptized so many congregations, and a Christian Church is obviously in existence in every tribe and almost every clan in this area, one then has to ask: what is the purpose of this vast ingathering? Is it just to make numbers? Is it just to create worshipping communities which will hold services weekly and pay pledges, and build chapels? *This, I feel, is our strongest temptation.* If we do this we make of the Church an idol. The Church must exist not for itself but for the life of the world, and for new life for all.

I then went on to talk about the signs of a person being a true Church member, and of congregations really being cells of the Kingdom. We should see, I wrote, that our members:
1. Know what it means to be a Christian in their daily work,
2. Know what it means to have a Christian home,
3. Witness to others,
4. Study the faith in groups and as individuals,
5. Take an active part in the improvement of the communities in which they live.

In other words, we should not be content with members who are merely Church-attenders, but we should strive for Christians who are 'a light to the world'.

The new life in Christ, which is God's goal for everyone in His mission, is a life of mature discipleship. God's plan for all those who are saved is that they should themselves participate in His mission to the world, until every man is brought into God's presence as a mature individual in Christ.

STUDY SUGGESTIONS

REVIEW QUESTIONS
1. What false views of the Christian faith are we likely to give when we (a) have a long catechumenate (b) demand extensive intellectual learning and memorization from our catechumens?
2. What difference if any is there between completing a catechumenate and 'passing out' from a school or college?
3. Read Phil. 3.13–14. What do we learn from this passage, about what we should expect of people before and after baptism?
4. Are we commissioned by the Lord to be policemen of the Christian

lives of our converts? What is our responsibility to the converts before God? If we have discharged our responsibility well, who will be judged if the convert backslides?

DISCUSSION AND RESEARCH TOPICS

5. Read the following passages and compare the teaching about idolatry which they contain with the use of the word 'idolatry' in your area.
Exod. 20.4–6; Exod. 32; Deut. 4.25–31; Deut. 5.8–10; Deut. 9.16; 1 Sam. 5.1–5; 1 Kings 18.20–40; 2 Kings 17.7–18; Isa. 2.5–22; Isa. 10.10,11; Isa. 44.9–20; Ezek. 20.27–32; Hos. 8.1–14; Hos. 9.10. Have Christians been condemning the same kind of thing in your area as the Old Testament writers condemned in Israel and the surrounding nations, or is there a difference? Is what people have been practising in your area idolatry, or is there another way of describing it?

6. What is the difference between telling converts to forsake all idols, and proclaiming the all-sufficiency of Christ?

7. For what reasons do some Christians go back to pre-Christian religious practices? Is there anything the Church can do to help them? Is their backsliding always their own fault? If not, whose fault may it be?

8. What needs to be achieved in a catechumenate?

9. Should catechumens be examined before baptism? By whom? What should the examiner look for in them before he certifies that they are ready for baptism?

10. Is it right for the Church to demand a baptismal fee from converts? What impression does this convey? What is the difference between a fee and a thank-offering? Give reasons and examples to support your answer.

11. How soon should new converts who have been baptized celebrate the Lord's supper?

12. Should the Church have a separate category for 'newly baptized', different from full Church membership?

13. (a) For what reasons do some Churches require Confirmation as well as baptism, as the sign of full Church membership and admission to Holy Communion?
    (b) What does the rite of Confirmation or Admission to the Lord's Supper mean in your Church?
    (c) What significance does it have for one who joins the Church and is baptized as an adult?

16. Training in the Faith

Not long ago the signboard outside the little Presbyterian Church which I attend was changed. Previously it had listed the ordained clergyman of the parish as 'the Minister'. But that clergyman had second thoughts. Instead, he put this line on the board:

Ministers: All Members.

And then his name was listed on a new line, entitled:

Teaching Elder.

In much of their work ordained ministers are, or ought to be, 'teaching elders' or 'teaching ministers'. This is one of the most important parts of their special ministry to God's people. The ministry of Christian education does not simply mean running the Sunday school or preparing catechumens. Christian education is a central task of the ordained ministry, and it is an essential part of the training for ministry of all God's people.

BUILDING UP THE LAITY

To neglect the educational ministry of the Church to its own members would be like letting the air slowly leak out of your bicycle tyres. The ministry of the Church would slowly settle down to the bare rims of the wheels. If any member of the Church is not a learner, then he is a less effective Christian, and the ministry of his Church is impoverished. Instead of a ministry of people who are growing every day in discipleship, the Church's ministry becomes that of a tired, clerical minority, with a few lay trustees.

Thus when we talk about the ministry of Christian education, we are immediately concerned with the ministry of the laity. Christian education is what builds up that ministry, the ministry of the people of God.

Much has been written about Christian education, and a great deal of what has been written is very good. We shall not attempt here to summarize what has been written. Our concern in this chapter will be to *interpret* the ministry of Christian education as an essential part of the total ministry of every district pastor.

We shall not, however, assume that the pastor ought to be the only Christian educator of the district or parish, in the way in which he is usually the only administrator of the sacraments. Rather, his work in Christian education ought to include two roles:

1. His own leading of Christian education, in other words, his teaching, and
2. His training of leaders, both to teach in the Christian education programme of the Church, and to carry out other functions.

THE PASTOR AS TEACHER

It is very important that every pastor should himself teach at least one class of adults. Nothing in pastoral work will stimulate his mind more, nor force him to continue his own Christian education as much as doing this. In addition, his own class or classes can be models and pilot projects of the sort of Christian education for which he is training teachers. If a man does not himself try out the programmes which he devises, he will never learn whether they work or not, nor how and where to improve them.

In other words, the pastor should not limit his teaching to 'the highest level' of Christian education. He should not teach only Church leaders, nor only the secondary-school educated people in the congregations. He should be involved in teaching at least one class of the most ordinary people of his district, and he may well discover, as Jesus did, that it is to the 'babes' that God has given the greatest understanding of His truth. Whatever the pastor expects others to do, he should himself be seen doing. He should not let it appear that he thinks such work is for his 'small boys'.

THE PASTOR AS TRAINER OF LEADERS IN THE FAITH

The pastor should train leaders, both to teach classes like those which he himself teaches, and also to exercise other functions within the body of Christ.

Obviously his first need will be to train leaders for Catechetical classes and Sunday school. In some Churches special Lenten or Advent programmes are held, and there may be a women's Bible class or a men's study group. There may also be opportunity for religious instruction in the day schools. Perhaps, if the congregation is small enough, the whole congregation can itself be the class, provided the people are similar enough in their degree of education and needs. A once-a-week evening class which all members would be expected to attend might be the best.

In one village in Thailand the pastor suggested that anyone who wished should stay in Church after the Sunday morning service, and ask him for an explanation of anything in his sermon which they had not understood. Soon this became a regular teaching period, which anyone in the village was welcome to attend and listen to, whether they were Church members or not. Lay worship leaders also could usefully hold such 'question and discussion periods', but they would need some training for it first.

The pastor should train teachers or leaders for each sort of class which is to be held, and he should go and observe these teachers, once he has trained them, as they carry out their teaching. Then, either individually or in groups of teachers, he might be able to give them advice, or work out with them some of their problems. His job is not to do their work for them when he visits—he could only do that very rarely—but to help them to do their work better. They can then go on to teach in an improved way every week.

The pastor will also have to train local Church leaders, council members, presbyters, or deacons (depending on what the Church calls them), finance committee members, stewardship education committee members, youth workers, and the like. How best to do this will vary with the situation and the place, and we shall discuss it later (see pp. 109–114). First we must consider the *nature* of the classes which ought to be held, whatever the group being taught and whatever the subject of instruction.

CHRISTIAN EDUCATION BY DISCUSSION METHOD

Whatever the sort of class, it ought not to be thought of as a time for the leader to show off everything he knows—as though the members were empty vessels whom he has to fill. The best learning, psychologists tell us, is *active* learning, not passive learning. It is learning in which the learner is actively involved as a subject in the learning process, and not just as an object to be taught. The leader needs to recognize that each member of the class has something to contribute to the learning process, just as he himself has a contribution to make.

Truth, we remember, is dynamic. It is alive. It is something that *happens* in interpersonal relationships and in actual changing situations. Truth does not merely consist of ideas or facts which have to be learned. People come to know the truth of the gospel through wrestling with it, and the teacher and his class need to wrestle together in the pursuit of truth.

The role of the leader is twofold.

1. First he will serve as an enabler (or 'midwife') of good discussion, helping the group members to express their thoughts and feelings and experiences.

2. Secondly, he will serve as a resource person, trained in the historical faith, who can share his knowledge with the people, as they need to learn of the accumulated wisdom of the Church.

In order to explain this, we gave the following instructions to our group of study leaders in Chereponi when we presented them with a series of Bible lesson outlines:

'These outlines are meant to help you to lead the members of your group to discuss the Bible themselves. The less talking you do, and the more talking your group does, the more successful you will be as a discussion leader. Do not allow the discussion to come back to you each time someone in the group has spoken. Don't let the discussions become question-and-answer sessions. Encourage the members of the group to address each other with their remarks, rather than to address you. Don't talk too much.'

There are certain sorts of lessons which fit this method of education better than others. The lesson outlines we devised were constructed in order to follow this method of education. We started with a brief introduction to the subject, given by the leader himself (not more than one minute), followed by prepared questions which he could use to help the people start talking about the subject. This method helped them to recognize for themselves some of the problems involved. Many of these 'discussion-starter' questions were quotations from things which the people themselves were saying about the subject, or from traditional proverbs or religious ideas concerning that same subject.

After the discussion had got going and some questions had been raised (usually ten or fifteen minutes), the leader would introduce the Bible lesson for the day. The outline provided him with a short exegesis explaining the context of the passage, and some of the technical points. Then he would be shown how to relate the Bible passage to the previous discussion which the people had been having, and to encourage the people themselves to relate the Bible teaching to the things which they had been talking about before. These questions were all 'open ended': i.e. they were questions which had no simple, easy, factual answers, but, rather, questions which required people to think and to express themselves in the light of Scripture. They were questions whose purpose was to stimulate good, hard discussion to help people gain new insights and new understandings.

After such discussion, the lesson ended with a memory verse which summarized the main biblical teaching on the subject of the evening, and with a hymn related to that subject. Finally, there were prayers by members of the class.

Each successive lesson began with a revision of the subjects discussed in previous lessons, together with a recitation of the related memory verses. The people's learning experiences could thus be summarized quickly and recalled whenever required.

This method was devised especially for work with illiterate people, but it can equally well be used with literates. It was wonderful how much illiterates were able to learn in this way. They often showed much more understanding of the matters we discussed than did our literate middle-school leavers.

WHAT SHOULD BE INCLUDED IN CHRISTIAN EDUCATION?

Another question to consider is the content of lessons. What subjects should be treated in Christian education classes? In Chereponi, we concentrated almost entirely on Bible study, but this need not be the only sort of class. The faith is relevant to *all* areas of human life, so there is no reason why there should not be classes in economics, ethics, politics, and agriculture, as well. We had some good classes in civic education.

'Christian education' is, in other words, the education of Christians—it need not just be education in 'Christian' subjects. All subjects can be Christian subjects if studied by Christians who are students of 'the whole gospel for the whole man'.

We have so far been discussing the training of the congregation—what Roman Catholics call 'the formation of the laity'—as it applies to adults. Appropriate lessons will be needed for children and young people, as well. The pastor must prepare leaders to do this training also. Perhaps he can get advice or even active help in doing this from any local schoolteachers who have themselves been trained in up-to-date methods of teaching young people of various ages.

STUDY SUGGESTIONS

REVIEW QUESTION

1. What is Christian education? How is it related to the ministry of the laity?
2. Who is responsible for educating the people of God in the faith?
3. Why is Christian education *not* like teaching people how to type or how to grow tomatoes or how to spell?
4. What should a pastor who visits a class which is being conducted by one of his trained workers do, if the worker seems to be teaching in the wrong way? How can he do this in such a way that he will not undermine that worker's authority?
5. What will happen if a pastor spends all his time training the whole congregation instead of training teachers who can share this work with him?
6. Make a list of the different sorts of Christian education that a pastor should be involved in. How many hours a week do you estimate he should spend at this work and in his preparation for it?

DISCUSSION AND RESEARCH TOPICS

7. What are suitable subjects for congregational classes in Christian education?
8. What are the advantages of the discussion method in learning?

9. A certain pastor said: 'If I train others as leaders in the congregation, the mass of the people will look to them for help and authority, instead of to me. I shall be undermining my own authority as pastor.' How would you reply to that pastor?

17. Training for Service

The second sort of training which the pastor needs to do is the training of people whose gifts may not be for teaching others, but rather for leadership in administration, or in counselling, or in some service to the community. In other words, the various 'officers' and 'servants' of the Church.

The pastor will need to conduct regular, ongoing, 'in-service training' for these paid Church workers, helping them to upgrade their standards in theology, Bible study, and other subjects. In some areas he may need to teach them either a local language or a *lingua franca* that will be a help to communication. He may need to train them to do other sorts of work, such as literacy or adult education.

The one subject for in-service training on which we concentrated the most in Chereponi was sermon preparation. In a regular weekly session, we pastors and the evangelists did our sermon preparation together. We took the lectionary scripture lesson which was to be used throughout the district that week, and the pastors did an exegesis of it for the evangelists. Then we discussed together how we could do an exposition of it for the congregations and preaching stations. Many of our voluntary preachers also came and participated in these sessions along with the evangelists.

THE USE OF LAY LEADERS

Many pastors in African or Asian districts and parishes find that they do not have enough trained professional workers or teacher catechists to look after their congregations well. If they do not train additional voluntary leaders, the congregations are deprived of regular nurture in the faith, since a pastor, catechist, or evangelist may only be able to conduct services for any one congregation once in two or three weeks.

After six years of work in Chereponi we had twenty-three congregations all wanting to have Sunday services, and thirty-one additional weekday preaching stations. But we were only two pastors and five evangelists who could staff them. Nevertheless, each congregation and

Besides teaching his congregation the pastor must train local leaders if the work of Christian mission is to succeed (pp.104 and 114).

Top-class athletes need a wise coach as well as many hours of hard training in order to enjoy success – like Said Aouita of Morocco, seen here winning a race at the Crystal Palace.

What can the coach and the pastor *not* do for the people they train?

preaching station had a service led by a trained leader every week. How did we do it?

Five years earlier, fourteen months after we began work but before we had baptized any village congregation, we called for candidates for our first leadership training course. We asked for two younger men from each of the villages where we were working. In some cases we got none, in some cases just one, and in one case three. We began with twenty candidates.

I felt that if these local leaders were to be trained to work independently of pastors and evangelists, they would have to learn to read. At that time 99 per cent of all Chokosis over the age of fourteen were illiterate, and most Chokosis speak only their own language (which had never been written down). So our course consisted of three parts: literacy; Biblical instruction; and 'practical theology', i.e. ethics and the conduct of worship. It was a one-month residential course, followed by sessions on market days (every sixth day) for the remainder of the year.

Twenty people started the course, but by the end of the month there were only eight remaining. However, we kept going. The endurance of those eight was most impressive. At the end of the year we had a public recognition ceremony for our first trained leaders.

Our rough literacy materials had been part of the problem: many got discouraged at how slowly they learned. We improved the literacy manuals each year until in the fifth year they were fit for printing. By that time, people were able to learn to read simple books before the end of a month, or even to learn in their villages before coming to the course, so that they were already literate or semi-literate when they arrived.

In the second year we had two such courses, in different areas of the district, and twenty-three people got certificates. In the third year we had three courses, in which many more were trained. In the fourth year we were able to introduce advanced courses for those who had previously finished the first course, and an additional beginners' course. In the fifth year we did the same.

The outcome of it all was that, as we went along, we developed a group of about sixty people who could read and teach others to read, and about twenty-five who could lead services and give catechetical instruction either in their own village or in nearby villages. Several of them became effective evangelists, who were the first to bring the Gospel to new villages. Four of them were employed as temporary paid evangelists, working in five to seven villages, until such time as we could get enough seminary-trained evangelists.

The result of it all was that, even when we had twenty-three congregations, the fact that we had only two pastors and five evangelists did not mean that we could hold services in only seven (or, if each paid worker did two, fourteen) villages on any given Sunday. Every village had a service, and most of the services were led by people who had never been to school.

By translating Scripture lessons for every Sunday and holy day of the year and cyclostyling them, we were able to put into the hands of each leader, a 'Bible', which, as I have said, we studied together each week.

We also put into their hands a simple liturgy and order of service, which helped them in the conduct of worship (see Chapter 19).

DEVELOPING TRADITIONAL LEADERS

Besides the teaching of reading and leading of services, however, some sorts of leadership were needed which these trainees could not exercise, either in their own village congregations or elsewhere. Their average age was twenty-one or twenty-two, and therefore most of them did not have the authority in their own villages which older men would have had.

When the congregation chose their presbyters, they usually chose men of about thirty-five or forty years of age, and women of thirty to sixty. I had indeed hoped that they would choose some of the household elders or local clan elders as presbyters, i.e. the 'formal leaders' mentioned in Chapter 7 (p. 38). They tended, however, to choose not formal leaders but informal leaders, or opinion leaders, usually one from each section of the village.

I came to see later that this was a pattern which the Chokosis often followed in choosing men to represent them outside of the village. As they had done in other areas of life, so did they do with regard to Church government. The presbyters whom they chose knew how to work closely with the village elders on purely local matters, so that the village elders occupied a position of 'informal leaders' in Church affairs.

Our job was to train the men and women whom they had chosen to lead them. The thirty-five to forty-year-old presbyters did not easily fit into our previous leadership training programme. Most of them were shy of learning to read (although we told them they need not be, and two men actually managed to complete the leadership training course). We needed, therefore, to add to our existing leadership training programme a second one, designed especially for the presbyters and Church mothers, who were almost all illiterate.

It is sometimes suggested today that people who cannot read cannot be taught. But this is obviously mistaken. Very complex tribal and national cultures are 'taught' all over the world among peoples to whom reading and writing are unknown. And the Christian religion itself spread throughout Europe and parts of Asia at a time when 99 per cent of the people of these areas were illiterate. Some useful training methods which do not require the use of reading are described in Hans Ruedi Weber's booklet, *The Communication of the Gospel to Illiterates.*

In Chereponi we did not have literacy classes for the presbyters and Church mothers, but in these shorter courses (usually two or three days, twice a year) we used non-written methods of instruction. We had the same Bible discussions and classes in worship and ethics as for the younger leaders, but we adapted our methods to their needs. We used more visual aids. We also used role-playing techniques, asking one person, for example, to play the role of a husband who had just had a serious argument with his wife, and different people in turn played the role of a presbyter trying to bring him to reconsider his unforgiving attitude. Afterwards, we talked about which actor did the right thing, which one approached the man in the most effective way. Or else we had one man play the role of a Church member who had been back-sliding, and the others acted in turn the role of a presbyter trying to counsel him. We focused on actual problems which the presbyters and Church mothers experienced in their life and work, not on abstract theories or doctrine. (Appendix 5, p. 200 shows a sample plan for such a presbyters' retreat.)

The presbyters and Church mothers were thus trained to be more effective in their leadership of the local congregations. By this training they were also made more effective members of the district session, i.e. the quarterly conference of all the Church leaders, pastors, and evangelists, which, in the Presbyterian system, exercises the highest authority in the district. They came to understand that they *were* the leadership of the Church, that this was *not* the missionaries' Church, but *theirs*, and they they were responsible to lead it. I shall be forever grateful for the wisdom and the insights which they expressed in these meetings.

After I returned to America, I came across these words by a Maryknoll Father, J. A. Grassi, which express very well the philosophy of the Church and of Church leadership which we tried to put into practice in Chereponi:

> From the very nature of the Church as the People of God we see the heart of any hope to create new Churches that will be self-supporting and self-extending. The Church will only become a missionary Church to the extent that the contribution and gift of each person is encouraged and developed. This will only happen when the Christian community itself studies how it can be a community of service to the world, and when it arrives in a democratic manner at the decisions necessary to mobilize the talents of each and all.
>
> However, this will only happen in practice when the missioner or priest avoids the traditional paternal role of making all decisions

himself. His function will be that of forming Christian leaders, rather than that of taking over Christian leadership. This means that he will adopt the role of catalyst, forming men with the Word of God so that they will be able to make responsible decisions for the world, rather than delegating this to someone else.

THE PASTOR AS 'MIDWIFE'

A pastor and teacher is a midwife, not a mother giving birth to a child. The people to whom he ministers are the mother: they are the ones who will bring forth the child, the new life in Christ which is coming to be in their society and culture.

The pastor—and the professional missionary—do have a definite responsibility. They must bring the message to their people and must transmit to them everything that they will need in order to be part of the Body of Christ. But they cannot do for the people what the people must do for themselves. They cannot give birth to the baby. If they try to do so, they run the danger of making the people *their* disciples, rather than disciples of Christ.

The pastor must encourage the people *themselves* to respond. He must help *them* to allow the Spirit to fashion them. He must equip *them* to live as God's saints. He must make *them* aware of, and develop in them, the Spirit's gifts to them for mission. *They* are the ones who need to take the initiative in Christian mission. The pastor's role is to nurture and to feed and to train that initiative. But he cannot kick the ball for them. He can't even make the kick-off. When the whistle has blown for the match to start, the trainer and coach must get off the field.

As pastors in Christian education, we have to ask the Lord to guide us to know what gifts He has given His people for ministry, and how we may best help to develop them. The gifts which God has given will differ from place to place, and so will the problems and opportunities for developing them. Our task is to devise a programme of Christian education which fits the whole of the local situation in its total social and cultural context, and then to mobilize all the human and physical resources we have to run the programme.

STUDY SUGGESTIONS

REVIEW QUESTIONS

1. For what different sorts of leadership can lay people be trained to help their pastor?
2. (a) Describe some ways in which people who cannot read or write can be taught the Faith.

(b) Describe how they can be taught to exercise leadership and other forms of service.
3. What is the chief purpose of Christian education?
4. Read 1. Cor. 3.5–11. What do we learn from this passage about the pastor's role in Christian education?

DISCUSSION TOPICS

5. What are the different categories of leaders in your Church who need to be trained? Are there some sorts of leadership for which people have not yet been trained, but should be? If so, which should be given priority?
6. Is it better to have paid workers than voluntary leaders in a Church? Give your reasons, with examples.
7. What are the advantages and disadvantages of awarding certificates to those who have completed certain courses?
8. What can be done to encourage every member of the Church to be a learner?

PART 5
THE MINISTRY OF ENABLING WORSHIP

18. Developing an Authentic Worship Life

THE PASTOR AS ENABLER

Some people think that the chief task of an ordained minister is to lead worship services. They see the minister as a preacher, an administrator of the sacraments, a leader of the liturgy, a performer of ritual. It is true that an ordained minister is, at different times, all of these things. But these four activities do not make up the whole of his responsibility for the worship life of the people of God. There is one thing the minister cannot do for his congregation: he cannot worship for them. And therefore the greater part of his responsibility for people's worship life does not concern what *he* does, but what he helps *them* to do.

There is a danger in many cultures that people will misunderstand the professional minister's role. They will think it is like that of the fetish priest—i.e. that he is someone who performs sacred rites *for* the people. But creative Christian liturgy, which is not simply translated from a liturgy developed elsewhere, will show that leader and congregation are part of one people at worship.

In this chapter, therefore, we shall again consider the minister as an enabler—this time, as one who enables the people of God to worship more meaningfully. Once again we shall see the minister, not primarily as a doer, but as one who helps others to do. His job is to equip the saints for what *they* are called to do, as ministers in their own right. The words, 'You are the king's priests' (1 Pet. 2.9) were addressed to the whole people of God. So it is all the people, and not just the minister, who are called to worship God. To understand this we must understand what is meant by the word 'worship'. And we must understand the relationship between 'worship' and 'worship services'.

THE MEANING OF 'WORSHIP'

The word 'worship' simply means 'giving worth' (i.e. praise and honour) to God. A 'service of worship' is simply an outward expression of the everyday inward meaning of our lives, in which we show by visible and spoken signs that we live in fellowship with God.

The wise men who came from the East to find the new-born King whose star they had seen held a worship service when they had found Him. They bowed down before Him, opened their sacks, and brought out the most precious gifts they could find: gold, frankincense, and myrrh. They offered them to Him, and bowed in awe of His Majesty.

When we speak about worship, this is the picture we should have before our minds—the example of peoples coming from afar to Christ the King, offering him the greatest gifts their lands can offer, and making adoration in the way their spirits move them.

God created man, not out of any need of His own, but out of His great love. He chose to exist for man, in order that man might have life and enjoy His creation in unity with Him. There is nothing that people must do in order to become acceptable to God, no rites they must perform, no rituals they must act out. That would not be Christian worship. Instead, Christians are called to receive in thankfulness God's gift of fellowship with Him.

This was God's intention from the creation, and, even though man rebelled and chose to reject Him, God has once again made it possible. For Christ has come to bring man into the New Covenant with God. He has done everything which needs to be done. What man has to do is simply to accept this, to live in it, to enjoy it, to be one with God. To live in such a way *is* to pray, it *is* to worship.

Thus in a worship service we show whose we are; we show why we live as we live; we show where our life has come from and where it is going.

There is no fruit without a seed, and no fruit without a tree that bore it. Neither is there any human life without God who creates and redeems it, nor any human life of service to God without an inward 'seed' of thanksgiving and praise.

In this chapter we discuss the worship service and not the whole life lived in worship. But they cannot really be separated. Therefore, when we consider services of worship, we shall always have man's total worship of God in mind.

PASTOR AND PEOPLE

The question we have to ask is: How can a pastor help his people, through their common worship, to give spoken and visible expression to the life they have in Christ? To answer this question we need to know who those people are. And we need to know whether the pastor belongs to the same tribe or nationality as the people? Have they had similar cultural experiences? Have they shared the same sort of education?

If the pastor and the people are from different backgrounds, how can he be sure that what *he* sees as meaningful worship will be meaningful to the people themselves? How can he make it authentic in terms of their own experience? Clearly he must not see the people merely in his own image. But how can he overcome the difference?

One answer that has been given, in mission-established Churches in many parts of the world, is that forms of worship ought not to be developed locally. According to this way of thinking the liturgies which have been developed once and for all in Europe have universal applicability. So the pastor in his seminary training studies them; and later, in his ministry, he introduces them to his congregation. According to this understanding, worship is a European art in which non-Europeans must be trained. The pastor does not train his people according to his own ideas of worship, but in patterns of worship developed over the course of history in Europe.

Recently, however, many Church people in Africa and Asia have disagreed with this understanding of worship. For worship to be authentic, these people say, it must be 'indigenous', that is to say it must develop in the culture and in the ways of the Christian community who are doing the worship. Africans cannot be expected to worship according to European ways. Africans must worship as Africans, Americans as Americans, and Asians as Asians.

But, others reply, if all nations are to worship in their own ways, how then can their worship all be Christian? Must Christian worship not be 'catholic', i.e. the same everywhere?

The problem is, therefore, how to allow a form of worship to develop which will be at one and the same time 'indigenous' (i.e. rooted in the local life of the worshipping community), and also 'catholic' (i.e. rooted in the life and traditions of the whole Christian church of all times and all places). If we have a worship service which is only indigenous, it will be a 'local' or 'parochial' form of Christianity—not really part of the world Church's worship. If, on the other hand, we have a form which is only catholic, it will not be the deepest possible religious experience for that particular community which is using it.

A service of common worship for a Christian community must incorporate what is common to all the members of that particular Christian community. But for it to be a Christian service of worship it will have to incorporate what is common to the whole Church everywhere. It must be related to the total experience of those who have come to God in Christ through all times and in all places.

Another way of saying this is to say that human beings are everywhere human. They are the ones created by God for fellowship with Him, who have fallen from fellowship and become strangers to God, and who have been reconciled to God in Christ. But every human being in the world, besides being human, also belongs to a particular culture.

As we have seen, each culture is distinct. No two cultures are the same. The people who belong to these cultures are therefore also distinct. All people share some things with all mankind. But they share other things only with members of their own culture, or perhaps with members of similar cultures. And some things they share only with particular groups—with other women, or other young men, or other farmers, or other members of their clan or family, or other citizens of their nation. And, finally, some things concerning people are true of them only as individuals (see p. 30).

PUBLIC WORSHIP

In preparing services for common worship (as opposed to private devotions) we cannot really deal with those things which are only individual. At the most, we can in common worship have periods of silent prayer, when individuals can make their own petitions and confessions and thanksgivings to God, or we can give opportunities for individuals to make requests, and for the congregation to pray for them. But a common worship service cannot be tailor-made to suit all the different individuals in the congregation.

Common worship consists primarily of those things which the group who are worshipping share as a whole, or which sub-groups within the larger group share as a whole. These shared things, out of which common worship arises, are those things which:

(a) all human beings, including all Christians, share in common;

(b) all members of the particular group share in common; or

(c) a mixture of the two: i.e. things which people *share* with all others, but which they *express* in their own different cultural ways which are common to the whole group that is gathered for worship. These cultural ways are not common for Christian groups in other parts of the world.

For example, all men throughout the world receive the fruit of their agricultural labours from God. And all men who receive something from another person upon whom they feel dependent, express thanks to the one by whose grace they feel they have received the gifts. All Christians believe that it is God who is the supreme Giver of all good things. But (1) God does not give the same gifts to all, and (2) not all men in all cultures express thanks in the same way.

Thus in a prayer of thanksgiving for the fruits of the harvest in Africa, it will not be appropriate to give thanks 'for the wheat from which we get the flour for our bread'. Nor, in many parts of Africa, is it suitable to have an instruction that: 'After the people have brought their offerings and placed them on the table, they kneel and the pastor places his hands downward upon the offerings, and he reads the following prayer.' In many parts of Africa a table would not be large enough for such offerings, nor would it be a place where the people would think of placing gifts of unprocessed food. Secondly, in some areas, for the pastor to place his hands *downward* on the offerings would be to curse and reject them—when making a gift it is customary to put your hands *under* it with your palms facing upward!

For these reasons, those Churches are wise who allow for considerable freedom in worship. Then new liturgies can develop which will be appropriate to the worship lives of the communities which use them, and at the same time be faithful to the central historical traditions of the Church. It is impossible for any one liturgy to fit all Christian societies everywhere.

In a very diverse society, such as that of Ghana, which contains many different sorts of congregations, those liturgies are probably best which are developed locally in congregations or in districts. In such a society the pastor ought to be given freedom within certain guide-lines, to work with his people to develop an authentic Christian worship life. He may need to become a composer of new liturgies.

This is a difficult task, especially if the pastor is not by birth or experience a 'man of the people'. But it may need to be done, and, with God's help, it can be done. In the next chapter we shall discuss some ways of doing it.

STUDY SUGGESTIONS

WORD STUDY

1. (a) What is the meaning of the word 'worship'?
   (b) What is the relation between 'worship' and a 'worship service'? Give examples to support your answer.
2. (a) What is the meaning of the word 'catholic' as used in this chapter?
   (b) In what other ways is the word sometimes used?
3. What is the meaning of 'indigenous'?
   Give some examples of things in your country which are *not* indigenous.

REVIEW QUESTIONS

4. What is the chief difference between common worship and private devotions?
5. What is the role of an ordained minister in regard to his people's worship?
6. Can a worship service be both 'catholic' and 'indigenous'?

DISCUSSION AND RESEARCH TOPICS

7. What would you reply to someone who said: 'If God is One, and if the Church ought to be one, then all Christians and all Churches ought to worship in the same way'?

8. 'According to this understanding worship is a European art in which non-Europeans must be trained.' (p. 118). What is your opinion?
9. Give some examples of worship practices in your own Church which are *not* indigenous. Do you think they are helpful?
10. Find out all you can about the worship practices of people of other religions in your country.
    (a) Do you think that some of these practices help people to worship God better than some of the worship practices in your Church? If so, describe them and say why you think they are helpful.
    (b) In which ways do any of these practices *hinder* people from worshipping God? Give examples.

19. Developing Liturgies

Those who compose liturgies must be sensitive to the local culture. A pastor does not have a mission from God to impose his own cultural ways, or cultural ways which he has learned from other nations or tribes, or his own private ideas of what is desirable. The congregations whom he serves are responsible members of the body of Christ. They must not be regarded as mere objects of the pastor's activity. They have a right to be the active subjects in their own worship lives. As we have seen, they have their own culture and their own ways, and God will lead them to express their religious feelings in ways which suit their own particular ways of life. But with God's help the pastor can enable them fully to be their own people.

PASSING ON THE LIFE OF THE SPIRIT

How can the pastor do this? Harry Boer, a missionary who has worked for many years in Northern Nigeria, suggests ways in which to enable people to develop an authentic, indigenous, Christian worship life:

> How can we pass on the life of the Spirit without also passing on the forms in which we ourselves received it? We shall not succeed simply by neglecting these forms. What we must do is to distinguish carefully between the life of the Spirit itself, and the particular forms and practices through which we have experienced it. We must also recognize the particular cultural, religious, and social background of the people to whom we minister the life of the Spirit. When we

121

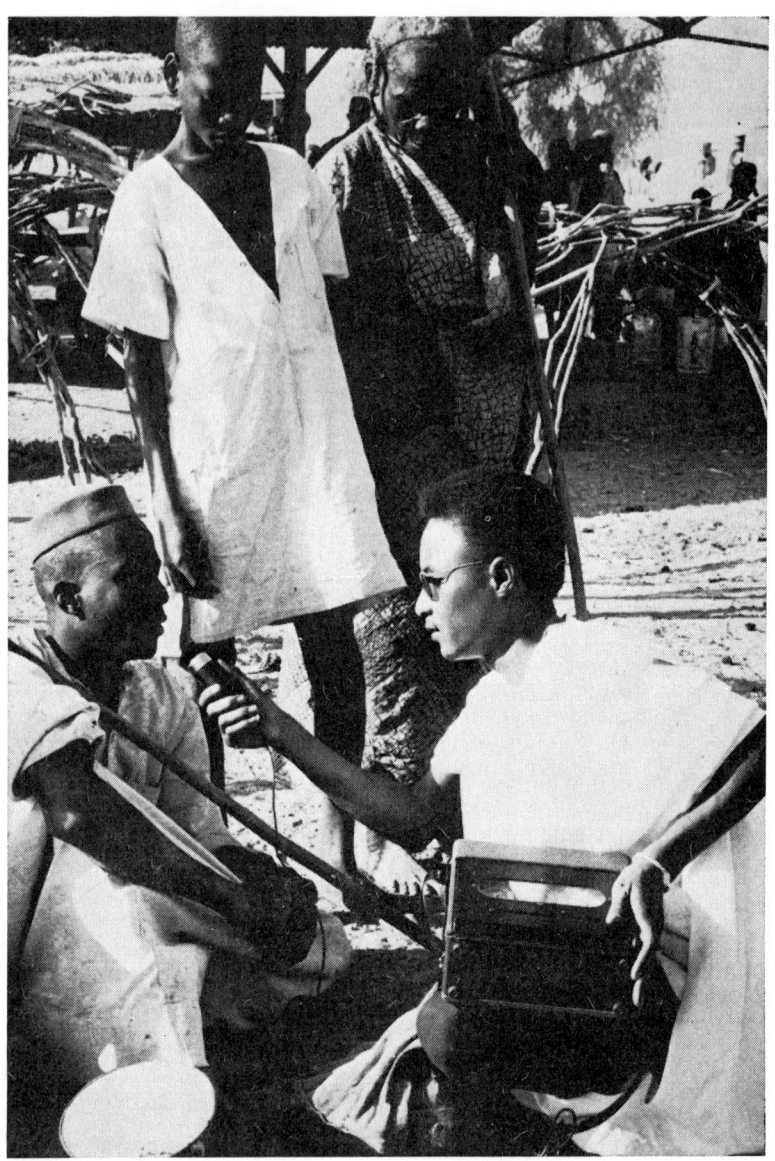

'People who have the life of the Spirit working in them must express it in ways that belong to their own character and situation' (p. 123).

A radio reporter in Nigeria invites people to express their feelings and ideas about the political life of their country, to be broadcast in a radio programme.

How can a pastor help Christian people to do the same in their worship life?

recognize these distinctions, *new* forms and practices can be created which are partly ours and partly theirs. Through these new forms the Spirit can work effectively in the life of the new Christian community, and the new community can best express its own spiritual life. This will be the result of *common effort*. The missionary will recognize that people who have the life of the Spirit working in them must express it in ways that belong to their own character and situation. And those who have newly come to Christ will recognize what can be helpful from the experience and insight of the Church which has ministered Christ to them.

In the end no one can really make a liturgy, or even a prayer, for another person. He can make a liturgy which the other will recognize and perhaps be able to use. But if another person has made it without his co-operation, it will not be *his* liturgy. The prayers will not be *his* prayers. The sensitive composer of liturgy is better able to develop a liturgy which 'fits' the society which is to use it than is an insensitive composer, i.e. one who does not even stop to ask questions about how these people may differ from his own people. But, all on his own, no composer from outside will be able to develop, for example, a truly Nuer liturgy for Nuers to use, nor a truly Malay liturgy for Malays to use, no matter how sensitive he is.

It may happen, however, that a Yoruba Christian, for example, is put in the position of having to develop a liturgy for a newly Christian people in Northern Dahomey. He may wish to refuse, but it may well be that there is no one else who could do it. The people in question may be totally illiterate, or literate only in their own language. As one who can read and write their language, as well as other languages in which liturgies have previously been written, the Yoruba Christian has a responsibility to the new Dahomeyan Church. He cannot deny this.

But this does *not* mean that he can do the work *for* the people of that Dahomeyan tribe. He can do it *with* them, but not *for* them. His responsibility is, first, to help them to know how other Christian communities have prayed and worshipped. He can show them how his own fellow Yoruba Christians, in his own Church, have worshipped, and how Yorubas of other denominations have worshipped. He can tell them how he has heard Ewe Presbyterians and Ibo Catholics worship; how he learned in seminary about French and British and American worship. He can tell them about the worship of the Early Church.

NO ONE 'RIGHT' WAY

When he shares this experience with the Dahomeyans, what he is really saying is: 'There is no one "right" way to worship, beyond what Jesus told the Samaritan woman about worshipping "in spirit and truth". People throughout history and throughout the world have worshipped in many different ways. I cannot tell you which way is right for you. I can share with you what I feel, and what my Church feels. I can tell you why some of these ways appeal to us, and others don't, and why *we* think some of them are right and others are wrong. I could try to analyse for you what seems to be most common in all these forms of worship, i.e. those things on which they all seem to agree. We could try some of these different ways of worship, and see how you feel about them. You could share some of your own feelings and thoughts about how you feel you ought to worship, and make suggestions about things I've not spoken of. Perhaps then Christians in other parts of the world will learn something important from the way in which *you* worship. Would you be willing for us to do this for a year or two? Perhaps by then we'll have some idea of the forms you'd like your worship to take— or maybe you'll decide that you don't want to fix any one permanent form.'

At that point, if I were that pastor, and the people had agreed, I would go on to suggest that they should have two regular sorts of Sunday worship:

1. worship which includes the Lord's Supper, and
2. worship which doesn't, perhaps because they wouldn't have a pastor every Sunday to administer it.

Such services as baptisms, marriages, burials, dedications, etc, would be special services. The most important services to consider at the start would, however, be the regular ones.

Then I would go on to explain how, in normal Sunday service, in addition to the singing of hymns and the reading and preaching of the word, most Christians usually want to approach God in five different ways:

1. *adoration*, i.e. the praise of God,
2. *confession* of sin and request for pardon,
3. *thanksgiving* for God's general and special acts of goodness,
4. *intercession*, i.e. coming before God in the interests of another person, to ask God's help for that person, or for other groups, and
5. *petition*, i.e. asking God for help or blessings for ourselves, and for communities of which we are a part.

These, I would tell them, are different sorts of prayer. Most Christians have found that a good service needs to include them all.

THE CONTENT OF WORSHIP

Probably the people would then ask what should be the content of the adorations, confessions, thanksgivings, intercessions, or petitions. But I would say: 'I can only tell you by giving you examples from my own home Church or from Scripture. And you must only use them as examples, not as your own prayers. What you need to do now is to ask yourselves: "What do *we* want to adore or praise God for? What do *we* want to confess to God? What are *we* thankful to God for? What prayers do *we* want to make before God on behalf of other people or on behalf of ourselves?" '

Perhaps they would say: 'You can do it for us. We are new in the faith. We know nothing.' I would remind them of some of the prayers I had heard them making in the past, whenever I called on them to pray during a service or evangelistic meeting. 'What you have to do now,' I would say, 'is just what you were doing then. Do you think you need a special language, or a university degree, to be able to pray? Prayer is talking to God, that's all. If you can talk to your father, you can also talk to God. You've *been* talking to him that way. God *is* our Father.'

Of course, if I had not been listening to their prayers carefully, or asking them to pray, I wouldn't have been able to say that. If I had not been trying to listen sensitively to their conversations and questions and concerns, I might not have known what things worried them or made them happy or made them feel secure. Yet, in my continual dialogue with them through the months, that had been my responsibility to them, to be as sensitive as I could be. Now it has become my task to reflect back at them what I have heard them say, to help them recognize the ways in which they ordinarily show their individuality and their culture. They themselves may not be aware of these things, because they are too close to them. Now, however, they need to be aware of them, so that they can compose a liturgy which 'fits' them, which will be *their* particular liturgy, in harmony with the larger Church's liturgy.

THE LORD'S SUPPER

I would also tell the people about the things which are usually done at an observance of the Lord's Supper:

1. the reading and exposition of the Scriptures,
2. intercession for the whole Church and the world,
3. an offering,
4. thanksgiving for creation and redemption,
5. speaking the words of Christ's Institution of the Sacrament,
6. prayers for the Lord's coming and for the showing of His Kingdom,

7. the Lord's Prayer,
8. the breaking of the bread,
9. the distribution of the elements,
10. the eating and drinking in communion with Christ and each member of the Church, and
11. the exhortation to Christian service.

(This list and much of the following explanation of the Lord's Supper are taken from the findings of an interdenominational study team which met in the USA in 1970.)

Then I would explain to the people that some Christians call this sacrament 'the Lord's Supper', thus emphasizing its connection with Jesus's last supper, and some call it 'Holy Communion', thus emphasizing the theme of our unity with Christ and with one another. Others again call it 'the Eucharist', thus emphasizing the theme of thanksgiving for what God has done for us in Christ. But whatever name is used for it, it has at all times in the history of the Church been central to Christian worship. It is the service by which God's people both receive and witness to the reconciliation accomplished by Christ. It is the service in which all Christians together participate in the oneness of His redeemed and redeeming community.

I would explain that this sacrament is not only something which the Church does, but something which God does as well. God once again seals His word with the visible signs of His love—the signs of Christ's body and blood. And we, by partaking in faith of the bread and wine, receive Christ into our hearts once more. It is really Christ who in the Supper gives Himself to us, as He promised, according to Revelation 3.20. He is the one Mediator and High Priest of the New Covenant. The priest or pastor who gives us the bread and the wine is ministering to us in Christ's name. He is authorized or recognized by the Christian fellowship in which the service is held. The priest or pastor is our minister and he is Christ's minister, and through his actions it is really Christ who is ministering to His community. Christ is the Host. The pastor and the priest are only the stewards.

WORSHIP AS WITNESS

It is important to remember, too, that the Lord's Supper is not directed only toward the Church. The Church is called, through this sacrament, to 'show forth' the salvation of God in Christ. That means to show it forth to the world. This is a missionary sacrament, a sacrament directed to the whole world. It is not the closed rite of a secret community. As joyful witnesses to the risen Lord, we offer to all people in their needs the hope we have in Christ. We look to the day when, after Christ has put all things in subjection to Himself, He will subject Himself to God the Father, so that God may again be all in all (1 Cor. 15.28). Through this sacrament we look to the completion of God's salvation of the world.

I would also explain that it is not absolutely clear from the Gospel accounts whether the Last Supper took place on the day of preparation for Passover, or during the festival of Passover itself. For this reason some Christians believe that the Lord's Supper should be celebrated with unleavened wafers (see Exod. 12.14–20), while others think that it should be celebrated with ordinary bread.

I would also point out another difference in practice, i.e. that some Churches use red wine (to symbolize more directly the blood of Jesus), while others use white wine, and still others use unfermented grape juice. In some parts of the world, where grapes are not found, various local drinks have been used.

What is important is not that Jesus used special things at the Last Supper, and that therefore the sacrament will not 'work' if we use different things. On the contrary, Jesus used the most ordinary food (in His country's case, bread), and the most ordinary drink (in His country's case, wine), and He made these ordinary things holy. As Christians we are not called to live an extraordinary life, a life with all kinds of strange rituals and practices. We are called to consecrate ordinary things, to live a life devoted to God right where we are. The greatest gift we can offer to God in thankful praise is ourselves (Rom. 12.11). It is through the bread and wine that we make a sign to God that we are offering him ourselves. It is through the bread and wine that God makes a sign to us that He is offering us Himself. And it is by eating and drinking those signs together that we come into renewed unity with God and with our fellows in the Christian community.'

After saying all this I think it would be my duty to stop, unless the people asked me special questions. I do not in conscience feel that I could go on to say: 'You *must* observe the Lord's Supper, now, in the following ways. You *must* have a preparatory service the day before. People *must* come to have prayer or confess their sins to the pastor or presbyter or priest during that week, they *must* bring an offering of so much money, they *must* all wear white clothing.' I would not say: 'There should be three hymns, the Lord's Prayer should come between the Scripture exposition and the Words of Institution, the pastor must not . . . the people should . . . etc., etc.'

LITURGY MUST BE SPONTANEOUS

I could not give such detailed instructions because, after saying all that I have said, I must recognize that if the communion liturgy is to be truly

127

indigenous *it must be a liturgy which the people make, in harmony with the Church universal.*

Bishop Peter Dery of the Roman Catholic Diocese of Wa, in the Upper Region of Ghana, a native Dagati himself, was asked why he permitted the women to give a traditional Dagati ecstatic shout at the close of the eucharistic celebration. 'It is a spontaneous action on their part,' he said. 'That is the only way we need to judge it. This is their spontaneous response, in joy, to receiving the sacrament. This is how some Dagati women express their Christianity.'

To attend a Catholic mass in the Wa Diocese is to experience truly indigenous worship. I have never seen a more African expression of Christianity, and, after having witnessed it, I am sure that it is a Dagati expression *of Christianity.* With traditional music, traditional instruments, and traditional chants and shouts, the Gospel of Jesus Christ is celebrated week after week in Dagatiland.

WHAT IS 'FOREIGN'

The example of Bishop Dery is important. It may be that in reading this chapter some people have said: 'This doesn't apply to me. I am a person of the same tribe and nationality as the people to whom I minister. He is talking about those who work among foreign people, or among new Christians.'

But is it really true that what has been said in this chapter does not apply to your situation? Suppose you are a theological college-trained pastor, going back to serve your own people. You find them perhaps using a liturgy brought by the Germans in the last century, or one brought from another tribe with a different culture. Although you are familiar with it, you may recognize that it does not truly express the people's own religious experience. You may perhaps see that many of the people are leaving the Church to join the sects. And although you may feel that the sects are being syncretistic (see pp. 75f), and have incorporated too many pagan elements into their worship, you may also recognize that in some ways their worship is truer to the culture of your people than is the official German Christian liturgy of your Church.

Perhaps you will then ask what you should do. It may well be that, like Bishop Dery, you are not yourself one of the people. You went away to a secondary school when you were twelve. You have lived away from home, except for vacation, for eleven years or more. You know few of the legends or proverbs of your people, and you know little of the meaning of their customs connected with birth, marriage, or death.

Are you, then, so very different from the outsider—the missionary to a foreign people or the Christian from one tribe who goes to another tribe to be a pastor? The answer is No. And the answer is that you too must be a learner and a fellow worker *with* your people. You cannot compose a liturgy *for* them, though you may help them to come to develop their own appropriate indigenous forms of Christian worship. As a theological college-trained man, you can offer them guidance, help, and insight from what you have learned of Christian tradition throughout the world, and from your new understanding of the Scriptures on which all liturgies should be based.

Like the men serving as pastors outside of their own cultures and societies, you can help the people to feel free to do new things, to change, to find forms of worship life which truly suit their culture.

STUDY SUGGESTIONS

REVIEW QUESTIONS

1. Why can a pastor not compose good liturgies by himself, for the Church to use?
2. What must be the attitude of a pastor who has to help his people to make a liturgy for themselves?
3. What two special kinds of knowledge does a student gain in his theological college training, which will enable him to help his people compose a suitable liturgy?
4. List the different sorts of prayer traditionally found in most Christian services, and describe them.
5. What are some of the different names given to the Lord's Supper, and what does each of them mean?
6. What, by tradition, are the parts of a Lord's Supper observance?

DISCUSSION AND RESEARCH TOPICS

7. Read Matthew 26.26–30. Notice how Jesus refers to two events, separated in time.
   (a) What are these two events?
   (b) In what way does this show that the Lord's Supper is not simply a memorial of Christ's death?
   (c) What else does the Lord's Supper point to?
8. Compare 1 Cor. 11.23–26 and Luke 22.14–20.
   (a) What are some of the differences between the two passages?
   (b) Why do you think there are these differences?
   (c) Are the differences really important?
9. Suggest five things for which rural people are thankful, for which urban people may not be.
10. Suggest one or more sorts of petition which the people of your own nation and culture might offer to God, which Europeans would not.

11. What things might the people of a village like to confess, which educated people probably would not feel a need to confess?
12. What happens in a Church whose people have had foreign liturgies imposed on them?

20. Indigenizing Worship

There is a risk in composing new liturgies. But no new life comes into being without risk. We have to be careful, however, to distinguish between different sorts of risk. There is the risk of 'syncretism' (see p. 75), which happens if the Gospel is hidden or distorted by being mixed with practices which belong to other religions. And another sort of risk, which missionaries sometimes fear as much, is that 'our' new Christians will decide to follow forms different from our own tradition. We fear that though we are Presbyterians, they will adopt a Lutheran or Apostolic way of doing things. We fear that they will say to us: 'We have heard your explanation of why you do these things your way, but the Methodist approach makes more sense to us in this one matter.'

We do have to remember our responsibility to give mutual advice and admonition to one another. If we honestly feel that the people are distorting the faith by their liturgical adaptations, we must say so, and explain why, even though we don't have final authority over them. But we must also ask ourselves whether we have a commission from the Lord to insist that they do things in the way in which Norwegian Lutherans or Luo Catholics do them. Are we so sure that *our* way is the only right way? Are we sure that our tradition is correct in this particular respect?

When we had our first harvest thanksgiving service in Chokosiland, after I had said a prayer of thanksgiving in presenting the offerings of the people, one of the congregational leaders said to me: 'You have spoken to God. We would like to speak to our fathers.' At that time my Chokosi was still far from perfect, and I thought he had said: 'We would like to have one of our fathers also speak' (i.e. pray). I said I saw no objection, but he went on to call the names of the ancestors one by one tell them about the offering and ask them for their blessing! I was shocked, but when I got back home I started to think what this meant.

I wondered whether there was some special connection between a harvest offering and the ancestors. I investigated, and found out that at the harvest time Chokosis do feel a special sense of dependence upon their clan ancestors. The ancestors were the first to settle the land, and they farmed it before the present generation did. It was *their* land, and so, in a way, the fruits which the people now derive from it came from them.

A CHRISTIAN EXPRESSION OF THE PEOPLE'S FEELINGS

Could we in faithfulness to Christian revelation express liturgically this sense of fellowship with the ancestors that the people feel at harvest time, I wondered. Could we give it a Christian expression? As Christians we know, of course, that the produce of the land comes from God, and that the land itself belongs to God. But it is also in a sense 'our fathers' land'. It is through the land that people everywhere have a feeling of unity with the founders of their 'fathers'' nation.

This idea, I noted, is found in the Old Testament as well. The land of Israel, from the time of Abraham on, was always 'the land of the promise'. God had promised the land to Abraham and his descendants. And when the people went out of Egypt to take possession of the land, He became known as 'the God of Abraham, Isaac, and Jacob', i.e. the God who had made His covenant, or promise, first with them.

In their harvest offerings the Israelites recited a confession of faith which began: 'A wandering Aramaean was my father' (Deut. 26.5). And Jesus himself had said to the Sadducees that, as God was called the God of Abraham, Isaac, and Jacob, he was not a God of the dead, but of the living (Mark 12.27). And so, in some sense, Abraham and Isaac and Jacob were not dead but living. It was through the *land* of Israel, the land promised to their ancestors, that the nation of Israel have always felt connected in the closest way with their ancestors.

What was wrong with the Chokosis' prayer, I felt, was not the sense of community they had with their ancestors, but the fact that the prayer was addressed *to* the ancestors, rather than to God. Could we not, I wondered, have a prayer which would express this sense of community with the founders of the clan, but which would be addressed not to the founders themselves but to the God who is 'the Father of us all'?

The next year, when I led the prayer, I prayed something like this:

Oh, God, our Father, and the God of our fathers. You have blessed us from the beginning of time. We thank you for our life, for health, and for the land on which we live. These fields that we have farmed, our fathers have farmed before us. And they have left them to us, and we have farmed them this year, and they have brought forth plentifully. We have come to present our thank offerings to you, for we know that all these gifts have come from you. You are the one who has caused the rain to fall, and the sun to shine. You are the one who has made the guinea corn germinate and grow and bring forth its grain. You are the one who has blessed us with the strength to do all this work.

On this day we are mindful of our fathers. They have left us, and we know that they have gone to you, and they are with you, and you know them better than even we do. We ask you to bless them and to bless us and to give us unity one with the other, so that in the day of Christ's coming we may all be gathered together in your kingdom.

We began to use prayers like this in other villages. And we continued. No-one again asked: 'May we also pray to our fathers?' The human need for a sense of harmony and continuity with one's ancestors was satisfied in a Christian way.

CHRISTIAN SUBSTITUTES FOR LOCAL RITES

Besides this matter of the ancestors, there were other ways in which we provided 'functional substitutes' for the Chokosi religious practices, i.e. rites which provided a Christian way of doing what had previously been done in a non-Christian way. In this way we avoided the danger of syncretism.

In the South of Ghana there has always been disagreement between the Church leaders in their official positions, and the ordinary Church members, on the subject of libation. Libation, as Dr C. G. Baeta of the University of Ghana has explained it, is a rite by which the living come into communion with the ancestors by making a drink offering. This (1) lifts the living to a new height, and (2) brings the ancestors closer to the living, so that (3) communion and communication between them can take place in a realm halfway between their usual places of being.

Libation is performed on all important occasions, to solemnize the occasion during regular annual festivals, as a form of annual communion, and at births and funerals. Dr Baeta even saw libation being poured by a man from whom the E.P. Church was buying land for a new secondary school. The man, he explained, had to 'get permission from the ancestors' before he could sell the land.

The position which almost all the Churches have taken on the subject is that libation is worship offered to the ancestors, who are regarded as gods, and that therefore it is an anti-Christian act. Church members have been forbidden to participate in it.

But people have not taken much notice of the prohibition. The newspapers often carry announcement of Catholic, Methodist, and Anglican funerals, which include both libation at the home and a thanksgiving or memorial service at the church. Libation is not often advertised in the case of Presbyterian funerals. But few Presbyterian pastors would deny that libation is often secretly performed when they are not present.

'Libation is performed on all important occasions. . . . Church members have been forbidden to participate but have not taken much notice of the prohibition' (p. 132). In East Asia where belief in evil spirits is strong, incense is burned to keep them away, and to procure blessing, for example on the site for a new building.
Do any practices in your own country show strong needs that people feel? Could the Church find Christian ways of answering those needs?

The Chokosis, with whom I worked, were a tribe of the Southern type (an Akan tribe) but they lived in the North of Ghana, where libation is not widely practised. Would the new Chokosi Christians, I wondered, be just as unwilling to give up libation as the Akans in the South? What could we do to provide a functional substitute for it?

CHRISTIAN FUNERALS

The Chokosi congregations had taken to the use of *pito* (a slightly fermented drink made of guinea corn) for their communion wine. It was this same *pito* that was customarily used in libation. In the funerals of mature people, on the eighth day after a death (if there was guinea corn available), and at the second funeral, libation was poured to the one who had just died. The people would pour a calabash of *pito* on the man's grave, and then, after speaking to him, would share the rest of the pot or pots themselves. It was a kind of communion between themselves, following the communion of all with the recently deceased member of the clan.

Catholics and Anglicans, I recalled, sometimes had memorial eucharists, which they offered to God in the name of a departed Christian. Why could we Presbyterians not also have memorial communion services? I asked. Why could we not have them at the very same time at which libation would normally be poured? Why could we not use the very same *pito*? Would this be an acceptable functional substitute for the Chokosis, that could replace the practice which we found difficult to reconcile with our Christian faith? Well, we could try!

As it turned out, the first Christian funeral we were involved in was that of old Dibolo, the headman of Mayamam, the village where almost everyone had been baptized. It was, in one way, an excellent opportunity, because not only the dead man, but also his whole household and village, were Christians. In another way, it was frightening, because this was one of the most important funerals to take place in Chokosiland for many years, and people would come from many villages.

I met with members of the family and the local session and said: 'How are we going to observe the funeral?' They described what they had planned. I mentioned the possibility of a memorial communion service, at which special prayers would be said for Dibolo, and where we could use 'Dibolo's *pito*' for the celebration. They said it sounded fine.

Everything went on, much to my amazement, just as planned. A very meaningful communion service was held in the chapel. Several representatives of the community participated in the leading of prayers. We celebrated the Lord's Supper, and no libation was poured on Dibolo's grave. There was no need to—we had provided a substitute.

From that time on we made it a regular part of every Christian burial that on the eighth day a communion service would be celebrated—sometimes in the deceased's compound or at the graveside, sometimes in the chapel.

In some cases we met opposition from relatives who were not Christians, because they still wanted to pour libation. It was therefore important to get people to say, while they were alive, that they wanted to have a memorial communion service rather than a libation when they died. So we discussed it regularly in meetings of local congregations and at the district session.

Many of those who were not Christians were quite impressed with our Christian funerals. As in other parts of Ghana, when people witnessed a Christian funeral, it made them say: 'I want to become a Christian so that when I go I'll have a service like that.' We tried to encourage people to care for the widows and children of the departed, rather than spend large sums of money, food, and livestock on the guests and on the graveclothes. We took special offerings for the widows and children. We encouraged Christians from other villages to come to the funeral, to express their unity with their Christian brothers in the village where the death had occurred.

We were not as successful in providing substitutes for other local funeral rites, such as placing food and water in the graves, sacrificing animals over the legs of the departed before burial, etc. About all we were able to achieve by the time I left was an understanding that Christians would not be asked to perform these things. People in many places still went on doing them. But as more and more people become Christians and as a Christian consciousness is formed more and more, these practices also will probably be transformed so that they are in keeping with a Christian view of life and death.

John Taylor, who has also thought a lot about the problem of a truly Christian expression of African feelings and relations concerning death, has suggested a form of prayer which can be useful in the Christian remembrance of the dead. Here is an English retranslation of our Chokosi version of it:

Our Father God, you who hold all men in your hand, those who are alive as well as those who are no longer in the world, as well as all the places where they are, we beg you on behalf of him whose name and dwelling and desires you know, and we give thanks to you as we are in remembrance of him at this moment. Speak to him, Lord, you who have sympathy upon us all; tell him how we love him, and accept the prayer that we ask for him, through our Lord Jesus Christ. (*The Primal Vision*)

We used prayers like this quite often, and always specifically mentioned the name of the one on whose behalf we were praying.

One thing which I heard quite early in my ministry in Chereponi influenced me strongly in the direction of not forgetting those whom we in the West think of as 'the dead', but whom Africans think of as 'the living dead'. In a Konkomba village in which we were working it became apparent that the young men were attracted to the Church, but that the older men were becoming concerned lest their sons became Christians. I tried to assuage their fears, to assure them that they, too, could become Christians, but that, even if they didn't, they had no reason to fear personal loss if their sons were baptized.

'You Christians,' one old man said, 'say God has commanded men to honour their fathers and mothers. But you yourselves do not believe that. You take young men away from their fathers, so that they no longer respect them, and you take the living away from the dead, so that they no longer give them honour.'

'That is not true,' I replied. 'We teach the young men to respect their fathers. Just because they become Christians does not mean they will cease to be good sons. Quite the contrary.'

'What about our fathers who have gone before us?' he asked.

And I realized that I had no answer. From his point of view the departed ancestors, too, were 'fathers'.

'Why are you so impious as not to give them their due respect?' he asked. 'Does God's commandment to honour our fathers not apply to them?'

Why did I have no answer? 'What about our fathers who have gone before us?' I continually asked myself for the next several years. The Church in Africa must answer this question, and must express the answer not only in words, but also in its liturgical life, in its worship.

In Ghana we did two other things to show in our liturgical life the concern we had for 'those who have gone before':

1. We observed All Saints' Day (November 1) by holding in each village a service of Remembrance for all the members of the congregation who had died in the previous year. We remembered them by name, and remembered also those who had died before, and affirmed our unity with them;

2. We included in every regular observance of the Lord's Supper a thanksgiving for our fellowship with those who had gone before us in the faith, especially those Christians in the congregation who had recently died.

Except in the harvest thanksgiving, however, we did not really face the question of our relation to members of the village who had died who were not Christians. Nor did we really face the question of the whole company of the 'living dead', and our relation as Christians to them. These questions also need to be faced, however. Canon Harry Sawyerr deals very fully with this problem in his book *Creative Evangelism*. Sawyerr's opinion is that God is not only the Father of the Christian dead, but also 'potentially the Father of the ancestral dead'. He points to the traditional Christian practice of the veneration of the saints, and he notes that, among those listed in the Letter to the Hebrews, for example, many 'questionable' saints are found. What the writer to the Hebrews seems to be saying is that Gideon, Samson, Barak, Rahab, and others are 'made perfect' through us. ('In the deathless society of the people of God they draw upon the treasury of life to which more enlightened generations have since contributed their experience of the love of God.') Sawyerr feels that

> by praying for the unconverted ancestral dead we may help them to discover the love of God wherever they may be, and in so doing find the means of attaining eternal salvation.

Whatever we may think about statements like Sawyerr's, we must admit that non-Roman Catholic Christians are only just beginning to face up to the problem of what has been a real omission in their liturgical worship.

HEALING

Another important failure of omission in many of our services is being pointed out to us forcefully these days by the so-called 'healing Churches'. Once again, whatever we may think of the approach which many independent African Churches take to healing, we cannot say they are wrong to be concerned with problems of sickness and health. We in the traditional Churches have been much too willing to leave 'medical matters' to our Church hospitals, as if healing were a purely physical concern. Christians of the mission-established Churches present themselves to the Africans as total Western materialists. Most doctors nowadays, however, through their Christian medical workers' fellowships, recognize the fact that sickness is not always the result of viruses and other infections. It is the *man* who is sick, not just his lungs or his stomach, and it is to the man that we must minister, not just to part of his body. Man is a unity, which includes both the physical and the spiritual, as Africans always knew, and healing means the 'making whole' of that unity.

It is not sufficient, therefore, merely to utter vague, general prayers 'for all the sick and their needs, that thou wilt minister to them'. We need to make opportunities to pray for particular individuals, by name and in person. And we need to do this not only in Sunday services but at other times. Services of intercession and prayers for healing are not expressly forbidden by any of our Churches. And they can be held not only in chapels or churches, but in peoples' homes. We need to discover those among us who have the gifts of healing and use them. We need to develop simple liturgies of intercession for the sick, involving possibly the laying on of hands and anointing with oil, both of which are accepted Biblical practices.

THE CHURCH YEAR

Finally, we need to consider the 'Church year'. Regular observance of the cycle of festivals of the historic Church—Advent, Christmas, Epiphany, Lent, Easter, Pentecost—not only provides a convenient framework for all our worship. It grounds it firmly in the history of salvation, in God's work of redemption in Christ. By observing the Church year we are: (1) guarded against the temptation 'to do the same thing Sunday after Sunday' and 'preach the same sermon week after week', and (2) able to dramatize the Gospel. The Christian faith is not a timeless expression of an eternal truth. It refers to events which have taken place *in* time. It witnesses to a God who acts in time and history, and who is making all things new.

The Church year does not mean that Christ dies again every Good Friday, nor that He is reborn every Easter Sunday, nor that the world waits as if He had never come every Advent, and receives Him all over again each Christmas. The Greeks believed in dying and rising gods, who died each year as the winter came, and rose each year as spring arrived. Our God died only once, but He is alive and will never die again (Rom. 6.9–10). But to *remember* His death dramatically at one special time each year, to remember His entry into Jerusalem and His last supper and His washing of the disciples' feet and His trial and crucifixion and burial, is to remind us that these were events within history. To remember His ascension dramatically once each year is to remind us that Christ is now with the Father because of what happened that day. To remember the descent of the Spirit dramatically once each year is to remind us that the Spirit is still among us, and to point us toward the mission we now have. To remember Christ's first advent dramatically each year is to direct us to hope for His second coming, and to remind us that God is moving through history to accomplish His purpose, that history has a goal.

The Church year is a way of showing Africans who, according to John Mbiti, think of time as going from the 'now' of the present to the 'then' of the eternal past, that in Christ their history has been converted. We all live now in a present which is moving toward a future, the future of Christ. This prepares them, Mbiti feels, to live fully in the changing world which they see everywhere around them, which their idea of the 'then' could never enable them to do. In other words, using the Church year is not just a matter of rules and regulations. By living the liturgy we become better prepared to be responsible agents in God's world, and to play the part He plans for us in history.

STUDY SUGGESTIONS

REVIEW QUESTIONS

1. (a) Why is it important to avoid syncretism in our worship?
   (b) In what ways can it be avoided?
2. Why is it good to observe the Church year?
3. Which of the traditional Jewish festivals do we know that Jesus took part in?

BIBLE STUDY

4. Read Deut. 16.1–3 and Luke 22.7, 8.
   (a) What do we learn from these two passages about the usefulness of 'Festivals of Remembrance'?
   (b) What events in the history of your people could be commemorated as a way of worshipping God?
   (c) What possible dangers, if any, do you see in this kind of 'historical' commemoration?

DISCUSSION AND RESEARCH TOPICS

5. What, if anything, does the liturgy in your Church say about the dead? Does it include the non-Christian dead? Should it? Give reasons for your answer.
6. (a) What sort of intercession for the sick, if any, is included in the liturgies now used in your Church?
   (b) Does your Church follow the Biblical practices of the laying on of hands or anointing with oil? If so, why? If not, why not?
   (c) Do you think these practices are helpful?
   Give reasons for your answer.
7. What is the difference between (a) praying to the dead, (b) asking the dead to intercede for us, (c) praying for the dead, and (d) remembering the dead in prayer and thanking God for them? Which of these do you feel Christians can rightly do?
8. (a) Do your people fear the dead? What does the Church say to them about such fear? Do the answers which the Church gives satisfy them?
   (b) Do your people fear witchcraft? Do they try to get protection against it? If so, why do they not rely on the help of the Church?
9. What chief lessons can the Church learn from (a) traditional religious practices, (b) practices of sect Churches?

10. Do you think that people in urban areas, who have neither farms nor gardens, should hold harvest festivals?
Give reasons for your answer.

11. For what traditional observances in your area has the Church provided 'functional substitutes'?
What others could it provide?

PART 6
THE MINISTRY OF
DEVELOPING STEWARDSHIP

21. Response and Responsibility

One of my closest friends in Ghana was the Roman Catholic priest whose district overlapped mine. We both had been working for some time in a certain village which had several sections. We had more or less arrived at an agreement that the Catholics would work in one of the sections and we would work in another. Our Presbyterian work had been going on longer than his, and a short time after this unofficial division had been arranged, we had thirteen young men ready to be baptized. The Catholics did not yet have any candidates for baptism.

TWO WAYS OF WORKING

One of the first decisions of our young congregation after they were baptized was that they would like to build a chapel. They shared this decision with me. 'Oh, do you think you need a chapel?' I asked.

'Yes,' they replied. 'If we have a place where we can all gather and invite other people to come, it is better than if we continue to meet in one of our rooms. The people will then know our meeting is open to everyone, and not just our own private affair.'

'That sounds good,' I said.

'But will you help us?' they asked.

'Help you?' I answered. 'How?'

They talked among themselves for a while. 'If you can get us some aluminium roofing sheets,' they replied, 'we can do the rest.'

'You mean you will make the foundation and floor, make bricks, build the walls, buy windows, and buy boards for the roof, and plaster the building?' I questioned.

Once again they spoke among themselves. 'We want you to get us a bag of cement for the floor and the boards for the roof.'

I made a quick calculation. 'The money I can get will be enough for the roofing sheets and a bag of cement. I can't get fifteen pounds to buy the boards.'

'Fifteen pounds?' they asked. 'Where could we ever get so much money?'

'I don't know,' I said. 'Maybe you should start saving now and then by next year you will have the money.'

They were discouraged. So I went on. 'But I noticed Waja's room,' I said. 'He roofed it with aluminium and yet he didn't buy boards. He used straight limbs from the local trees. Couldn't you do your chapel that way? You haven't planned a very big building, you know.'

They decided it was a good idea, and they would do it that way. Two months later, the chapel was completed. The Moderator of the Church came from the South and dedicated it. They were very happy. It was probably the smallest chapel the Moderator had ever dedicated, but it was theirs.

In the meantime Father Joseph had told the people of the other section of the village that he would like to help them build a chapel. He would provide the masons and carpenters and the cement to make proper building blocks (ours had been made of baked mud), and a concrete floor. He would have his carpenters make windows, and he would buy boards, sheets, and nails for the roof. They could show their co-operation by providing some hand labour for making the bricks and by having the women fetch water. They agreed. The chapel was built.

The Catholic chapel was very impressive. It could have held four of ours inside it! When it was completed, the young man in that section of the village collected money for the dedication celebration. That was the only money they paid, as I understand. All the rest came from Catholics in America.

And the rains came, and the winds blew. The wind blew the roof off the Catholic chapel and it also blew a quarter of the roof off the Presbyterian chapel. Immediately the storm was over, two young men set off on bicycles to the town to inform Father Joseph: 'The wind has blown the roof off your chapel!'

Twenty-four miles away, in Chereponi, I heard nothing. Six days later I arrived on my weekly visit to the village. I saw the damaged Catholic chapel and I looked anxiously towards our chapel. I saw the place where the missing sheets used to be, and then I saw most of the sheets, stamped back into shape and resting neatly under some bricks. The young men had been able to save enough of the sheets so that they only needed to buy two new sheets and some nails, the evangelist informed me.

'Why haven't they informed me of this?' I asked him. 'Oh, they are collecting money to go and buy the sheets, and then they will come to ask you to send the carpenter. They've collected some yams—each member has given a bundle—and Kwame and his brother are taking them to Garimata market to sell.'

What a difference there is between the two groups of people, I thought. Father Joseph's people are willing to co-operate with him, but to their mind it is *his* work and not theirs. All that these people, on the other hand, are asking me to do, is to help them to do *their* work. It really is their own! I realized.

GIFTS OF THANKS

That was what I hoped it would be, and what I always hoped the work of the Church would be in Chereponi area. In all matters of money, I tried to work in such a way that the work would be the Chokosis' own. After I had been in Chereponi only three months, and had received many gifts of welcome, I all of a sudden stopped accepting them as personal gifts. This must have seemed very strange to the people. But I was, after all, doing the work of God and not my own work. If people, in response to that work, wanted to give me a gift, I should regard it as a thank-offering for the hearing of the Word.

So that is what I told people each time they gave me some yams, or some eggs, or a chicken or guinea fowl: 'Thank you very much,' I said. 'I must tell you how I appreciate this gift. I am, however, paid by the Church for the work I am doing. I would like, with your permission, to regard this as a thank-offering to God for the work. I believe that the work is very important. And I can see by your gift that you do too. So I would like to use your offering for the work of the Church.' Then I would explain how we needed exercise books and chalk, and money to repair our bicycles, and kerosene for the lamps we used at night during meetings, etc.

In this way the people learned that someone had to pay for all the things we used in the work. They learnt that we did not just pick money off trees like pawpaws, and that the work could not go on without the gifts and the loving support of people who believed it was important.

I would then sell the gifts (often to my own wife!), record the proceeds, and use the money for the work. We didn't get much—usually just two or three pounds a month. But our budgets weren't high either. I never accepted money from our American mission for our regular work. The regular budget came from my 'pastor's grant' from the Southern Ghana Church. Our total programme budget during those first two years was only about two hundred pounds a year. So if we got thirty pounds from individual and village thank-offerings the people were already doing a lot for the support of the Church.

LIMITING 'OUTSIDE' HELP

Of course if I had asked for more money I could have had it. Each year the Africa secretary of our mission headquarters in America asked: 'How much should we budget for Chereponi?'

143

'Nothing,' I replied.

'But you must be able to use something,' he answered.

'How can you, on the one hand, tell me to make myself dispensable as soon as possible, and, on the other hand, try to tell me I should accept budget money from America?' I objected. 'Will the Ghanaian pastor who succeeds me have those funds to call on?' I asked. 'Why should I use what he will not be able to have?'

I knew that if I did not take that attitude, the time would come when people would look back to 'the good old days' when A. C. Krass was pastor and money flowed like milk and honey. They would think what a shame it was that a Ghanaian pastor had had to replace him. They would become 'pauperized', and think themselves poor unless help was coming to them from outside.

'No,' I told the Africa secretary, 'I will not use anything for the work that my successor will not one day have.'

'Maybe we could see that he got it also,' he replied.

'No,' I answered, 'even then it wouldn't be good. Even if he could have it, it would not really be good for him to have it. It would not be good for the new Christians here to have Americans doing for them what they could be doing for themselves. They will never be able to support a big programme, so we shouldn't start off with one. *We should only start a programme that they themselves will one day have the resources to carry on.* If the Church in Chereponi area in the year 2000 will not be able to pay more than six evangelists, we shouldn't take on more than that now. If the Church in 2000 will not be able to have a mobile cinema van, we shouldn't have one now. If the Church in the year 2000 will not be able to provide free literacy materials, we shouldn't give them away free now. If the Church in 2000 will not be able to build chapels for congregations, we shouldn't build them now. We should only do what we know they will one day be able to do.'

I was really sharing with him the insights I had just gained from an exciting book by Bishop V. S. Azariah, the first Indian Anglican bishop, called *Christian Giving*.

'Therefore I will not accept anything from our mission,' I went on, 'for the regular, ongoing work of the Church here. I will not accept anything that will have to be repeated year after year. I will only accept help for extra things, things that, once bought, will not need to be bought again.' Azariah would not have accepted even that.

So we got a small annual grant—larger than we requested—of two hundred pounds a year at first, and then later one hundred pounds, and then nothing. We used this to buy, among other things, a typewriter with vernacular letters, a cyclostyle machine for duplicating literacy books (but not the stencils or the paper or the ink—those would have to be provided from the regular budget, because we would always need

'It would not be good for the new Christians to have foreigners doing for them what they could be doing for themselves' (p. 144).

Indonesian students demand independence rather than American aid, even though it means harder work for everyone—including the children, like this boy with his heavy load of harvested rice. But Jesus said, 'It is more blessed to give than to receive.' In what circumstances is it right for poorer Churches to 'bless' richer ones by being ready to receive help from them?

more of them). We bought roofing sheets to help congregations to roof their chapels and cement to help them make foundations, but we did not build chapels for them. And some of the money was used to pay travel costs to help blind and disabled people to get to rehabilitation courses.

In some cases, I may not have used the money wisely. Sometimes the people expected us to repeat an item which I had thought was a once-and-for-all-item. I bought a couple of bicycles for the use of some of our newly-trained leaders, to help them to get to other villages to preach or teach literacy. It later turned out that this led others to expect that, if they did well, they also would get bicycles. This was a mistake on my part. I later turned to using the little money available, not to buy bicycles, but to repair old, broken ones which the young men or their families already had, in order to enable them to get where they needed. Perhaps even that was too much.

USING LOCAL RESOURCES

The point was this: We did not use the American money for everyday kinds of things because it seemed better for the work to be done less efficiently, less rapidly, and in a more primitive manner, *but done with local resources*, than for it to be done effectively, rapidly, and with handsome equipment, but only with the extensive help of outside funds. It seemed better that the local vernacular Christian newspaper should miss an issue entirely because there were no funds to buy stencils and ink, than to see a permanent supply of stencils, ink, and paper purchased with American funds. If the paper didn't appear, then it was sad, indeed. The new literates had nothing else to read in their language. But it meant that everyone would ask, 'Where is the *Gong-Gong*?' We could then say: 'The offerings have not been sufficient for us to buy paper this month,' and this gave them a new reason to be faithful with their offerings.

It seemed better, when we had our leadership training courses, to have the students complain, after the money ran out, that there was not enough meat, than for us to use outside money to buy meat. It was better for them to sleep in a building of local construction and with a grass roof, which their fellow villagers had built, than to sleep in a fine, modern building built with American money and by paid masons and carpenters.

Many of my colleagues, both in our mission and in others, disagreed with me about this question of money. But I never met one who could answer the following question: *If you are going to start by using foreign funds, how are you going to stop without its being a terrible let-down?*

146

Therefore, the policy always was to consider, as well as we could, what the Chokosis themselves would one day be able to provide and *to provide no more than that.* Up to that level we would use 'foreign' funds, i.e. funds from Southern Ghana, only if my successor also would be able to call upon them. And we should do so only if the people in Chereponi would (a) realize right from the beginning where those funds were coming from, i.e. from offerings of other Christians in the South, and (b) start to exercise some stewardship themselves, for the sake of the work.

STUDY SUGGESTIONS

Review Questions

1. (a) What was the difference, from the point of view of providing money, between the Roman Catholic priest's way of working in Chereponi, and the way of the Presbyterian missionary?
   (b) Do you agree that the Presbyterian way was better? Give reasons for your answer.
2. (a) What may happen to a Church which relies on money from richer Churches for its regular expenses?
   (b) What may happen to a Church which relies on money from richer Churches to pay for the new work it wants to do?
3. In what ways can people who do not have much money still help the work of the Church?

Discussion and Research Topics

4. Find out where your own Church gets its resources from. If it gets any help from outside, is it free to use the money in any way it wishes?
5. 'The goal of Church development should be Churches which support, govern, and propagate themselves without the intervention of Churches from elsewhere.' Do you think this is right? Do you think it is possible? Give reasons for your answer.
6. If a Church needs outside help do you think that help should be given for special purposes only? If so, what purposes?
7. What should a Church do when it has achieved full self-support?
8. 'It is more blessed to give than to receive' (Acts 20.35, AV).
   Do you think this means that God 'blesses' a Church which gives help to poorer Churches more than He 'blesses' the poor ones? If not, what does it mean?

22. Developing Local Stewardship

At first the Church hardly ever received money from the Chokosis. The average Chokosi man only had about fifteen pounds of cash going through his hands in a whole year. Instead we received gifts in kind. These were not to be sneered at. Their value was much higher than what the people could have afforded to give in cash.

Chief among these gifts were the large harvest thanksgiving offerings made by whole villages. The Chokosis themselves had an old tradition of tying up a large bundle of guinea corn to give to a poor widow or blind old man at the harvest time. They responded most enthusiastically to our request that they show their thanks to God at harvest time for the food He had given them that year, and for the hearing of the Word. They said we were reviving their harvest custom which had fallen into disuse, and would bring a bundle of guinea corn or a bowl of millet or soup-makings. We found that we got enough food from those thank offerings to be able to feed all the young men who came for leadership courses for three whole months. All that we needed to add from the district treasury was oil, salt, meat, and sugar.

Even after some people had been baptized, we still were shy about asking for money. The educated members of our congregation in Chereponi town, it is true, paid money, but we did not expect that the villagers could do that.

STARTING A PLEDGE SYSTEM

The Church in Southern Ghana had a 'pledge system'. Each member would be asked in January how much he or she would promise to give each month through the year. Each would then receive a card on which the pledge would be recorded, and the gifts would be checked off until the whole amount had been given. I admired the system, but I felt that the Chokosis were too poor to use it.

However, after trying without success to find ways of supporting a greater share of the budget locally, I decided to suggest to the District Session that we introduce the pledge system after all. The Presbyters and Church mothers had many questions. There was a long, hard debate, but at the end the following minutes were recorded:

The district pastor explained the pledge system and the Session agreed that it would support this move, provided:

(a) pledges of as little as one penny per month be permitted,

(b) those who could not afford even that would, upon explaining this, be excused,

(c) those who could not pay at a given month could make up their arrears before the year ended.

It was not a very promising beginning! But we started. That was November 1966. In 1967 we received about fifty pounds in pledges. By 1970 we were able to count on receiving almost four times that much. A penny became the pledge of only an old widow or a pregnant woman. Everybody else had increased their giving to anything from threepence to two shillings a month.

A LONG-TERM PLAN

Perhaps some diagrams will help to explain what we were aiming at. Diagram 5 shows the total budget of the Church in 1967. The dark part is the proportion of the whole which the local people raised. The dotted lines show the proportion they would have been able to raise in each succeeding year, if the budget had remained the same (which it didn't).

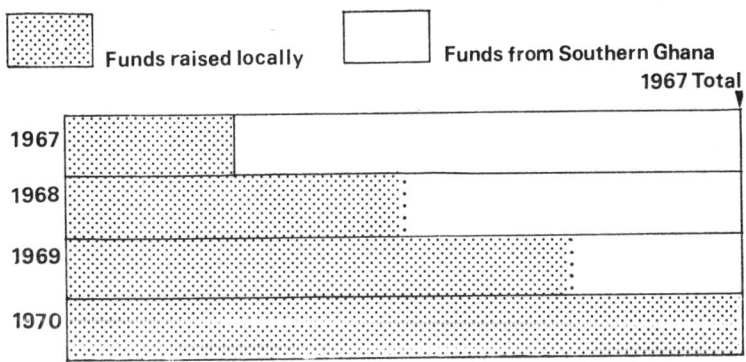

DIAGRAM 5

In the first year, they raised enough money to cover the cost of our whole programme of work, but not salaries. In the second year they raised enough to pay the salary of one of our informally-trained evangelists. In the third year they were able to pay the programme budget plus the salary of one evangelist. In the fourth year, they were able to pay the salary of two evangelists, and in the fifth year they would have been able to pay the salary of both evangelists and the programme budget. We could expect more money each year, because people were learning to give more, and also more people were being baptized.

As the Church grew in numbers, so did its work of mission. So we had to employ more evangelists and another pastor, and to increase the programme budget, to cope with the greater size of the work. As the local gifts grew, so did the total budget. The dark part of Diagram 6 shows the proportion of the 1970 budget which the people were able to support, and the dotted lines show what the funds they had pledged could be expected to support in future years.

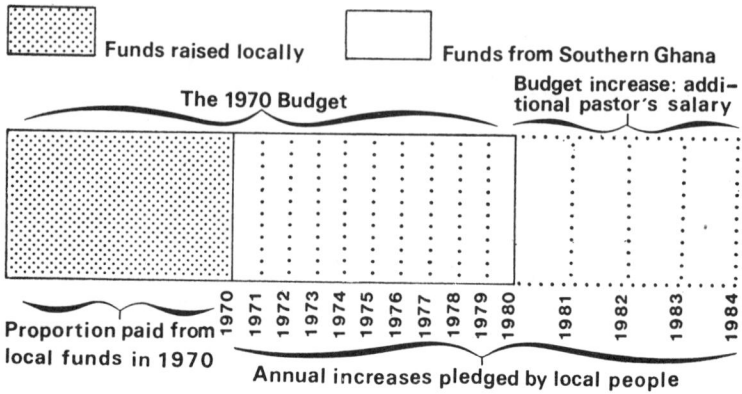

DIAGRAM 6

Even if the whole salary of another pastor were to be needed before the people had been able to raise the whole amount needed to cover the previous budget, that would not stop them being able to grow into full responsibility for the work of the Church in their districts by 1984.

Our goal was that the Chokosi and Komba and Konkomba Churches should support the entire work themselves, without any help from outside. And by means of the pledge system they aimed to do it by steady annual increases until such time as they needed no more help. Recognizing what their financial condition was it seemed unlikely that they could do this in less than fifteen years.

This may seem very slow. What governments, after all, have fifteen-year plans? But governments also receive outside help, and most five-year plans are followed by second and even third five-year plans.

Our programme was a slow one, but it was a programme which avoided two evils: (1) pauperization and (2) strangulation. To 'pauperize' people (make paupers out of them), means to do for them what they should do for themselves. The result is that they learn to think of themselves as being unable to cope with life without being aided. To 'strangulate' people means not giving them enough air to breathe. As we saw in the last chapter, Father Joseph's early way of working (he later changed quite a bit) seemed likely to pauperize people. It kept them from facing the problems they needed to learn to face.

The Assembly of God programme in the same area, on the other hand, seemed likely to risk strangling the Church. As soon as the

Assemblies had trained a pastor, they put him in charge of a congregation and told the congregation to support him But the young congregations simply were not able. Pastor after pastor ran away because they just could not feed and clothe their families on the tiny offerings which they received from the congregations. Those Churches were deprived of the leadership they needed at an important time in their lives. The new Christians did not receive the nurture they required. The Church, as a result, did not grow, but shrank.

DEVELOPING A PROPER BALANCE

The important thing is to strike a balance. A programme of shared stewardship both recognizes the newness of the Church, and also respects its autonomy. It expresses the financial responsibility of the older Church to the younger (for a time), but also challenges the new Church to take a proper share of that responsibility on its own shoulders, not 'some day', but from the very beginning. Such a programme forces the Church to work unhesitatingly toward the time, not too far distant, when it will not only have its own life to support, but will also be called on to engage in mission to others.

'It is more blessed,' our Lord said, 'to give than to receive' (Acts 20.35). So we must not deny to our new brothers in the faith the blessings of being called on to give. But neither can we simply say: 'The financial responsibility is yours now. You've been baptized. Support the work yourselves.' Those who have plenty should help those who are in need, so that neither will be rich and neither will be poor, but all will be equal (2 Cor. 8.13–14). In other words, the missionary's responsibility is not only to see that the Word is planted and germinates, but that it gets enough water and sunlight to grow until it too can bear the fruit of maturity.

But not all who read this chapter will be working in newly-developed Churches. And not all congregations have either the freedom, which that sort of situation offers, for developing stewardship programmes from the start, or the difficulties which such beginnings always present. In Churches which have been established for some time, different questions need to be asked, for example the following:

Where does the Church get its support? Do the members themselves raise the money that is used? Or is it provided by a body overseas or from a central Church treasury? If they are self-supporting, is the money which they raise enough, or does the Church really need more money to run a proper programme? Have the members been trained in good stewardship habits? If not, what new programmes of stewardship education, and new systems of financial organization, can be planned in consultation with the people?

Perhaps the sort of work which the Church is doing already makes too many demands upon the people, and they cannot really raise more money than they are at present giving. Perhaps the answer will be the difficult one to which Bishop Azariah came, that certain sorts of work should be stopped. Perhaps some of the salaried positions should instead become 'tentmaking' ministries, in which Church workers will serve part-time while earning their own living in part-time jobs. This decision is usually a difficult one to make, but it is often the only way in which the people can stop being 'pauperized', and become responsible for their own work, beggars in no man's house.

Whether the situation is a new one or an old one, it is worth trying to follow the basic principles of stewardship laid down in this chapter. God's people must support God's work, at a level appropriate to their economic means. Whatever work is done in a given area in God's name ought to be the people's own work, which they themselves support and direct.

INDEPENDENCE AND INTERDEPENDENCE

There is, however, an extreme to which these arguments should not be pushed. The ultimate goal of each congregation is not total self-support so that each separate district or congregation becomes totally independent of all others and stands on its own feet alone. The goal which Scripture presents to us is *interdependence* To the same people to whom Paul wrote: 'Everyone has to carry his own load' (Gal. 6.5), he also wrote: 'Help carry one another's burdens' (Gal. 6.2). And from those people he took an offering to help the poor in the Churches in Judaea.

As Christians our goal is not self-sufficiency, but mutual responsibility. I am not being responsible to you if I have the means to support myself but do not do so, but rather expect you to support me. Nor are you being responsible to me if you support me even though I have the strength to support myself. And if I have the means to help you while you are struggling, I am not being responsible to you if I say, 'Stand on your own two feet,' at a time when you are not yet strong enough to do it.

A relationship of mutual trust and responsibility between richer and poorer Churches is needed to guarantee:

(a) that the total resources of God's people in all places will be available for the needs of God's work in each place, and

(b) that the resources will be applied to the situation in each place in ways that respect the dignity of all God's people.

In the secular world, as the proverb goes, 'he who pays the piper calls the tune'. In the Church, however, the richer must find ways of making their resources available for whatever tune the poorer chooses to play, which will not result in the poorer being regarded as 'small boys'.

'The goal which Scripture presents to us is interdependence . . . not self-sufficiency, but mutual responsibility' (p. 152).

During an election in Tanzania, when people lined up to register as voters, President Julius Nyerere (standing fifth in the line) joined the queue. The people were dependent on him as leader of the government, but he in turn was dependent on their votes. In what other ways, besides financial ones, are 'older' and 'younger' Churches mutually dependent on each other?

If the older and richer churches can give their aid without demanding obedience in return, then there is no reason for the ones who receive to look to the givers for direction. Those with longer experience may and ought to give advice, in the spirit of fellowship, but they should never seek to dominate those whom they help by their gifts.

In this also we all need to trust the Holy Spirit, who is the power behind the Church's mission. We must let Him use us, but we must never try to take His place. Missionaries and evangelists are not the power behind the mission, He is. As Christians we are all merely stewards of the mysteries of God (1 Cor. 4.1–2), and what is required of us is that we should be faithful. For some, faithfulness will lie in teaching others also to be faithful. For some, faithfulness will lie in receiving that teaching, so that all may be stewards of what God has given. And the greatest part of any teaching will be found in example and in sharing one's experience. What new Christians see existing Christians doing, they too will learn to do.

STUDY SUGGESTIONS

WORD STUDY

1. Look up the word 'pauper' in a dictionary.
   Then give an example from everyday life of people becoming 'pauperized' in circumstances which have nothing to do with the Church.
2. What do you understand by the phrase 'mutual responsibility'?

REVIEW QUESTIONS

3. What happens if a new Church is left to support itself too soon?
4. (a) What three conditions were laid down for the pledge system when it was first introduced by the Chereponi District Session?
   (b) Do you think any other conditions might be needed for stewardship schemes in different situations?
   (c) What, if any, are the dangers of a pledge system?
5. In what ways is a Church which supports its own work likely to be 'freer' than a Church which receives foreign help?

DISCUSSION AND RESEARCH

6. (a) What sorts of financial help, if any, do you consider less harmful to the selfhood of the Church than others?
   (b) What benefits might come to a Church if it stopped receiving funds and personnel from overseas?
7. (a) What are the advantages of 'tithing', or proportionate giving?
   (b) How can pastors encourage such giving by Church members?

8. Read Matthew 25.14–30; Luke 3.10–14; Luke 12.48b; 1 Cor. 4.1–2; 1 Cor. 9.
   (a) What do we learn from these passages about the qualities of a good 'steward'?
   (b) What other qualities, if any, does the Church need in its 'stewardship' of God's gifts?
9. What theological objections can you think of against Church taxes or fixed 'Church membership' fees?
10. Should the pastor himself handle Church funds? If not, who should be responsible for them?
11. (a) Find out what systems of regular and pledged giving, if any, are practised by the Churches in your country, and whether they are successful.
    (b) Find out what proportion of their income, if any, the Churches in your country give to poorer Churches.
12. What are the advantages and disadvantages to a Church or group of Churches, of organizing some 'central funds' for distribution, as well as local funds.
13. 'Perhaps some of the salaried positions should become "tent-making" ministries, in which Church workers will serve while earning their own living in part-time jobs.' (p. 152). Read Acts 18.1–5, and then say why a 'part-time' ministry is sometimes called a 'tentmaking' ministry.
14. (a) At what period or periods in a Church's history can money from richer Churches stimulate its life?
    (b) At what period or periods can money from richer Churches strangulate a Church's life?

23. Concern for Economic Development

When the first missionaries from Europe and America began work in many parts of Africa and Asia, they tended to become 'multi-purpose' missionaries. They preached the Gospel, which they had been commissioned to do, but they also transcribed languages, developed literacy materials, started schools, set up hospitals to cure the sick, took part in agricultural development, settled disputes, and often judged court cases. Many of them began local industries. The Church was doing, and paying for, much of the work for which governments are responsible today.

A missionary who goes out from Europe or America to Africa nowadays, or an Asian who is a missionary to another Asian country, or an African working in a land which is not his own, is in a very different position. He is nearly always sent out to do a particular job, just as many others in the place where he works have been sent out to do their particular jobs, as policemen, agricultural extension workers, doctors, public health nurses, teachers, literacy workers.

And the same is true of the pastor serving in his own country, among his own people. He is just one among many different specialists. What is his relationship to them? Do he and the government teacher of agriculture have anything in common? Are there any ways in which they are called to work together? Does the ordained minister have any direct concern with economic development, or public health, or modernization, or secular education? Is he concerned with the development of new nations, or with making the world more fit for men to lead a fully human life? Or is he only concerned to preach the Gospel and to look after the people who come into the Church?

THE CHURCH AND 'DEVELOPMENT'

A missionary working as a district pastor may receive conflicting advice from different people.

One 'expert' on the subject will tell him that a missionary who does his work in the way the Apostles did, will not concern himself directly in improving people's living standards. His immediate job is not that of changing conditions, and certainly not that of doing what the government ought to do. His job is simply to train Christians who will see it as part of their Christian responsibility to help solve their country's social, political, and economic problems.

But another 'expert' will say that in the new countries of the world 'evangelists' should also be concerned with material development and with the 'humanization' of the world. They will say that the work of Christianity and that of 'civilizing' or 'humanizing' will only succeed if they go hand in hand. So the missionary must discover and help forward whatever forms of economic development seem to fit in with God's plan of salvation, and sometimes Church funds must be spent on this sort of work.

Which 'expert' is the new missionary or the new pastor to believe?

When I myself began work in Chereponi, I was told that the preaching of the Gospel began only two years earlier, but there had been a government health centre for four years, schools for ten years, an agricultural extension service for fourteen years, a veterinary service for even longer, police even longer than that, and no one could remember when taxation started and the first roads were made. It was not the Church's job to 'pioneer' development. So the immediate question I had to ask myself was: what is the relation between the work I am here to do, and the development of the Chereponi area?

People who ask this question today find no simple answer to it. Some say that evangelization must wait until economic development has first taken place. 'A man with an empty stomach is not interested in the Gospel.' And others say that the only proper concern of Christians is to save people from damnation, and that development is of no real value.

But both pastors and missionaries may have to decide quickly how they will answer. In Northern Ghana, for example, people did not simply wait for me to make up my mind theologically. The Assistant Education Officer, a Protestant Christian from Southern Ghana, visited me shortly after I had begun working in a few villages. 'I want you to help us,' he said. 'You have contacts with some of the villages where we are trying to get parents to enroll their children in school. We want you to help us to convince them that they should enroll them.'

What was I to do? From his point of view the answer was simple: the Church in Southern Ghana had always been involved in education. It had founded and managed many schools. So he thought that I, as a pastor of the Church working in the North, would of course be interested in helping the government to do this 'Christian work', even though the government no longer permitted Churches to open their own schools and all new schools were government schools from the start.

Could I have said: 'We're not interested in government schools. We have our work to do and you have yours, our job is not to help you do yours'? Did the name 'Local Council' or 'E. P. Church' before the word 'School' make all that difference?

RELIGIOUS OR SECULAR?

At about the same time the question came to me again from another source. We had been preaching in the village of Mayamam for about six weeks. The response was tremendous. We could feel that the people were ready to accept the Gospel. Each time I finished preaching I would, however, ask: 'What questions do you have? Is there anything you don't understand or find hard to accept?'

'If someone comes to you and gives you good news,' old Dibolo, the headman, replied, 'are you going to ask him "Is it true?"'

Each week he continued to reply in the same way. I had been preaching about the God of love, who did not wish to remain distant from His people, but wanted to help them to a fuller, happier life, and that was why He had sent His Son Jesus to them. This was indeed good news to the Mayamam people, and they recognized it as such

But the sixth week was different. 'We have a question this week,' Dibolo began.

I was nervous. I expected objections to what we had been preaching, some religious difficulties which the Gospel presented to the people of Mayamam. Perhaps they were not ready to accept the Gospel after all.

'What is your question?' I asked, worried.

'Yesterday they ate the fish,' Dibolo replied.

'They ate the fish?' I asked, not understanding what this could mean.

'The stream bed dried up and they ate the fish that were left at the bottom. We have no more water in the village.'

'Where do you get water now?' I asked. He pointed to a place a mile and a half away in one direction.

'The women have to walk that far for water?' I asked, unbelieving.

'For about a month they will get water there,' he replied, 'but then that stream will dry up, too, and they will have to go twice as far in the other direction to a river.'

I made a quick calculation. Until the rain came, twice a day the women would have to go six miles for water. Twelve miles a day for two pots of water. I was astounded.

But this was not a very 'religious' question. I could have replied: 'I am here to preach the Gospel. I am asking for questions about the Gospel, religious questions. You should take questions about secular matters to the government.' But could I really? Were these not religious questions to them? Did they not arise in response to the Gospel I had been preaching about a God of love who cared for His people?

THE BIBLE'S TEACHING ABOUT MATERIAL GOODS

Once again we must turn back to the Scriptures for help in seeing what we should do. The first thing we need to note is that writers in the Bible did not distinguish between 'sacred' things and 'secular' ones, nor between what is 'spiritual' and what is 'worldly', in the way in which people do today. Even words like 'blessing' and 'peace' mean in the Bible far more than simply 'spiritual blessing' or 'inner peace'.

'The Lord has greatly blessed my master,' Abraham's servant said to Laban, 'and he has become a man of power. The Lord has given him flocks and herds, silver and gold, male and female slaves, camels and asses.' (Gen. 24.35 NEB). When he used the word 'blessing' he used it to mean 'material' goods like animals and precious metals and servants.

In the Bible there is no separation between 'internal' or spiritual peace on the one hand and 'external' or worldly peace on the other. External peace is regarded as a sign of spiritual peace, and spiritual peace leads to peace in the world (see Psalm 122.6–7).

Thus a Church which is faithful to Scripture and announces 'the peace of God, which passes understanding' must not be concerned only with 'peace of heart'. It must be concerned with the total peace which in Hebrew is described by the word *shalom*. According to the Bible it is

God's will to bring about this sort of peace among all His people, and so His Church must involve itself in this work of peace. 'The Church,' Professor Hoekendijk tells us, 'is, nothing more, but also nothing less, than a means in God's hands to establish *shalom* in this world.'

So it is wrong for the Church to say: 'Our work is only spiritual. We are not concerned with material things.' If the Church is concerned with peace, this means that it must be concerned with relations between man and nations, with 'secular' affairs. Our ministry is to the world. As Christ understood His life, so Christians must understand theirs. They exist as His Church only to serve, to be there for others. The prophetic words which Isaiah used to describe the coming ministry of the Christ describe also the sort of ministry that we should aim at:

The spirit of the Lord God is upon me
because the Lord has anointed me;
he has sent me to bring good news to the humble,
to bind up the broken-hearted,
to proclaim liberty to captives
and release to those in prison;
to proclaim a year of the Lord's favour . . . (Isa. 61.1–2 NEB).

The Church which has as the central line of its common prayer 'Give us this day our daily bread' cannot pretend to be just a 'spiritual' Church. Christian faith and African traditional religions have this in common, that both are concerned with this world. Neither is 'other-worldly', they both value the life which people live now. Whatever it is that makes a man suffer, or a woman cry out for joy, whatever it is that makes a baby cry or brings pain to an old woman, whatever it is that threatens a community or builds up the life of a village—these are the things with which both African religion and Christian faith are concerned.

Christians, however, have a much greater reason than people of African traditional religions to be involved in the development of the world. According to the Hebrew-Christian tradition, God is not only a distant creator, but is involved personally at every moment in continual creation and redemption of the world. Because God is active in this way, Christians believe that what they do to develop the world, they do in partnership with God. This is part of the good news which Christians have to proclaim: 'God is working his purpose out in the history of the world.'

We can see that this is true when we look at the life of Jesus. Understanding His ministry as He did, He did not just preach and forgive sins. He was also active. He healed the sick, and fed multitudes, and ministered in other 'secular' ways. When He sent His disciples out, both before and after His resurrection, He sent them out not only to preach and teach, but to heal the sick and raise the dead (see Matt. 10.8; Mark 16.15–18).

As we read the Acts of the Apostles, we see evidence that the apostles too understood their work as not only that of preaching and teaching and establishing Churches. They also healed and provided for the poor.

And in the New Testament letters, we see that the early Christians felt it was their duty to work for the peace of the world (e.g. 1 Tim. 2.1–3; 1 John 2.17; Jas. 3.13–18). They did not understand peace as just 'internal' peace. They thought of peace in the full, rich sense of Old Testament *shalom*. They had to represent the cause of justice and right. Their work had to serve the cause of reconciliation between human beings, not only the cause of reconciliation between God and each individual person. Their faith did not concern only 'spiritual' things. It concerned life, reality, human existence, creation. They thought of Jesus just as the Chokosis did, as the Improver and Restorer. They thought of Him as the one who makes the world a better place to live in, the one who creates community and brings life.

Thus we cannot separate clearly that with which the Church is concerned, from that with which the Church need not be concerned. But this does not mean that there are *no* distinctions to be made. We can think of all Christian work as evangelization, and all service as witness. But there are different sorts of service. The Church's mission is one, but, as we saw at the beginning of this Guide (p. 2), there are different ministries. And some of these ministries concern the world as well as the Church. We shall consider these in the next chapter.

STUDY SUGGESTIONS

WORD STUDY

1. (a) What do Bible writers usually mean by the word 'blessing?'
   (b) What is the meaning of the Hebrew word *shalom*?

REVIEW QUESTIONS

2. Is the Church's responsibility towards the people different in places where the government is not working for health and welfare, from its responsibility in countries where the government is actively working to improve the life of the people?

3. What continuing responsibilities does the Church have for 'humanization' of the peoples' lives when the government is actively working for the development of a more human society?

4. The central petition of the Lord's prayer is 'Give us this day our daily bread' (p. 159).
   What does this fact teach us with regard to the Church's ministry?

5. Is the Church's ministry of healing no longer needed when governments have established hospitals and clinics?

6. If your Church maintains hospitals or schools, what reasons are there, if any, for its continuing to do so, even when the government is prepared to take them over? What are the chief reasons *against* its continuing to do so?
7. If your Church runs schools or hospitals does it use them as 'bait' to catch converts and influence people? If so, do you think this is a good thing? Give your reasons.
8. If pastors also manage schools, what effect does this have on their pastoral work?
9. What, if anything, can a Church do to influence Christians in government service to carry out a Christian ministry in their work?
10. Ought pastors to preach about worldly things?
11. Does the social service work of any Church you know deserve the adjective 'selfless'?

24. Service to the Community

'There are many forms of work,' Paul said, 'but all of them, in all men, are the work of the same God.' (1 Cor. 12.6 NEB) But he went on to say that 'A body is not one single organ, but many . . . You are Christ's body, and each of you a limb or organ of it.' (1 Cor. 12.14, 27), and he listed the various sorts of ministry undertaken by the body (see p. 3).

GOSPEL AND SERVICE

In this book we discuss most of these ministries separately, but some people find it helpful to think of them as falling into three groups, or categories:

1. The ministries which in Greek were called *kerygma*, involving proclamation and direct evangelism.

2. The ministries of *koinonia*, or fellowship, i.e. the ministries which help to equip and strengthen the Church by teaching, pastoral work, administration, and ecclesiastical organization.

3. The ministries of *diakonia*, i.e. works of humble service to others.

It is the same Church which exercises all these categories of ministry, though different people within the Church exercise each specific ministry. The Church can never say, 'We are not called in this age to perform works of service,' or 'At this time in history our task is not to preach the Gospel.' The Church has to do all of these things all the time. The Church is responsible to the Holy Spirit to use all the gifts which He gives, and not to choke any. So it is responsible to see that all of its ministries are being carried out. None of them can be complete without the others. Good stewardship involves spending our resources as well as gaining them, and the resources we have to take care of include time as well as money.

According to the New Testament, the ministry of the Word, which is a part of *kerygma*, has besides its own function, the function of holding together the various other ministries, and making them one. As we saw in Part 3 and as Harry Boer has written, the proclamation of the Gospel is therefore not simply one activity among many in which the Church of the New Testament engaged. The *preaching* office is the *central* office in the Church.

TEAM MINISTRY

I found this to be true in Chereponi, where we became involved in many sorts of ministry. It was through our team's weekly study of the Word that each of us came to see the place which he had in the total ministry of the Church. We saw that all our different ministries— health, agricultural work, literacy training, preaching, and pastoring congregations—were part of God's work of bringing new life to the Chokosi people.

The Church did not everywhere integrate its various workers as closely as it did in Chereponi. We in Chereponi were a pilot 'team ministry'. Many agriculturalists and health workers, however, worked independently of the pastors and catechists, some from choice and others by assignment.

One agriculturalist, however, Robert Thelin, after working for some time in an area where there was no village Church work to which he could relate his own, was reassigned to our team in Chereponi. And he discovered that in those villages where the Gospel had been preached the people were much readier to try new agricultural methods and to engage in self-help projects than those in his former station. He saw that the Word *had* brought new life. People had been freed from their fears and anxieties. They had new expectations. He saw that you can indeed preach the Gospel to people with empty stomachs! The Chokosi villagers were poor but they had heard the Gospel. The Gospel gave them hope. They greeted him with enthusiasm.

And just as Bob Thelin's agricultural ministry was strengthened by the ministry of the Word, and by the work of the Church's literacy workers, so were our ministries of the Word and of fellowship completed by his demonstration of love, compassion, and service in action.

WHAT SORT OF SERVICE MINISTRY?

As I talk to Africans today I get the feeling that most of them are glad that the era of the 'one-man team' missionary is ended. That way of working belonged to the colonial period. There are many books written by such missionaries, books with titles like *Uplifting the Xhosa, Bringing Civilization to the Yoruba,* or *Christ's Servant among the Dark People.* But no one seems to read them anymore. For one reason, some of the authors of these books were rather imperialistic in their outlook. They show the missionaries as heroic figures, 'delivering' the Africans from 'darkness', 'barbarism', 'devil-worship', 'bondage', etc. Not many missionaries in Africa today would want to be like them, nor would Africans or Asians who are themselves missionaries to people who are for the first time hearing the Gospel!

Today, much more is known about the history of Africa and Asia than was known a few generations ago. People are no longer so sure that the Western world represents 'civilization' and Africa 'barbarism'. They are not so confident that Western technology will provide all the solutions to the world's needs, nor that the solutions will be found quickly. Most of the governments of developing countries are working hard to bring good health, formal education, and improved techniques of agriculture and animal husbandry to their people. So Western missionaries are less tempted to play the role of God today than their predecessors were.

There may be areas in which a government is overburdened, or not yet able to function, where it requests the Church's help. And the Church and its missionaries should be happy to give such help. But most governments now regard the work of social and economic improvement as their responsibility, and no longer rely on the Churches for help in providing such services.

If missionaries and Churches fear the day when their help will not be needed, it may be because they are doing the work for the wrong reason. Perhaps they fear that if they do not control schooling, they will get no converts; perhaps they have been using their hospital work as a means of getting new members. Perhaps they fear that if the people become independent they will no longer be interested in the Church. Maybe they are committed to 'rice Christians' because they are afraid that if they have no 'rice' to offer, they will get no Christians.

The Churches need to look at the relationship between preaching and service in a new way today. We have to recognize where we have been wrong in the past, and see how we can avoid making the same mistakes in the future.

For some people, therefore, these are trying times. 'Can we bring people into the Church without loaves and fishes?' they wonder. It seems that God is testing His Church to see whether it can be faithful to its ministry, now that He is pruning away some of the 'signs' which it has used to 'win people to the Kingdom'. He wants to see whether His Church can understand service in a new way: selflessly.

The answer depends upon whether or not we are willing to follow the teaching of the New Testament with regard to ministries of service, and avoid using our service to control people.

'You have received without cost,' Jesus told His disciples, 'Give without charge.' As Jesus himself gave, out of pure love, so are we called to give, expecting nothing in return. Our service must be a witness to the Kingdom, in which the selfish (ourselves) are made selfless, the unloving are made loving, and the unconcerned learn to be concerned. 'If I by the finger of God cast out demons,' Jesus said, 'then the Kingdom of God has come upon you' (Luke 11.20). If we are able to perform ministries of service which truly liberate people from poverty, ignorance, oppression, fear, and sickness, it will only be the power of God that we do it. But if we *are* able to do these works by God's power, then it is a sign that the kingdom of God has come: God is reigning.

CHURCH AND GOVERNMENT

The Church needs also to recognize that other bodies are doing these works of liberation as well—governments, voluntary organizations, secular agencies, international bodies. And if these bodies truly liberate people by their work, then they too do it by the power of God, *whether they recognize the fact or not*. God is working through them, and we ought to rejoice to see the signs of God's Kingdom in them.

'The wind blows wherever it wishes,' Jesus said. 'You hear the sound it makes, but you do not know where it comes from or where it is going' (John 3.8). The Holy Spirit does not work only through our Churches. We should recognize that when the Holy Spirit works through the Churches it is in order that all mankind may see God's work, and may respond by doing likewise. 'Let your light so shine before men,' Jesus told the disciples, 'that they may see your good works and give glory to your Father who is in heaven' (Matt. 5.16). What better way is there for governments and secular agencies to give glory to God than to do what God wills? The Church does what God has shown it in order to teach all men to do the same. To insist that the Church must always be the one to serve in this way is to claim the glory for ourselves and not for God.

Rather than seeking to be God for men, the Church's job is to be a light to nations, showing the way toward things which the nations themselves can do. When the Church has seen a need and pioneered the way to meet that need, and others then follow its lead, it can leave that work to them, and move on to new ministries.

Many Christians in Africa and Asia are coming to recognize that this is true of formal education. The Churches pioneered the way, but governments, with far greater resources, are able to do the work more effectively today, and the Church ought graciously to withdraw. Some Churches accept this in regard to health work also. Churches were the first in most lands to establish hospitals, but they found it difficult to continue supplying and staffing the hospitals. Most governments have more adequate resources for this than the Churches.

SOME NEW MINISTRIES OF SERVICE

This does not mean that the Churches have no place in educational or health work. It does mean that they ought to ask what their *new* responsibilities are, and what creative new sorts of service ministry should be added to their traditional work. Here are at least four:

1. The Churches have a responsibility to *provide a chaplaincy* for the Christians who work in government institutions, helping them to see their responsibilities as Christians to be creative yeast among their fellow workers;

2. The Churches have a responsibility to *represent the people's needs* to government, to insist that governments should meet human needs well, devise the best possible educational and medical programmes, and administer them well and honestly, with social and economic justice, and at rates that all can afford to pay.

3. The Churches have a responsibility to *remind governments of the best insights of traditional culture.* Unfortunately in many parts of the world people have equated progress with Westernization. They have copied Western ways, mistakenly thinking that 'what is done in London, or New York, or Paris, is best.' Many educated people in Africa, for example, feel little attachment to their own culture, and believe that in order to modernize, they must de-Africanize. This is to 'throw out the baby with the bath water.'

An educational system which assumes that pupils must become 'Europeanized' in order to be educated betrays the indigenous local or national culture, and is based on a lie. A medical system which only treats people's physical needs without recognizing the spiritual background to these physical needs will leave too many people uncured.

The Church can play a constructive role by representing the truly indigenous elements which should not be discarded as 'uncivilized' by those who direct education and medicine.

4. The Churches have a responsibility to *meet needs which governments*

165

and secular agencies cannot meet, either by filling in the gaps, or by doing new and different things. For example, the government may be so occupied with curative medicine that it can do no preventive medicine. The Church can then start a pilot programme of preventive medicine and health education. Or the government may, by its health policies, be helping more people to live to a riper age, but has not time to help parents to plan their families. Those Churches who believe that it is right to do so can then help with family planning. The government may be able to run teachers' training colleges well, preparing people to teach mathematics, history, and every sort of course with efficiency, but may not have developed any programme to train school counsellors and vocational advisers. Perhaps the Churches can offer the services of experts, or run short courses to train teachers in these skills. The Churches have many creative possibilities in these fields in addition to their long-recognized responsibilities of providing school and college chaplains.

Before it embarks on any such programme, however, the Church first needs to ask the question: is there any other agency which we could persuade (and perhaps help) to do this task? Only if the answer is 'no' should the Church itself undertake it.

INTEGRATING MiNISTRIES AND MISSIONS

It is important, too, that the Church should *integrate* its ministries of compassion and service with its preaching and pastoral ministries. The relationship between its different activities needs to be well thought out and well planned. The various ministries of service to the world must not be regarded as 'extras' simply because they may change with changing times. Their importance for the whole mission of the Church, and especially in developing countries today, was summed up clearly by a conference of the Protestant and Catholic Churches of Botswana, Lesotho, Malawi, Tanzania, and Zambia in 1971 (see Appendix, p. 199).

Some readers may have wondered how I answered the questions about co-operating with the government which the Assistant Education Officer and the people of Mayamam asked me (see pp. 157–158). Briefly, the following is what I did.

REASONS FOR SAYING 'NO'

To the A.E.O., I basically said 'No'. I explained that for two reasons I could not in good conscience help him to enroll the children in school. To do so would conflict with the Church's mission to the people.

1. First, it was important that the Church should not give the impression that it was a European institution for 'educated' people only, and

allied closely with Western-type schools. The people were very suspicious of our intentions on that point. By connecting ourselves too closely with the schools, we might frighten people away from hearing the Gospel. The Gospel does not demand that Africans should become Europeanized; it is for everyone, whether they are educated or not.

2. Secondly, because of the way in which schools in the area functioned, I could not in good conscience recommend to all parents that they should send their children to school. The schools were too far removed from village life. They did not prepare the children to live happily and usefully within Chokosi society, but tended to separate them from it. The teachers showed little sympathy for the parents' needs and hopes. They often tried to separate the children from their parents, so that those who went to school became unruly and disobedient at home. Many teachers felt no responsibility to see that the children returned home to help with house and farm work after school and at weekends, but instead persuaded the children into serving them in their own houses. In addition, this gave parents the impression that if their children were educated they would easily get jobs, which was not true, because there were no jobs.

I was, however, willing to try to get one or two pupils to enroll from each village, because it was useful for a village to have in it someone who could read notices and tax receipts, and interpret for the leaders when they needed to communicate with outsiders in English. But I would not encourage all the parents to enroll their children. The Assistant Education Officer accepted this limited help; he, too, hoped that the Ministry of Education would one day make schools more related to African village life.

A TEMPORARY MINISTRY

To Dibolo and the Mayamam people I did not say 'No', but promised to find out what help the government could give in getting them a bulldozer to make a dam. I went to the district and regional offices of the Ministry of Social Welfare and learned that no help could be had in less than a year. There was only one functioning bulldozer in the whole of Northern Ghana at that time, and it was booked to work in twelve other places first. And there was no dynamite available for blasting wells.

I reported this to the people, and also told them that a group of Christian students from the South had asked for a work project in the North. If the Mayamam people were interested, these students could come and work with them by hand to make a small dam, and the Church would help by supplying shovels, pick-axes, and headpans. They were not easily convinced, but, three weeks later, after much discussion, the project started. Six weeks after that the village had a small reservoir.

The next year the government sent a bulldozer. The people contributed voluntary labour and the Church paid for the fuel. The bulldozer worked, very badly, without good direction from the district office, for four weeks. Then it broke down. When it was repaired, after four months, the government took it to another village for three months before returning it to Mayamam. By then the rainy season had begun and it could not work.

Because of these and similar frustrations, the Church decided, after much agonizing discussion, to accept a bulldozer given by Churches in the United States, to work under Church direction, in order to alleviate the water problem in the Chereponi area. The villagers pay for the fuel, and the Southern Ghana Church pays for the operator's salary. Maintenance is provided by international aid funds. We were not altogether happy about this solution, but we felt that in the circumstances, the Church's responsibility to meet human needs meant that it could not simply say: 'We cannot help you. That is government's responsibility.' The bulldozer ministry could form part of the Church's total ministry in the area. But we hoped that it would be a temporary ministry, which the government would soon take over.

We saw that the Church needs to exercise careful stewardship in financial matters. So also it needs to exercise stewardship in its use of people and other resources, and to undertake only those ministries which can contribute fruitfully to its total mission.

STUDY SUGGESTIONS

WORD STUDY

1. (a) Describe each of the following sorts of ministries:
   kerygma, diakonia, koinonia,
   and give examples from your experience.
   (b) How are these ministries related to one another?

REVIEW QUESTIONS

2. 'The proclamation of the Gospel is not simply one activity among many' (p. 162).
   What is meant by this statement?
3. (a) What is a 'team' ministry?
   (b) In what sorts of situation do you think that a team ministry can be most successful?
4. Describe one chief way in which the methods used by Western and other missionaries today differ from those used by missionaries in the past?
5. List three 'wrong reasons' for which the Churches have in the past undertaken works of service.

6. (a) What do the Church's works of liberation and government's works of liberation have in common?
   (b) What extra reason do the Churches have for doing works of liberation, which governments do not have?

DISCUSSION AND RESEARCH TOPICS

7. (a) List four sorts of new service ministry which the Churches can undertake in developing countries.
   (b) What other possible sorts of new service ministry can you suggest?
   (c) What new service ministries might be particularly useful in your own country?
8. The agriculturalist Robert Thelin discovered that people who had accepted the Gospel were more ready than others to accept new agricultural methods.
   (a) Describe any similar instances you know, of people who have been encouraged to improve their conditions of life as a result of hearing the Gospel.
   (b) If you have not already had such experience, can you suggest possible examples?
9. In what ways may co-operation in government service projects sometimes conflict with the Church's mission to the people?
10. Give two examples of situations in which the Church ought *not* to co-operate with government.

PART 7
TAKING A LOOK AT OUR MINISTRY

25. Relationships with other Churches

Many people are at first amazed when they hear how the work of the Evangelical Presbyterian Church in the Chereponi area has progressed. They then begin to ask questions: 'Were there any other denominations working there?' 'Was yours the only Church to have a full-time work in Chereponi?' When they hear that the Evangelical Presbyterian Church was the only Church to have a full-time missionary stationed at Chereponi, then they say, 'Oh, your case is different! That's why you were able to be so effective. Our situation's not like that at all.'

And they are right. The fact that no other Church had a full-time work in Chereponi did contribute to the success of our work there. But it contributed, not to *our* success, but to the success of *God's* work in Chereponi. Since God wants all His people to be one (John 17, Ephesians, Colossians), His work is hindered when His people are divided among themselves and so divide the people to whom He sends them. If we are divided in our witness, our effectiveness will be reduced. After a particularly unsatisfactory example of competition between us in the village of Sanguli, Father Joseph once said, 'The Konkombas have enough divisions among them already. Don't you see that we are simply doubling those divisions? They are using their relations to one or the other of us as weapons against each other!'

CHRISTIANS OF OTHER DENOMINATIONS

Father Joseph was quite right. In the village of Kpeo there had been a long feud between the people on one side of the road and the people on the other side. Not knowing of this feud, I started working on the chief's side of the road. I always wondered why it was so hard to get people from the other side of the road to come to the chief's house. I finally gave up trying. Even when the people worked on a dam which the whole village needed very badly, those from the other side of the road didn't come.

Then one day I saw what they were waiting for. That day Father Joseph came along, stopped his car on the road, and went over to the houses on the other side of the road. Immediately the people came out. In other words, they wouldn't become Christians if it meant becoming the same kind of Christians as the chief's people. But if they could become another type of Christian and so could remain divided, then they would consider it!

Villages in Saboba area came and played one of us off against the other. In the Chereponi area villages played off Father Anthony (the Roman Catholic priest who worked there part-time) and me. What they were really saying was obvious: 'If you use your ability skilfully enough to provide us with food, bandages, old clothing, schools, medicine, and cinema shows, we'll become your kind of Christians and not his kind.'

When I let the flesh reign over me, I responded, in subtle ways, I am ashamed to say, by entering into undeclared competition with the Catholic priests for the souls of men.

I never used the food and clothing that way, it is true, but it was more difficult to refrain from giving a film show, when I knew that if I didn't use my film strips first, Father Anthony might bring a motion picture to that village and 'claim' the village for his Church. It is a fact that I never agreed to help a village build a dam *only* because it was a village which was responding to us, or which promised to hear the Gospel *if* I would help them. But I know that it was only natural for me to be more interested in villages whose people were interested in the work we were doing.

And in the early years I often found myself thinking, 'It really isn't the will of God that these people should become Roman Catholics and worship Him indirectly, through Mary and the saints. He would really rather see them worshipping Him purely (as Presbyterians!).' In that way I could justify my choosing to help the children in school A to get uniforms rather than those in school B (knowing full well that the parents of most of the children in school A were inclined toward becoming Presbyterians, whereas the parents of children in school B had been receiving the Roman Catholic missionary). What I publicly said, however, was: 'We don't give uniforms to children in order to get them to follow us. We give them to all the children in a school, regardless of whether they have any attachment to our Church or not.' (It just so happened that we didn't have enough to go around, so why not give the uniforms we had to those who had been showing more interest?)

THE TEMPTATION TO 'USE' PEOPLE

There is a word to describe all this: *manipulation*. It means using people as if they were things, employing skilful ways to get them to act less freely, to get them to do what *you* want. Some people simply call it 'bribery'. Other people say 'techniques of creating rice Christians'. The fact is, people *asked* us to do these things—for they tried to use *us*, just as we learned to use them. But, whoever started it, the effect was the same: people 'came to Christ' for unworthy reasons. And what we discovered almost every time was that a person who comes to Christ for the wrong reasons does not become a real disciple. When the gifts cease to flow, he ceases to be a Christian. If you start a relationship by buying people, you have to continue to buy their affection, for if you stop buying, they stop selling.

Fortunately Fathers Anthony and Joseph and I got to know one another, at least socially. So we discovered that sometimes a village was trying to 'buy' two of us at the same time. We learnt what the people were trying to do to us. And—when we were honest—we saw how we ourselves were trying to manipulate them in order to compete with one another.

And there were other interesting things that we discovered from meeting with the Roman Catholics.

'What did you preach about today, Father?' I would ask over lunch.
'About Christ the Good Shepherd,' he replied.
'You mean from John 10?' I would ask in amazement.
'Yes,' he replied, 'that is our lectionary reading for today.'
'But that's our lectionary reading, too!' I exclaimed.

Or they would ask me, 'How do you prepare people for baptism?' and I would explain. 'You know,' they would say, 'that's very similar to our new catechetical approach!'

I learned about the changes taking place in the Roman Catholic Church as a result of the Second Vatican Council. They in turn learned how Presbyterians had been influenced by union negotiations, by the liturgical movement, and by the World Council of Churches. In many ways, we discovered, we were becoming more like one another.

WORKING TOGETHER

We learned to care for one another, and became interested in each other's problems. We decided to work together at a common translation of the Lord's Prayer and the Apostles' Creed. We borrowed hymns from one another, and compared liturgies. We shared tools for self-help projects, and carpenters, and seeds, and bandages, and then literacy materials, and still later our bulldozer. We got a permit for dynamite, and they had a licensed blaster, and we started to co-operate in making wells. We made our Bible translations available to them, and they lent us one of their best catechists to help us do more. The biggest surprise of all came to the people in the villages where we had been competing, when my car was out of order and I appeared in Father Anthony's green Volkswagen which he had lent me.

What happened in the end was, however, different from what this growing co-operation might suggest. The Catholic Church left practically the whole work among the Catholics to us Presbyterians. Father Anthony himself would have left the work to us entirely. But his society was unwilling to see it simply given over to the Presbyterians. And so he maintained a kind of chaplaincy to those already Catholics, while continuing some work in the areas where we were not working.

Father Anthony had not been in good health, twice he had gone back to Holland on sick leave. When in Ghana he was always working partly in Chereponi and partly in Yendi, and felt he could never do the work in Chereponi justice. He saw that we, on the other hand, were able to staff the work well with catechists and lay volunteers as well as top leadership. 'You are able to minister effectively to the Chokosis,' he told me. 'Why should we even feel a need to be here?'

A NEW ATTITUDE

However, Father Anthony's attitude was really based not on whether they could staff the work or not, but on the new sense of the Church as a whole which we had gained in our working together. The Church—for him as well as for me—was no longer the E. P. Church or the R. C. Church but the Church of Jesus Christ.

I came to recognize this when Father Anthony attended our district anniversary service in 1968. Eleven men were baptized at the service, and when the pastor had completed the baptism, he asked all those previously baptized to come and give the new members of the Church the right hand of fellowship. Father Anthony joined the line. When he got around to me, he said, 'Congratulations on your new members,' Then he corrected himself saying: 'Congratulations on *our* new members!' As new members of Christ's one body, they belonged to his Church as well as to ours.

As Father Joseph said, when attending our chapel cornerstone-laying in Saboba: 'The time has passed when we need to think that the other's gain is our loss. If one of us gains, then all of us have gained. If one of us loses, then all of us have lost.'

AVOIDING COMPETITION

Father Anthony's action completed a much longer history. At first the Assemblies of God had also had a ministry in Chereponi. A missionary had been stationed there for eighteen months and then had left the mission to go home. While the Assemblies were arranging to replace him (which we didn't know, because we didn't talk to each other much in those days), I was assigned to become district pastor of Chereponi and Saboba for the E. P. Church. I had been working there for a year and a half before the women assigned to Chereponi for the Assemblies had the necessary funds to come. When they did we had already become well established.

The women came to visit me. I knew that they had two questions on their minds: Was I really a Christian? and Was the area large enough for both missions to work in? The first question they never asked me, but simply observed and listened to how I spoke about the work. They saw that we shared many concerns, chiefly the concern that the Chokosis would come to know Jesus Christ as Lord and Saviour. They opened up their maps and population census and asked if I would tell them where we were working. They found that we were working in almost every large village which could be reached by road. It would have been difficult for them to go by bicycle to the other villages, as they were middle-aged. As I seemed to be a Christian, could they, in fidelity to the Lord, really come and compete with us for the villages on the road?

They told us that we would learn their decision. They wanted to pray and learn the Lord's will, they said. Evidently they learned that it was not the Lord's will that they come to Chereponi. They applied to their council for reassignment I will never forget this most large-hearted Christian act of theirs.

It was as a result of this act of Christian unity, as well as Father Anthony's, that we came to be the only mission working full-time in Chereponi. *In other words, a situation came to be which might not have been.* Chereponi might have developed like so many other parts of the world, where rival missions compete among a small population. We avoided this by getting to know one another, listening to one another, sharing our deepest hopes, and finding our essential unity. Once we recognized that we all were Christ's, we recognized that the only important thing was that Christ be glorified, that people learn of His salvation and become part of Him. Whether they became part of Him as Assembly of God Christians or Evangelical Presbyterian Christians or Roman Catholic Christians was no longer important.

This essential unity of the Church in its witness to the Chokosi people has led to the tremendous success which the Church has been having there. The Lord has shown us that we must all be one, 'so that the world will believe' (John 17.21).

But this sort of unity may not seem possible where there are already two or more competing denominations. Is it realistic to suppose that Churches which have *already* become established will give up their work, so that another Church may carry it on for the sake of unity? It might be good, but it is not likely.

VARIOUS FORMS OF UNITY

But it is possible to recognize that unity has many forms, e.g.:

1. *Comity*, where different missions agree on who is to work in a certain area, or in certain sections within an area, or village by village, so as to avoid competition, is only one form of unity. And it is a rather negative form, though it does have its uses in some situations. Comity is bad when a Church is unable or unwilling to evangelize the area given to it, but refuses to allow any other Church to come in. Comity then means nothing but jealousy: 'This is *our* area and no one else can have it.'

But comity is a useful arrangement when (a) areas are too small to permit several missions to work, (b) the missions are not close enough in fellowship to one another to be able to work positively together.

2. *Joint action for mission* is a more positive form of unity, in which different denominations contract to work *together* in mission to non-Christians. There was an example of this in Yendi, when the Baptists asked the other Churches to join in an evangelistic crusade. 'We will hand out cards asking people to state which Church they would like to learn more about or join. We don't care whether it's ours or one of yours,' they said. But the Baptists' programme still belonged to one Church, it was not a programme started by the Churches contracting to work together.

In Dahomey, however, several Churches from different nations around the world have contracted to work together in mission. They have agreed that anyone who is baptized will become a member of the Methodist Church of Dahomey, which was already there. The other Churches seek no members of their own, but simply to bring more people to Christ. Where such joint action for mission is possible, it is certainly to be preferred to comity.

3. *Full organic union* goes further still, and Churches which previously were separated become one. There are many union schemes among Protestant and Anglican Churches in Africa and Asia today, ranging from the federal arrangement adopted in Zaire, to the full organic union which operates in India and Sri Lanka and is proposed for Ghana and other countries.

Church workers at the local level, however, have little say as to whether or when such schemes will come into being. Usually the most that is possible for them is to work out either a village-by-village or area-by-area comity arrangement, or a form of joint action for mission in certain sorts of work, e.g. educational work, health work, literacy campaigns, development, etc., and perhaps, if we trust one another as fellow servants of the Lord, joint evangelism.

Whatever co-operation we can achieve will come as we respond to the

'Co-operation will come as we respond to the prompting of the Spirit' (p. 175).
In many relief organizations, workers from nations previously at war with each other
labour together to ensure adequate food supplies, and help underdeveloped countries
to increase their resources. In Burma rice is weighed for storage; in Bihar a food-for-
labour programme gives occupation as well as relief.
In how many different ministries of service do the Churches in your country co-
operate with the government—or with one another?

promptings of the Spirit, who is not a Spirit of disunity but of peace (1 Cor. 12.13; Ephesians 2.18; 4.3; etc.). The Spirit flourishes where fellowship is strong.

Where we meet together with the workers and people of other denominations for social purposes, this may well be a beginning. As we work with them on projects of service to the community, we find ourselves forgetting the differences of belief and practice between us. What we do together for the love of God and of His people seems more important. Joint Bible study and discussion will carry us even farther as we discover what we share, and learn the reasons for other people's differing convictions. And when finally we bow our heads together before the same Lord in common worship we fully realize our unity. An example of this was our 'day of prayer for the conversion of the Chokosi nation', held in Ghana and Togo in alternate years, in which the Catholic Churches and the Evangelical Presbyterian Churches of the two nations and the Assembly of God congregation of Togo joined together in fasting and prayer. It was a wonderful experience of the unity of the Spirit, which led us to hope for regular intercommunion between our divided Churches, where we will come together at the Lord's table.

The important thing is that we should refuse to regard our present divided state as permanent, no matter how partially reconciled we may at any time be. We are on the road, no more, and we must always be going farther on that road, toward the unity which our Lord had in mind when He prayed 'that they all may be one'. Even along the way, though, we share real unity!

STUDY SUGGESTIONS

WORD STUDIES

1. What are the following?
   (a) comity
   (b) joint action for mission
   (c) full organic union.
   If you can, give actual examples of each.

REVIEW QUESTIONS

2. (a) What is meant by the word 'manipulation'.?
   (b) In what ways, if any, do the Churches in your country 'manipulate' people?
   (c) In what ways, if any, do others in your country (e.g. the government) 'manipulate' people?
   (d) Do you think it is ever justifiable to 'manipulate' people? If so, by what agencies and for what reasons?

3. If two Churches compete for new members in the same areas, what is likely to happen?
4. What sort of 'joint action' brings about the fullest realization of unity between Christians of different Churches?

DISCUSSION AND RESEARCH TOPICS

5. (a) What personal qualities are necessary to enable missionaries, local Church leaders, and ordinary lay Christians to work together with Christians of other Churches?
   (b) Do you think that (i) missionaries and (ii) local Church leaders need qualities different from those of ordinary Christians in order to work with people of other Churches? Do Church leaders and missionaries ever hold the laity back from greater unity with other Christians?
6. (a) In what situation is it easiest for people of different Churches to work together?
   (b) In what situation is it most difficult?
   Give reasons and examples to support your answers.
7. What would you reply to someone who said: 'The work of evangelization is so important and so urgent that it does not matter how many different Churches are at work in the same area'?
8. 'Usually the most that is possible is to work out . . . a form of joint action for mission in certain sorts of work' (p. 175). What other sorts of service suitable for joint action by Churches working together can you suggest, besides those listed?
9. Make a chart to show:
   (a) those places (districts, towns or villages), and
   (b) those forms of work in which (i) your Church works in union with other denominations (give the names of those denominations), (ii) you cannot in good conscience work with other denominations (again give the names of those denominations), (iii) you are not at present working in union with other denominations, but might do so in good conscience.
10. (a) Do the members of your Church regard members of other Churches as their brothers in the faith?
    (b) If so, those of which Churches, and why? Why not others? Do they believe that a man can be saved if he belongs to those Churches?

26. Our Attitude to People of Other Religions

There is another question which many of my Roman Catholic brethren asked me when they learned I was writing this book: 'What about our relation to those who are not Christians?' they asked. 'What should our attitude be to Muslims, and to those African traditional religionists who will probably not become Christians in the foreseeable future? And what about the many people in our midst who have no real religion?'

This question was asked out of a burning, out of an uneasiness of soul, an unwillingness to close anyone off from fellowship, out of a desire to attain the largest possible unity of all humanity. Pope John XXIII addressed his letter *Peace on Earth*, not just to all Catholics or even to all Christians, but 'to all men of good will'. In the same way, many Roman Catholic priests would like to see a unity wide enough to include the whole of humanity. I worked closely with one such priest in Yendi, who helped to bring about a larger degree of unity between Muslims and Christians than had ever before existed there. This was a goal well worth working for.

SALVATION BELONGS TO ALL

Many Roman Catholics, when they think about mission, have now ceased to regard the Church as 'the *ark* of salvation' and see it more as 'the *sacrament* of salvation'. They say that salvation is something larger than the Church. The Church is the sign of that wider salvation, but salvation exists in the world at large, and not only within the Church. Those who believe this, tend to reject the older doctrine which says: 'There is no salvation outside of the Church,' just as Protestants have long rejected it (especially as applied to any one particular Church) and prefer to say 'There is no salvation outside of Christ.'

Many Roman Catholics, too, now say 'There is no salvation outside of Christ.' But they feel that there may be unbaptized people who, even though they do not know Christ, or have seemed to reject Him, are nevertheless in a mystical way united to Christ, and are therefore saved through their union with Him.

The traditional reply of the Church to such a statement is that Jesus said, 'I am the way, the Truth, and the Life; no one comes to the Father but by me' (John 14.6). This is interpreted to mean that if a person has not truly come to Jesus Christ, he will not reach the Father. He will not be saved.

The Roman Catholic response to this is: 'We agree that Jesus is the Way, the Truth, and the Life. But we do not feel that even we in the

Church have come wholly into His way, nor that we know its every path or direction. It may be that others, in the intentions of their heart, in following their own religion, have come truly to walk in the way of Christ, even though they do not give it His name.'

They argue that the goal of the Church need not be to convert all men to Christianity or to seek to baptize all men, and that the Church has not failed if it has not convinced all men to become Christians. They say that this was a mistaken goal, and that only a few—the 'sacrament', the 'remnant'—need become Christian. These will then become the 'sign' for the others, pointing to where salvation is to be found, i.e. among all men of whatever religion, and not just in the Church.

These arguments arise out of very real concern and love for human beings. But in several ways they seem to fall short of the teaching which we find in the New Testament.

1. We are not responsible to judge who will or will not be saved (see Matt. 7.1). We can and should leave the whole problem of ultimate salvation in God's hands, and rest confident that He knows what to do about it. Our arguments will not advance His purposes. Our task is not to argue about matters concerning salvation, or to estimate the numbers of people who may or may not be saved, but simply to carry on our work, trusting that God will use us as He sees fit in the fulfilment of His purposes.

2. Arguments like those above usually develop in places and at times when (a) the Church has few first-generation Christians in it, (b) people of other religions have been showing great resistance to the Gospel. In most parts of Africa, however, and in many Asian countries, neither of these conditions is found. Where they are not found it makes no sense to import from other places arguments that do not concern the Church in its local situation. Where these conditions *are* found, we must still ask the people 'Why is there such resistance? Is it because of the people or because of our approach to them?'

3. William Carey's saying: '*Expect* great things from God, *attempt* great things for God' is as true now as ever. If we expect too little, we are likely to achieve too little. Why should we expect less than a tremendous response to the Gospel at this time in the world's history? Except for some areas, every sign points to a tremendous ingathering of the nations in many parts of Africa, and of Asia and the South Pacific. It is surely better that 'anonymous' Christians should become Christians in name. We expect those who consciously set out to serve Christ to become more fully Christian than those who do not acknowledge Him. So why should we not try to bring as many people as possible to know, accept, love, and serve the Master—and not only individuals, but families, villages, clans, tribes. In most places it is possible, and we should continue to aim high (see Matt. 28.19).

4. Those who argue that the Church need not try to convert all peoples to Christ seem to have taken out of its context the phrase 'sacrament of salvation' from the document *Lumen Gentium* (Latin for 'Light to the Nations') which is the 'Constitution of the Church' agreed by the Second Vatican Council. They use the phrase to compare the Church with the rest of humanity. They say that the Church *consciously* knows Christ, other human beings do not. But salvation belongs to them also. The Church is the sacrament, witnessing to salvation which is already in the world.

THE CHURCH:
SIGN AND INSTRUMENT OF SALVATION

But in the document itself the phrase is used to compare the Church as it is *now* in the world, with what it *will* be in the fulfilment of God's purpose. As 'sacrament of salvation', the Church is not only a *sign* witnessing to salvation, it is also an *instrument* of salvation. It points to union with God, and in its mission it must actively function to bring men into union with Him.

And the document emphasizes that the Church's task of bringing all peoples to Christ is more urgent than ever today, when the nations are joined together more than ever before by social, technical, and cultural ties.

There are many ways in which Christians can work together with people of other religions to help fulfil God's purpose for creation, just as Christians of different Churches can work together. Increasingly the Churches *are* joining in service projects which are organized by people of other religions or by secular governments. And there is no doubt that service of this kind does show forth God's love to the world. But the Church is not *only* a 'service agency'; it is an instrument in God's hands for the purposes of His work of bringing all mankind into renewed unity with Himself. If the Church rejects this task, and says it is enough for it simply to point to a salvation which can exist apart from explicit faith in Christ and baptism, then it is refusing to accept the task quite explicitly given to it, of extending the People of God throughout all the world.

The last chapter of the main section of *Lumen Gentium* has a passage which is well worth quoting in conclusion:

Christ, having been lifted up from the earth, is drawing all men to Himself (John 12.32). Rising from the dead (see Rom. 6.9), He sent His life-giving Spirit upon His disciples and through this Spirit has established His body, the Church, as the universal sacrament of salvation. Sitting at the right hand of the Father, He is continually active in the world, leading men to the Church, and through her joining them more closely to Himself and making them partakers of His glorious life by nourishing them with His own body and blood.

Therefore, the promised restoration which we are awaiting has already began in Christ, is carried forward in the mission of the Holy Spirit, and through Him continues in the Church.

Thus the Church is commissioned to 'Go to all peoples everywhere and make them my disciples, baptizing them in the name of the Father and of the Son and of the Holy Spirit, teaching them to observe all things I have commanded you.' (Matt. 28.19).

To do this task properly the Church must be one, but its unity is a unity in Christ. If it denies its essential difference from those who are not in Christ, its trumpet will give an uncertain sound. To love our neighbours, to be one with them as fellow men, does not mean that we cease to be who we are: disciples of the risen Lord who calls all men into union with Himself through His Church.

STUDY SUGGESTIONS

REVIEW QUESTIONS

1. (a) What do you understand by the word 'salvation'?
   (b) Do you believe that non-Christians can be saved?
2. In what ways does the argument that the Church need not try to convert *all* human beings fall short of New Testament teaching?
3. Read the following passages:
   John 11.35, 36; John 14.6; John 17.21, 22; Acts 10.34, 35; 1 Cor. 1.10–13; 1 Cor. 1.21–24; 1 Cor. 12.12–20; Eph. 3.7–10; Col. 2.28, 29; 1 Pet. 2.9, 10; 1 Tim. 2.5, 6.
   (a) What do they teach about the unity of the Church?
   (b) What do they teach about the way of salvation?
   (c) What do they show to be the role of the Church in God's plan of salvation?
4. (a) What is meant by the phrase 'a sacrament of salvation' as used of the Church?
   (b) In what document is this phrase used?
   (c) In what way is this phrase sometimes taken out of its context and what is it then used to mean?

DISCUSSION AND RESEARCH TOPICS

5. Does your Church expect, as Carey advised, 'great things from God'? Or is it comfortable with its present achievement, and if so does its lack of expectation cause it to attempt less? What more could it do to bring people of other religions to Christ?
   Give examples of some ways in which (a) individual Christians and

(b) the Churches as such, can work with people of other religions, or with secular agencies, to help fulfil God's purposes for the world.
7. What dangers, if any, do you think there are for Christians in working with people of other religions?

27. Evaluating Our Ministries

In the last two chapters we have taken a hard look at our ministries, and especially at the ministries of missionaries and ordained ministers to people as groups, rather than individuals. But there is one final question we need to ask: how can we *evaluate* our ministries? We need to ask this about our own individual ministries, and also about the total ministry of our Church.

Ultimately, of course, the only correct answer is that we cannot: only God will finally evaluate our work. Judgements which we make from within our own situation are bound to be shortsighted. Later, our judgement that certain actions were a 'failure' or a 'fruitful approach' may well be shown to be mistaken. Where we say 'there is real growth,' people may later wonder why we ever thought that there would be growth. And where we say 'we do not expect much fruit from this harvest', people may later wonder at our lack of faith.

When the Bremen and Basel missionaries who came to the Togo and Ghana coast in the nineteenth century evaluated their work, they had reason to be pessimistic. In the early years the number of missionaries who died of malaria and yellow fever was greater than the number of new Christians who were baptized. In some places the Church worked for fourteen years without a single convert. Yet the epitaph on the gravestones of one of those missionaries was: 'I know that my Redeemer lives.' She was affirming that her seemingly unsuccessful work had not been done in vain, for God had promised that His Word would not return to Him empty.

JESUS'S EVALUATION OF HIS MINISTRY

At one point in Jesus's own ministry the people of Galilee asked Him to evaluate His work, to show whether He really was the Messiah, as He claimed. They made their evaluation of it, and they were convinced that He was not the Messiah. If the Messiah truly came, they felt, everyone would follow him. But that was not the result of Jesus's work. He preached to all the people, but hardly any followed Him. How could He be the Messiah?

Notice how Jesus replied. He didn't say 'It is wrong to evaluate work of this sort.' What He said was: 'You're evaluating the work in the wrong way. You look only for quantity, for numbers. God does not look only for quantity. He looks for quality. He looks for lives which have been truly transformed by the good news of the Kingdom, and for what those lives produce. Have you never watched how a farmer plants grain? He sows a lot of seeds; he throws them out all over the ground. Some fall on the path, others on rocky ground, others among thorns. He doesn't expect those to grow. But the seed that falls on good, fertile ground, more than makes up for the seed that is lost. One little seed produces thirty or sixty or even a hundred grains. That's real growth for you. Judge whether I am the Messiah, not by whether everyone hears me, but by observing what happens to those people who truly receive my Word. There you will see really miraculous growth, and you will know that the Kingdom is present. Those people change and become new people. They become citizens of the Kingdom of God, enlisted in the task of bringing that same Word to other lives.' (See Mark 4.1–9.)

If we are to take instruction from Jesus, our evaluation will not be based simply on a 'head count' or on the numbers of 'souls saved' or 'Churches planted'. But that does not mean that we should either refuse to evaluate our work, or that we should consider numbers not worth counting. Jesus continually evaluated His disciples' performance ('I saw Satan falling as lightning from heaven!' 'Oh, men of little faith.' 'You will forsake me.' 'In the world those who bear authority lord it over their followers, but let it not be so among you.' 'Let the little children come to me.'). He corrected them, rebuked them, encouraged them, inspired them, trained them, led them, walked with them. And He made clear to them that they were always on the way. They had not yet arrived at the goal, and they must always strive on.

If we are to be faithful to Jesus, we too must always remind ourselves that we are on the way. We must examine where the way has led us, where we have walked in the wrong direction and need to change our course, and where we have been making progress and need to redouble our efforts.

We must persevere in our efforts to carry the message of the Kingdom to 'all nations' (Matt. 28.19). His words, 'I have other sheep which are not in this sheepfold. I must bring them, too' (John 10.16), and His intention to draw all men to Himself (John 12.32), remind us that the love of God embraces not only the Church but all creation (John 3.16; 1 Tim. 2.4). We cannot be indifferent to the fact that there are men who do not know of Him, or have not really heard His message, or who have rejected Him. It must burn our consciences and keep us from being comfortable within our own congregation and our own Church.

THE BASIS OF EVALUATION

In evaluating our work, therefore, we have to consider the question of its quality, and also ask ourselves questions about its quantity and future productivity. And we must always consider both questions together. Quantity is easily measured, but some readers may ask: By what standards do we measure quality? How can we judge success or failure?

In Chereponi we compiled forms for annual evaluation of the Church's work at the congregational and district level. These forms were based on the theology of mission and the ideas about ministry which are expressed in Parts I and 2 of this Guide, and which lie behind the whole work. Copies of these forms are given in Appendices 6 and 7 (pp. 201 and 206). With some modification, they could be used by other Churches in doing their own evaluations.

No such form can, of course, serve all Churches equally well, because different Churches organize their work in different ways. Any form has to be related to the particular situation in which it is to be used. The forms we used in Chereponi were related to the situation there. In other places people will want to ask other questions, and will not want to ask some of the questions we asked in Chereponi.

EVALUATION LEADS TO ACTION

It may be useful to examine in a little more detail the motives which led us in Chereponi to draw up these forms, and the principles on which we based them. The questions which we set ourselves were difficult questions to answer. But we recognized the need to attempt this difficult task, and also the need to do it annually.

All too often in the Church, the people who carry out studies of any movement are not the people who are active in the movement. Usually those who do the study are unrelated to the work itself. Perhaps they come from another country, or department, or age group. They may gain valuable insights, but quite often they do not share those insights with the people involved in the movement, or do not report back to them in a form which is meaningful or helpful. As a result, there is a division between the 'doers' and the 'studiers.'

Some of the social and anthropological studies undertaken by governments and universities and central Church agencies will be useful at local level. But each local Church needs also to undertake its own 'self-studies' to add to the studies which others do of it. Otherwise it is likely to go on repeating the errors of the past, and may continue for many years in unfruitful paths.

The Church in France is an example of this. For centuries the Christians

'How can we judge success or failure?' (p. 185).

Wherever people sow and reap they will gather in the grain with thankfulness; but, to make the most of the harvest, more work yet is needed. In Mexico, winter tomatoes are weighed and graded for export.

In what ways should we *not* try to measure the success—or failure—of the Churches' mission?

in France went on supposing that France was a 'Christian country'. They failed to see that the Church had long ceased to minister to the working classes, and that in recent times even the middle classes were growing away from Christianity. In the 1940s however, a book appeared entitled, *France—A Mission Field*. In it the authors showed that France was in very few ways still a 'Christian country', if it ever had been one. This shook the Church in France to its foundations. Such a revelation can only be shocking, but it can shock the Church into action. As a result of that book, many new things started to happen in France.

The letters to the seven Churches in the Book of Revelation were also shocking. But the purpose of the inspired writer was just to shock those Churches which needed shocking, to shock them into action. He was in a very real way doing an evaluation of their life and witness.

SEEING OUR WORK THROUGH OTHER EYES

The evaluation forms which we used in Chereponi include questions which I was asked by other bodies when I was a pastor, as well as the questions which we asked about our own work. When pastors, catechists, evangelists, or Church councils must answer, not just their own questions, but questions which others ask of them, they are forced to consider their work in a new light. Thus Churches who use the forms, or an adaptation of them, will almost certainly have to face questions which they have not previously asked, and will be enabled to see their work as other people from outside—concerned Christian brothers— would see it.

When Churches fill out forms such as these, they are writing their own history of the work. By continually asking: 'How does this compare to last year?' they can see where the Church has been going. They may, perhaps, discover that it has been going nowhere—that what they thought of as growth is just growth in numbers, or that the numerical growth is not due to an influx of new Christians, but is simply a result of transfers from other congregations and confirmations of children who previously were not included on the communicant rolls.

We can compare this sort of evaluation with what a shopkeeper does when the time comes round for stocktaking or inventory, and for preparing his annual accounts. He needs to know just how much he had, how much he has sold, and what it cost him, as well as what he has gained, in order to calculate his profits. If he wants to expand his business he needs to attract new customers. And if business is slack he needs to know the reason: is he failing to stock the goods people want, or to advertise them widely enough, are his prices too high? Or is it just because the whole country is going through a time of economic difficulty?

Evaluation of Church work is a sort of stocktaking, even though the good news is free for all who will accept it. Like a shopkeeper filling out his stock record or inventory, I discovered several things when I filled out evaluation forms. First, I found that many of those who had been baptized became inactive a year or so after baptism. This became a useful occasion to go and visit these inactive members, and in many cases, to reawaken their interest in the Church. And it was a good group exercise. I never did such visiting alone, but went around with the presbyters. This helped us all to come to a new sense of where the Church was.

One year we discovered, for example, that over half of the Christian community in our district was under the age of fourteen. But we had no regular programmes for youth and children. We had thus been ministering to less than half the Christian community. Before the survey, we had never realized that. As a result of the survey we could take steps to correct it.

Another aspect of such surveys is that they show up not only the work you have, but also the work you don't have. We were quite self-satisfied that we were working in many places, but we came to realize that we were *not* working in many more. We had thought it was a large work, but, as the Chokosis say, 'A big head will not be lacking in hair'. The work was big compared with what it had been a few years earlier, or compared with what it was in other districts of the Church. But even after 300 per cent growth, our Christian community still represented only ten per cent of the population!

This sort of evaluation is not easy to do. Like stocktaking it takes time and effort. But, as another Chokosi proverb says: 'The aftermath of taking the easy path is mourning.'

I was once informed by a colleague that, because of some stomach troubles, he had an appointment with the doctor. 'I hope he doesn't find anything wrong' I said. 'If there's something seriously wrong with me,' he replied, 'I certainly hope he *does* find it.'

If there's something seriously wrong with a Church, we need to find it, so that we can correct it.

ANALYSING FAILURE

But what if the final evaluation is: 'This work has been a failure?' Perhaps we can find comfort in saying, 'Don't let us be discouraged. Let us think of the first missionaries. They were afraid they had failed, but look at the Church now. We don't know what the outcome of our work will be, either. We must just persevere and try new approaches. One day God will lead us to the right one?'

But perhaps this may not be true. Perhaps the fault lies with our methods, or with our shortage of staff. And perhaps we, or the larger Church, if there is one, helping us, can correct it.

And there is also a chance that the fault lies not with the Church itself, but with the times. Perhaps the time is not yet ripe for effective work among those people. Remember that the Holy Spirit does not always work in the same way in all places and at all times. Perhaps He is not yet doing the work He one day will be doing among our people. If so, we are labouring in vain. 'Unless the Lord builds the house, they labour in vain who build it' (Ps. 127.1). We are in Bithynia but He wants us to be in Macedonia; the work in Bithynia or Asia will come later (see Acts 16.6–10).

There is another possibility also that we must consider, though it is not a happy one. Perhaps the fault in a particular place, say in one tribe or within one particular village, lies not with the Church, nor with the times, but with the people themselves. Maybe they *have* heard the message, but have rejected it, not thoughtlessly, nor because it has been presented in ways they cannot understand, nor because it is associated with another group or nation or clan or tribe they don't like, nor because they connect it with Western culture, but simply because they have rejected it. They have rejected Christ.

We may hide from this fact. We may deny it. We may continue to try new approaches. We may finally say, 'Because of their culture, it is impossible for them to become Christians, but if we carry on a medical or educational ministry we may be able to influence them to be a different sort of Muslim or African traditional religionist. We may help them to be better people.' But then we have to ask: 'Is that our commission? Is that what Jesus sent His disciples to do?'

Jesus sent His disciples to preach the Kingdom, to call men to a decision, to let them know the claim which God was making for their lives, to confront men with God's Word, incarnate in Him. Jesus sent His disciples to make disciples of all nations, to bring all men into a trusting, loving, hopeful relationship with God.

Jesus had no illusions. He knew that many would reject the message. His advice to the disciples was strong: 'If you come to a place where people do not welcome you or will not listen to you, leave it and shake the dust off your feet.' He was not telling His disciples to curse them, for he added, 'This will be a warning to them!' (Mark 6.11.)

There are times when we must, in all honesty, face up to the fact that people have rejected not us but Jesus Christ, just as those who accept us accept not us but Jesus Christ. 'Whoever welcomes you, welcomes me, and whoever welcomes me, welcomes the one who sent me' (Matt. 10.40). But 'Whoever rejects me and does not accept my message, has one who will judge him. The word I have spoken will be his Judge on the last day!' (John 12.48.)

We do not judge people—they judge themselves by their rejection of the Word of Life. But we have an obligation to let them know how serious their rejection of Christ is. Perhaps only this will bring them to repent. If we are too mild to give that warning we may have failed in our obligation to them.

This does not mean that we should do what one catechist I met did: preach one sermon and ask for a decision then and there. We must remember that the Jews to whom Jesus at first sent His disciples had much more knowledge of the history of God's dealings with men than many of the people to whom we go today. It may take a year or two or even longer, before we can know for sure that they have heard the message, that it has broken through all the cultural barriers and met them where they are, and that they have indeed rejected it. Just as we are not to be too quick to baptize people, so we ought not to be too quick to shake the dust off our feet. It should be the last thing we want to do. We should not do it until we have exhausted all the possibilities of communicating the message to them. But at a certain point we may have to face up to the fact that, much as we hate to say so, they have rejected the Gospel. And then we must act sternly.

In Chereponi we only did this twice, in the villages of Tombu and Nyangbande. In both cases we had preached for long periods of time. There was no visible response to our message. Finally we had to confront the people with their rejection of the Gospel. 'We have been preaching here for a long time, week after week,' we told them, 'and we have heard no one say he is ready to accept the Gospel and give himself to Christ. Many other villages are calling us to come and preach, and we have not had sufficient staff to be able to answer their requests. We cannot continue to come here and turn down the others when there is no good reason to do so. Tell us now; are you willing to accept the Gospel and become Christians or not?'

In both cases there was no response. Each time I went on, 'If the village as a whole is not willing to become Christian, are there no individuals who are?' No one replied. Calmly I went on: 'This is a serious matter and it calls for your decision. You have not been willing to make that decision. By not making a decision for Christ you have in fact been making a decision against Him. I must warn you how dangerous this is. We are going to stop the work here. However, if you change your minds and call us, we will always be ready to come back.'

We were never called back to Nyangbande. They continued in their hostility, not only to the Christian message, but to the people of the neighbouring village of Mayamam, who had become Christian. Eight months later, however, the old man in Tombu who had been most influential in getting that village to reject the Gospel came to see me and said, 'I want to be baptized. I know what I said before. I know everyone says I am the one responsible for your stopping the work in our village. I don't know what they think about the Gospel now, but I know what I do. Any time you are ready to come and baptize me, I and my wife are ready.'

We began their instruction in their own compound. Each week more people joined. On the eighth week I came to the village to find the old man on his deathbed, I baptized him and his wife there and then. The others continued to come. We moved to the headman's compound. More and more people joined the catechetical class. At the end of five months, over sixty people were joined to Christ in that village. I still believe that if we had not stopped the work when we did they never would have come to that decision.

All over the world there are missions which have been working for decades among people just as unresponsive as the people of Nyang-bande, always refusing to make the break our Lord told us to make. Their mission has failed, and yet they refuse to recognize it. At the same time many other tribes and peoples are clamouring for the good news, and the Churches have insufficient staff to bring it to them and insufficient labourers to nurture new Christians in their faith. If we are unwilling to heed our Lord's command, we bear a heavy responsibility. Whose mission is it? we must ask. Is it ours or the Holy Spirit's?

THE ECONOMICS OF GOD'S MISSION

Part of every evaluation is to discover which areas need reinforcement, and which areas of our work need to be cut out or sharply reduced. The 'economics of mission' is based on the fact of our limited resources, and our responsibility to use those resources as effectively as possible in the Lord's work. Without regular annual evaluations and resolute action following upon those evaluations, we cannot possibly do so.

But note that this evaluation of people's response is important only in connection with our fulfilment of the Great Commission. The Church has other responsibilities as well, responsibilities of charity and love and service, to bind up the wounds of men and heal their diseases, to spread enlightenment and work for a better, more humane world. It must mobilize its resources effectively to meet not only the Great Commission, but what we might call the Commission of the Parable of the Last Judgement as well (Matt. 25.31–46). But in feeding the hungry and clothing the naked we are not concerned about people's response. We need ask for no decision for Christ. We do these works out of selfless love. They may bring people to hear the Gospel, but if they do not, it is no great matter. That is not their primary purpose.

The Church cannot say to the people of villages like Tombu and

Nyangbande, 'As you have rejected the Gospel, we are withdrawing all aid from you.' Its aid is given without any strings attached. Even when the evangelizers shake the dust of a place off their feet, the agriculturalists and nurses and teachers and literacy workers may find good reason to stay there. There may be a good response to their work, and at a later time they may well be able to say to the evangelizers: 'We think you might come back now. There is a new responsiveness to the Gospel here.' Or they may never say so.

In the meantime, the evangelizers will have been working elsewhere, bringing in the fruit that is ripe for harvest, so that no time will be wasted.

The time is short to do all we have to do. While there is light we must work, and work as effectively as possible. By regularly evaluating our work, we shall be able to increase its effectiveness.

The sower in Jesus's parable did not go back to the seed that had fallen among the thorns to cultivate it again, nor did he go back to put more seed on the path or on the rocky ground. He was too busy harvesting the miraculous yield of the seed that had fallen into fertile soil.

STUDY SUGGESTIONS

REVIEW QUESTIONS

1. What do we learn from the Parable of the Sower about the sorts of response to the Word of God which we should expect from people?
2. Read the Parables of the Wheat and the Tares (Matt. 13.24–30), the Leaven (Matt. 13.33), the Mustard Seed (Matt. 13.31f), the Unfruitful Fig Tree (Luke 13.6–9), and the Seed Growing Secretly (Mark 4.26–29).
   What do we learn from them about evaluating our work?
3. What standards should we use to judge the success of the Church's work?
4. What standards should a pastor use to judge the work of his evangelists or catechists?
5. What standards should a pastor use to judge his own work?
6. Who should judge the work of a pastor?
7. To whom are Church workers responsible?

DISCUSSION AND RESEARCH TOPICS

8. A pastor once said: 'Every annual evaluation of the work of the Church should both begin and end with prayer.' What do you think he meant?
9. A congregation has completed its annual evaluation and has come to the conclusion: 'Our work has failed.' Make an imaginary chart

to show the possible reasons for its failure. List them under three headings: (a) poor work, (b) resistance by the people, (c) other reasons.

10. How can we judge others without making them feel we are rejecting them as persons? What is the meaning of 'brotherly criticism'?

11. What does the principle of 'Gospel not law' mean for the evaluations we do?

APPENDICES

Appendix 1: A Guide to the Understanding of a People's Religion

1. Do people belonging to this society believe that other beings inhabit the universe, besides human beings and the animals? If so, of what sorts are these beings?
   (a) Is there a supreme God or sky-God? Is he believed to have created the world? What are his names? (Give both proper names, and proverbial names, such as 'He who never disappoints'.)
   (b) Are there other gods? What are their names?
   (c) Are there any other non-human spirits besides God and the gods listed in (b)?
   (d) Are there any human spirits who are active in the world besides living people?
   (e) Do any animals have sacred power?
   (f) Do any inanimate objects, either in the world or in the heavens, have sacred power?
   (g) Does the earth have sacred power?
2. What is the relation between God and those powers listed in 1. b-g? Are any of them intermediaries between human beings and God? Are they all in harmony with each other? Or do they sometimes conflict? Are any of them evil powers, or are they all good? Can the powers act if God does not agree?
3. What are the different sorts of customary rituals performed by the people, and to which of the powers (1 a–g) are they directed?
4. Do all these rituals have the same purpose? Or different purposes? What are the purposes? Do people get life, or power, or blessing from them? Do they unite the community?
5. What specialized religious 'offices' does the society have (e.g. as priests, priestesses, owners of the land, diviners, mediums, sorcerers, medicine men, prophets)? Do chiefs, headmen, or heads of houses perform religious functions?
6. How does a person become any of these officers (as listed in (5))? Is there any object which a person can buy in order to become religiously powerful?
7. Is it only through specialist religious officers that ordinary people can come into contact with the spiritual powers? Or can people come into direct contact with the powers?

8. What are human beings composed of? (Body? mind? spirit? soul? different types of soul?) Which of these elements (a) die? (b) go to a different place when a person dies? (c) can become reincarnated? (d) can go out of a person when he is asleep? (e) may be associated with witchcraft? What kind of life can people enjoy after death? What type of relationships do the dead have with the living? Can the living do anything for the dead? Can the dead do anything for the living? Can the dead bring evil as well as good?

9. What are the important things which take place during burial and funeral observances? What will happen if these things are not done properly?

10. Do the people have any special rite of communication with, or remembrance of, the ancestors?

11. What special practices, if any, do the people have with regard to: (a) the birth of twins? (b) other sorts of non-normal deliveries? (c) the death of a woman in childbirth? (d) the death of an epileptic or a person with sleeping sickness? (e) the death of a person or the burning of a house by lightning? (f) the death of a person in an accident? (g) death by snake-bite?

12. Do the people have any special customary rites in connection with planting or harvest, or with the eating of the first fruits of a crop? With what spiritual beings are these rituals connected?

13. Which groups in society take part in each of the types of religious ritual? the clan? the tribe? the family? the village? a special group?

14. Are there any rituals or medicines useful against (a) evil spirits (b) witchcraft (c) black magic?

*15. What are 10 (or 5) *good* things?

*16. What are 10 (or 5) *bad* things?

17. Are there any puberty rites or initiation ceremonies or bush schools? What values are taught in them?

18. In what ways have the religious practices of the people changed in the last fifty years or so? Are these changes related to social and cultural changes of other types?

* These questions are best asked of many individuals or groups and the results tallied. Those responses which occur over and over again can be listed as 'dominant values' of the people. Check also those which appear less often. Does the dominant group recognize these as legitimate alternative values?

Appendix 2: Selections from A Catechism for Northern Ghana (Evangelical Presbyterian Church)

1. What is a Christian?
   A Christian is a person who believes that Jesus Christ is Lord.
   (2–8 Questions about the life, ministry, death, resurrection, commission and second coming of Christ.)
9. What is the Kingdom of God?
   The Kingdom of God is the rule of God over all creation.
10. When will this Kingdom be established?
    It already can be found wherever people have repented and placed their faith in God, wherever they live in love and work for the triumph of God's will. It will be completed when all mankind has heard the Gospel, and Christ returns to reign.
11. What should people do who believe the good news of the Kingdom?
    They should repent and be baptized as members of the Church.
    (12–15 Questions about the nature, constitution, and mission of the Church.)
16. Do Christians worship three Gods?
    Not at all. They believe that the Father, the Son and the Holy Spirit are one God, existing in the perfect unity of love.
    (17. The Christian doctrine of God the Father).
18. Are there any lesser gods through whom God the Father can be approached?
    No, Jesus Christ is the one all-sufficient mediator between God and man.
19. Must people follow all of God's commandments before they can be saved?
    No, people cannot be saved by their works or actions, because we have all fallen short through sin. But God in His mercy has given salvation to human beings as a free gift through Christ.
20. What can people do to thank God for the free gift of salvation?
    They can love God with all their hearts, and souls, and strength, and love their neighbour as themselves.
21. Do we achieve blessing from God by offerings, prayer, or fasting?
    No, we should not do these things in order to try to win blessing from God, but only to show thanks to God and to show love to our fellow human beings and to become more devoted to God.
22. Why do Christians not wash their hands and feet before praying?
    We do not believe that God is pleased with only external purification. We believe that we must ask Him to purify our hearts.
23. What do Christians believe about the dead?
    Christians believe that God is the God of the living and the dead.

Jesus's death was an offering not only for the living but for the dead also. People who did not have a chance to hear of the good news of Christ in their lifetimes have a chance to repent after they die.

24. Can we have communion with the dead?

In the Lord's Supper we believe we are united in one fellowship with all those who have lived and are living in Christ.

(25–27. Questions about the Lord's Supper.)

28. What does the Church teach us about our bodies?

The Church teaches us that our bodies are the houses of the Holy Spirit. We must therefore keep them clean and free from sin or unhealthy practices.

29. What does the Church teach us about our possessions?

The Church teaches us that all our belongings come from God, and that we hold them as stewards. They are not given to us only for ourselves, but also to help others.

30. Is a Christian required to give offerings to the Church?

There are no fees in the Church. Whatever we give we must give of our own free will, in order to show thanks to God.

31. What does the Church teach us about our families?

The Church teaches us that it is God's will that human beings should live in families. Parents are responsible to provide for their children, and to train them, and children should give respect to their elders.

32. What does the Church teach us about marriage?

The Church teaches us that God has instituted marriage for the lifelong fellowship of a man and a woman, that they should become one flesh and share all things in common.

33. What does the Church teach about government?

The Church teaches us that government is instituted by God for the order and welfare of human beings. Christians must give respect to all in authority and obey the laws of society. Christians must take an active part in the affairs of their society, and strive for justice and the welfare of all.

34. What does the Church teach about work?

The Church teaches us that it is God's will that people should work to earn their living, and that all work is sacred. Through their work human beings serve God and their fellows.

35. What did Jesus say was the greatest virtue of all?

The greatest virtue of all, for which all people should strive, is love.

36. What did Jesus promise to those who are persecuted for His sake?

He promised them comfort in their time of trouble and a place in His kingdom.

37. As Jesus has given His life for you, what would you like to do for Him?

Appendix 3: Suggested Standards for Adult Baptism

1. The person must be at least fourteen years old.
2. He should have received Christian instruction once a week for a minimum of three months and have attended worship or heard preaching for at least one year.
3. He should be able to answer (not necessarily by memory) questions concerning the central elements of the faith and show that he understands what he is about.
4. He should know the Lord's Prayer and Apostles' Creed by heart.
5. He should understand that becoming a Christian means leaving the worship of all except God in Christ.
6. He should understand that if he is already married he should remain faithful to his wife and not marry another, and if not yet married that he should marry only one wife.
7. He should understand that he is to be an active member of a Christian community by:
   (a) regular attendance at worship
   (b) regular financial support of the Church
   (c) sharing in the preaching mission of the Church
   (d) taking part in all voluntary work projects
   (e) continuing his Christian education after baptism
   (f) in all his life and work in the larger community, witnessing to Jesus Christ and the new life through his deeds.
8. He must show signs of a sincere desire for a new life in Christ and of repentance for all that has separated him from God.

Appendix 4: Extract from the Report of a Conference of the Protestant and Catholic Churches of Botswana, Lesotho, Malawi, Tanzania, and Zambia, 1971

(a) The greatest contribution that the Churches can make to the development of our nations is to spread the vision of the whole Christian Gospel. This includes an attitude of love and service to all mankind in the fullness of our humanity.

(b) Church leaders must be encouraged to preach the whole Gospel and this may be helped with deeper Bible study, with the distribution of some of the literature now available, and with meetings designed to study the needs of the whole man.

(c) In each country we need some people, both full-time and part-time workers, who can do the work of development animation both at national and local levels.

(d) We should all stimulate the formation of local (village or town) ecumenical committees for development, which should work within the community structures.

(i) The policy of setting aside one week each year (Christian Service Week?) when *all* the Churches in a country would pay particular attention to the demands of the Gospel in terms of service was recommended. During this week information can be shared, collections for development work taken, and service projects carried out; and local communities can be encouraged to take part in these activities ecumenically.

(j) We encourage each country as a matter of priority to develop projects amongst people at the grassroots of society, either in village or urban suburb, that build up the awareness of development possibilities. These projects should, where possible, be led by trained personnel and follow as closely as possible the principles referred to in the talk by Dr Charles Elliott which were:

1. Treat people as subjects, not as objects;
2. Work through existing group situations;
3. Work with the poor and oppressed at grass-roots;
4. Work in the home environment not in institutions;
5. Study the needs of the whole man.

Appendix 5: Outline for a Presbyter's Retreat

FIRST DAY

2 p.m.–3 p.m.	Approach to Marriage
3 p.m.–4 p.m.	Hymn Practising
8 p.m.	Bible Study and Evening Service

SECOND DAY

6.30 a.m.	Morning Service
7 a.m.–8 a.m.	Bible Study
8.30 a.m.	Breakfast
9 a.m.–10 a.m.	Duties of a Presbyter
10 a.m.–11 a.m.	Hymn Practising
11.30 a.m.–12.30 a.m.	Family Relationships and Child Training
1 p.m.	Lunch
2.30 p.m.–3.30 p.m.	The Relationship between a Presbyter and an Evangelist
4. p.m.–5.30 p.m.	How a Congregation can Support the Church Financially
7 p.m.	Bible Study and Evening Service

THIRD DAY

6.30 a.m.	Morning Service
7 a.m.–8.30 a.m.	Community Development and Civic Responsibility of the Christian
8.30 a.m.	Breakfast
9 a.m.–10.30 a.m.	Agriculture: The Stewardship of the Soil
11 a.m.–1 p.m.	Watch Literacy Work Demonstration
1.30 p.m.	Lunch and Departure

Appendix 6: A Guide for an Annual Evaluation of the Work in a Congregation

I. STATISTICS

1. ADULT MEMBERS

Basic facts
- (a) Number of confirmed members at time of evaluation
- (b) Number of confirmed members at time of previous evaluation
- (c) (Increase/Decrease) of . . .
- (d) Number of baptized adult members who are on inactive list
- (e) Number of enrolled adult catechumens
- (f) Others regularly attending service

Explanation of the facts
- (a) Number of deaths of confirmed members in the period
- (b) Number of transfers of confirmed members in the period
- (c) Number of members put under discipline since last evaluation
- (d) Number of members returned to full communicant status since last evaluation
- (e) Number of adult baptisms in the period
- (f) Number of confirmations of children becoming Church members in the period
- (g) Number of members admitted by transfer in the period

2. CHILDREN

Basic facts
- (a) Number of children at present on Church rolls
- (b) Number of children on the rolls at last evaluation
- (c) (Increase/Decrease) of . . .

Explanation of the facts
- (a) Number of children born to Church members during the period
- (b) Number of children previously on Church rolls who died during the period
- (c) Number of children not previously on rolls who died during the period
- (d) Number of children added to the rolls by transfer
- (e) Number of (infant baptism/dedication/blessings) during the period

3. Present ratio of adults and children in the total Christian community. Of the . . . members on the rolls, . . . are adults and . . . are children.

II. THE LIFE OF THE CHURCH

1. EVANGELISM

    (a) Have the unbaptized members of the village/town been confronted with the Gospel in this period?

    (b) Do the members of the congregation evidence a strong desire to share the Gospel with non-Christians in the village?

    (c) Have the members of the congregation engaged in sharing the Gospel with people outside the villages?
    with neighbouring villages? If so, which ones?
    with clan-related villages? If so, which ones?
    others?

2. WORSHIP

    (a) On how many Sundays in the average month is the service conducted by a member of the congregation?

    (b) How many members of the congregation can lead a service? preach? read the Scripture lesson? lead prayers?

    (c) How many people normally attend Sunday service? What percentage is men? women? adults? children?

    (d) Are any other services held during the week? Describe them.

    (e) How many hymns can the congregation sing?

    (f) Do the prayers and thanksgivings in the services come from the leader or arise out of the congregation?

    (g) Is there any dialogue or discussion during the sermon or at other times in the service or after the service?

    (h) Is there a special children's service or is there a children's sermon and hymn in the main service?

3. CHURCH LEADERSHIP

    (a) How many consecrated presbyters (Church mothers, deacons, or elders) are there at present? male female

    (b) Are any now on trial, awaiting consecration? male female

    (c) How many of these (a) and (b) can read and write?
    Do they make regular visits to homes of members?
    On a systematic, planned basis?

    (d) Do they do counselling? Pray for the sick? Help settle disputes? Handle congregational finances? Collect pledge payments? Attend district meetings regularly? Attend retreats or training courses at a district or presbytery level?

    (e) Are there any in the congregation who have completed a leadership training course? Are they able to function effectively?

    (f) Do all the local leaders meet together for prayer/discussion of Church matters? How often?

(g) Do the members of the congregation accept their leaders and co-operate with them? (comment).

4. CHRISTIAN EDUCATION

Adults:

(a) Is there regular adult Bible study or group discussion of the faith and/or practical problems of Christian living?
How often?
Who leads it?
Is there good discussion or simply one-way information-giving?
On the average, how many attend?

(b) Are the literate members of the congregation reading good Christian literature?

Children:

(a) Is there a Sunday school or other regular Christian instruction for children?

(b) How many are at present enrolled?

(c) How many were enrolled last year?

(d) (Increase/Decrease) of . . .

(e) Number of children in confirmation instruction (Church membership classes, catechism)

(f) Number of children in confirmation instruction at last evaluation

(g) Number who have since been confirmed

(h) (Increase/Decrease) of . . .

(i) Comments on the quality of Children's religious education

5. FINANCES

(a) List the ways in which the congregation raises funds/goods for its congregational programme and the amounts received this year and last year.

(b) List the ways in which the members of the congregation support the work of the larger Church and the amounts received this year, i.e.
number of people pledging
(increase/decrease) of ( ) since last year
number of people completing pledge payments
(increase/decrease) of ( ) since last year

(c) Do the members of the congregation work together to help the needy?
Do they do so individually?

(d) Are the congregation's worship facilities (place of worship and necessary furnishings) adequate? List any improvements this year?

6. Relations with other Congregations

(a) Has the congregation visited other congregations in the district this past year? Has it had visits from other congregations?

(b) Does the congregation ever exchange preachers with other congregations?

(c) Do members of the congregation attend funerals of Christians of other congregations who are not of their own clan? Have any Christians of unrelated clans attended funerals in your village this year?

7. Groups within the Congregation

Describe the fellowship/work/choral/service groups at present existing within the congregation, and the contributions they make to the life of the Church and of the larger world, and to the enrichment of the membership.

8. Christian Service and the New Life in Christ

(a) Are there any adult literacy classes in the village? Who sponsors them? Who leads them? Are the Church members involved in them? How many Church members have received functional literacy certificates in the past year? men women

(b) Does the Church provide any adult education opportunities other than literacy?

(c) Number of children of members who attend school

(d) Does the Church provide any educational opportunities for children who do not attend school?

(e) Has there been a programme of Christian home and family life work this year?

(f) Has there been a programme of agricultural development?

(g) Describe community development projects undertaken this year and the role of Church members in them. Credit unions? Co-operatives?

(h) Has the Church done anything in the area of health education and hygiene?

(i) Has there been any civic education this year?

(j) Describe any locally-sponsored non-agricultural industries.

III. PROBLEMS AND ACHIEVEMENTS

1. Describe any problems which have come up in the past year which are of special note, and state whether the problems have been solved or whether they are still in need of solution.

2. Describe what you feel are the significant achievements of the congregation in the past year.
3. What hopes does the congregation have for further growth in the Kingdom, the life of the Church, and the spread of the Gospel in the coming year?
4. What hopes and fears do you as the compiler have for the congregation?

Appendix 7: A Guide for an Annual Evaluation of Work in a Pastoral District

I. STATISTICS

1. UNIFIED STATISTICS

Totals of all the individual statistics of the congregations found in Section I of the Annual Evaluation of the Work in a Congregation (Appendix 6).

2. ADDITIONAL FACTS

(a) Total of villages in which there are baptized congregations . . . List them and put a * next to those which were not listed last year.
(b) Total of other villages in which preaching is regularly carried out. List them and put a * next to those which were not listed last year.
(c) Names of villages listed last year where work has since stopped.
(d) Names of additional villages with which contact has been made.

3. ANALYSIS OF THE CHRISTIAN COMMUNITY

(a) Men . . . % Women . . . %
(b) Adults . . . % Children . . . %
(c) List tribes included and, where relevant, the clans of those tribes.
(d) List tribes and clans of tribes which are not included and villages where they are.
(e) Are any of those in (d) now included in the list of preaching stations or has initial contact been made with them?
(f) Will the Church be able to minister to them in the near future, or should it ask for help from the denomination or from another Church?

II. THE LIFE OF THE CHURCH

1. EVANGELISM

Describe progress in the past year:
(a) How much of this has been the result of efforts by the Christians themselves?
(b) Would there have been more progress if the Church had been able to mobilize its resources more effectively?

2. WORSHIP

Describe the development of worship in the past year.

3. LEADERSHIP

   (a) Describe all leadership training programmes and their functioning in the past year:

   (b) Number of trained leaders now . . . as compared to last year . . .

   (c) Number of literate presbyters (elders, deacons, Church council members) . . . as compared to last year . . .

   (d) How effectively and independently would you say the local leadership of the congregations of the district operates?

   (e) Present number of pastors . . . evangelists . . . other full-time Church workers . . .

   (f) Does the Church need more such leaders? now? in the future?

   (g) Is progress being made toward the replacement of non-local paid leaders by local ones?

   (h) Do the leaders work well as a team? Or do they work separately?

   (i) Are paid leaders doing any tasks which could equally well be done by voluntary leaders?

4. FINANCES

   (a) Total support raised in the last year (not including congregational funds)

   (b) Total support raised in previous year

   (c) (Increase/Decrease) of . . .

   (d) Total operating budget (salaries and programme) for the year

   (e) Percentage of total operating budget now raised locally

   (f) Number of years before you expect the district will be able to be self-supporting

   (g) Number of people making pledges last year . . . this year . . .

   (h) Number of people completing pledge payments last year . . . this year . . .

   (i) Is there a district finance committee? Does it function well?

   (j) Is there a local treasurer? Does he function well? Is he given responsibility?

   (k) If the answer to any of the questions in (i) or (j) is 'no', state why.

5. GROWTH IN FELLOWSHIP

   (a) Have the congregations in the district come to enjoy a greater fellowship as Christians in the past year?

   (b) Have barriers of tribe been crossed?

   (c) Have barriers of clan been crossed?

   (d) Do you still see signs of tribalism or clannishness?

   (e) Do the congregations regard the district session (district council) as an expression of their own selfhood, or as a body which imposes policies from above? Do they have a sense of really participating in the decisions which are reached?

(f) Experience of wider fellowship:
with other districts of the denomination
with other denominations
with people of other religions

6. GROUPS

Do the fellowship/work/choral/service groups existing at the present in the district fulfil the needs of the members, and provide adequate means of witness and service to the larger community? To what extent do they involve Christians of more than one village working together? Describe their programme. What steps do you hope can be taken in the next year to improve these groups?

7. CHRISTIAN SERVICE AND THE NEW LIFE IN CHRIST

(a) Total involved in adult literacy classes in the district
Number who have received certificates for functional literacy in the past year
of which ... are men and ... are women; percentage of Christians now literate ...
Number of voluntary teachers ...
Is adequate Christian literature available for new readers?
Is any being developed?
Bible translations now available
Are any more being done? any simplified versions? portions? popular language versions?
(b) Adult education opportunities other than literacy
(c) Number of children of Christian parents attending schools ...
Percentage of children of Christian parents now attending ...
(d) Educational opportunities for children not attending school
(e) Christian home and family life programmes
(f) Agricultural development
(g) Community development projects, credit unions, co-operatives
(h) Health, hygiene, and sanitation
(i) Civic education
Are Christians participating responsibly and intelligently in the local political life?
(j) Locally-sponsored non-agricultural industries.

III. PROBLEMS AND ACHIEVEMENTS

1. List problems found in more than one congregation in the district, and indicate whether or not they have been solved and what steps are being taken to solve them.
2. List the achievements of the Church in the district in the past year.

3. What hopes do the people have for further growth in the Christian life in the next year?
4. What are your fears and hopes in the next year?
5. Describe ways in which the Church in the district is moving toward greater unity with other Christian denominations in the area.
6. Is the Church making the best possible use of the gifts of the Spirit to its members for mission? What about teachers and other government employees?
7. In how many schools in the district is religious instruction being given? ... out of a total of ...
   Is it being done together with other denominations or separately?
8. List problems which you experience in your work.
9. What resources do you need for your work which are not at present provided for you?
10. Other comments.

Key to Study Suggestions

CHAPTER 1

2. and 3. A dictionary may give you some help in answering these questions.
5. See p. 2, para. 7. 6. See John 13.1–17.
8. See p. 2, paras 5–7.
9. See p. 2, last para., and p. 3, paras 1–4.

CHAPTER 2

1. See whole section headed 'God's Plan' on pp. 5 and 6.
2. (a) See p. 6, numbered paras 1–5.
   (b) See p. 11, paras 4, 5, and 6.
4. (a) See p. 6, paras 1 and 2.
5. See Situation examples A, B, and C, pp. 8–10.

CHAPTER 3

2. See p. 16, last para., and p. 17, paras 1 and 2.
3. See p. 17, paras 4–7.
4. (a) See Acts 16.6–10. (b) See p. 15, para. 4.
5. See p. 18, para. 2.

CHAPTER 4

1. static, established, immutable, systematic, organized, fixed.
2. (a) See p. 20, paras 1–3. (b) See p. 19, last para.
   (c) See p. 22, paras 4 and 5.
5. (d) See p. 22, paras 3–5, for some suggestions.

CHAPTER 5

3. See especially p. 26, para. 1 (Famisa), p. 26, para. 2 from foot (Mayamam), p. 27, para. 4 (Sobiba).

CHAPTER 6

1. *Individual:* personal, separate, sole, single.
   Group: community, social, mass, corporate.
2. Two possible words could be 'tradition' and 'social structure'.
6. See p. 33, paras 1 and 2.

CHAPTER 7

1. (a) Based on p. 35, para. 4. (b) Based on p. 35, last para.
   (c) Based on p. 36, paras 3 and 4.
   (d) Based on p. 36, last 2 paras.
2. (a) See p. 36, para. 4. (b) See p. 36, para. 5.
3. (a) See p. 38, numbered paras 1–3.
4. See p. 37, last para.
6. See p. 38, last para., and p. 37, para. 1.
7. Based on p. 36, last 2 paras, and p. 37, paras 1 and 2.
8. Based on p. 40, last 2 paras, and p. 41, paras 1–3.

CHAPTER 8

2. Based partly on pp. 42–43, numbered paras 1–3, p. 45, para. 1.

CHAPTER 9

1. See p. 49, numbered paras 1–3.
2. Based on p. 49, numbered para. 3.
3. See p. 47, last 6 lines, and p. 48, lines 1–13.
5. Based partly on p. 51, paras 2 and 3 and last para.
6. See p. 51, paras 3, 4, and numbered para. 2.
7. See p. 53, last 2 paras, and p. 54, lines 1–11.

CHAPTER 10

1. See p. 58, para. 3.
2. (a)–(c) Based on p. 57, last 2 paras.
3. See p. 58, last para., and p. 60, para. 1.
4. (b) See footnote in RSV, or marginal note in any other annotated Bible version.
5. (a), (b), and (c) See p. 60, para. 4.
6. See p. 60, para. 2.

CHAPTER 11

1. See p. 64.   2. Based on p. 68, paras 2 and 3.
3. See p. 65, para. 4, and p. 72, para. 3.
4. See p. 68, paras 5 and 6.
5. See p. 68, para. 4.
6. Based partly on p. 67, para. 4.
10. See p. 64, para. 5.

CHAPTER 12

1. See p. 75, last 3 lines, and p. 76, lines 1–10.
2. See p. 73, last 3 paras, and p. 74, para. 1.
3. See p. 74, paras 2–4.

CHAPTER 13

1. (a) Based on p. 82, para. 1 and last para.
   (b) *Exegesis:* exploration, excavation, examination.
      Exposition: explanation, expression, expounding.
2. See p. 79, paras 1–3.
3. (a) See p. 79, paras. 4 and 5, and p. 80, lines 1–3.
   (b) See p. 80, para. 2.
4. See p. 79, para. 4, and section headed 'example' on pp. 80 and 81.

CHAPTER 14

1. See p. 88, paras 3 and 6.   3. See p. 93, paras 3–5.
4. and 5. See p. 90, last 2 paras, and p. 91, para. 1.
8. Based on p. 93, para. 3.

CHAPTER 15

1. See p. 100, paras 1 and 2.   2. See p. 100, paras. 2 and 3.
4. Based on p. 102, paras 1 and 2.

KEY TO STUDY SUGGESTIONS

6. Based on p. 98, paras 2–4.
8. Based on p. 102, para. 3.
9. See p. 99, para. 4, and p. 100, para. 2, last 5 lines.
13. (a) See p. 91, para. 3.

CHAPTER 16

1. See p. 104, paras 2–5.
2. See p. 104, last para. 3. See p. 106, paras 3 and 4.
4. See p. 105, last para., p. 106, paras 1 and 2, and p. 108, para. 3.
5. See p. 108, paras 1 and 2.
6. See p. 107, paras 2–6.

CHAPTER 17

1. See p. 109, ch. 17, para. 1.
2. (a) and (b) See p. 112, last 2 paras, and p. 113, paras 1 and 2.
3. See p. 114, para. 4.
4. See p. 113, last para., and p. 114, paras 1–3.

CHAPTER 18

1. (a) See p. 116, para. 4 and last line, and p. 117, paras 1 and 2.
   (b) See p. 117, paras 4–7.
2. (a) See p. 118, paras 4 and 5. 3. See p. 118, para. 3.
4. See p. 118, para. 6, and p. 119, paras 2 and 3.
5. See p. 117, last 2 paras, and p. 118, paras 1 and 2.
6. See p. 118, para. 5.
7. See p. 119, last 2 paras, and p. 120, paras 1 and 2.

CHAPTER 19

1. See p. 121, ch. 19, para. 1, and p. 123, paras 2–4.
2. See quotation at foot of p. 121 and top of p. 123.
3. See p. 129, lines 5–11. 4. See p. 124, last 14 lines.
5. See p. 126, para. 2.
6. See p. 125, last para., and p. 126, lines 1–6.
7. (a) Jesus referred to (1) His coming death; (2) His own resurrection—and that of His disciples.
   (b) The Lord's Supper points also to God's offer of salvation to all who will turn to Him.

CHAPTER 20

1. (a) See p. 130, ch. 20, para. 1. (b) See p. 130, ch. 20, para. 2.
2. See p. 138, para. 2.
3. See e.g. Mark 14.12–26; John 7.1–15; John 10.22–26.
7. Based on p. 131, paras 2–5.

CHAPTER 21

1. See section headed 'Two ways of working', pp. 141–143, especially p. 142, last 2 lines, and p. 143, lines 1–3.
2. (a) See p. 144, lines 8–13 and 17–22, and p. 146, para. 3.
   (b) See p. 146, paras. 4–6.
3. See p. 143, paras. 2–4.

KEY TO STUDY SUGGESTIONS

CHAPTER 22

2. Based on p. 152, paras. 3–6.
3. See p. 151, para. 1.
4. (a) See p. 148, last 5 lines, and p. 149, lines 1, 2.
5. See p. 150, para. 5.   6. Based on p. 154, para. 1.

CHAPTER 23

1. (a) and (b) See p. 158, paras headed 'The Bible's Teaching . . .', and p. 159, lines 1–4.
2. See p. 157, para. 1, and p. 159, paras 3 and 4.
3. See p. 156, para. 5.   4. See p. 159, para. 3.
5. See p. 160, paras 2 and 3.   10. Based on p. 159, para. 2.

CHAPTER 24

1. (a) See p. 161, numbered paras 1–3.
   (b) See p. 162, para. 1.
2. See p. 162, para. 2.   3. (a) See p. 162, paras 2–5.
4. See p. 162, last para., and p. 163, paras 1 and 2.
5. See p. 163, para. 4.
6. (a) and (b) See p. 164, para. 3.
7. (a) See p. 165.
10. Based on p. 166, para. 2, and numbered paras 1 and 2.

CHAPTER 25

1. (a), (b) and (c). See p. 175, numbered paras, 1, 2, and 3.
2. See p. 171, last para.   3. See p. 170, para. 2.
4. See p. 175, last 8 lines, and p. 176, paras 1 and 2.
8. See p. 172, last 13 lines, and p. 173, lines 1–7.

CHAPTER 26

1. Based on p. 179, paras 3–6, and p. 180, paras 1 and 2.
2. See p. 180, numbered paras 1–3, and p. 181, numbered para. 4.
3. See also p. 179, paras 4 and 5, and p. 182, para. 3.
4. (a) See p. 179, para. 3.   (b) See p. 181, para. 1.
6. Based on p. 181, para. 4.

CHAPTER 27

1. See p. 184, para. 1.
2. We learn that all our work is measurable and will be judged by God.
3. See p. 185, para. 1 (and Appendix 7).
4. See p. 184, para. 2, and p. 188, para. 1.
5. See p. 184, paras. 3 and 4 (and Appendix 6).
6. See p. 183, ch. 27, para. 1.
7. See p. 191, para. 3.

Index

215